SHAKESPEARE: THE PLAY OF HISTORY

CONTEMPORARY INTERPRETATIONS OF SHAKESPEARE

Published by Macmillan

Derek Cohen
SHAKESPEAREAN MOTIVES

Martin Elliott
SHAKESPEARE'S INVENTION OF OTHELLO

Graham Holderness, Nick Potter and John Turner
SHAKESPEARE: THE PLAY OF HISTORY

Murray J. Levith
SHAKESPEARE'S ITALIAN SETTINGS AND PLAYS

Lachlan Mackinnon
SHAKESPEARE THE AESTHETE

Peter Mercer
HAMLET AND THE ACTING OF REVENGE

Further titles in preparation

Series Standing Order

If you would like to receive future titles in this series as they are published, you can make use of our standing order facility. To place a standing order please contact your bookseller or, in case of difficulty, write to us at the address below with your name and address and the name of the series. Please state with which title you wish to begin your standing order. (If you live outside the UK we may not have the rights for your area, in which case we will forward your order to the publisher concerned.)

Standing Order Service, Macmillan Distribution Ltd, Houndmills, Basingstoke, Hampshire, RG21 2XS, England.

Shakespeare
The Play of History

GRAHAM HOLDERNESS

Tutor in Literature and Drama
University College of Swansea

NICK POTTER

Senior Lecturer in English
West Glamorgan Institute of Higher Education

JOHN TURNER

Lecturer in English
University College of Swansea

MACMILLAN
PRESS

First published 1988

Published by
THE MACMILLAN PRESS LTD
Houndmills, Basingstoke, Hampshire RG21 2XS
and London

Companies and representatives
throughout the world

Printed in Hong Kong

British Library Cataloguing in Publication Data
Holderness, Graham
Shakespeare: the play of history.—
(Contemporary interpretations of Shakespeare)
1. Shakespeare, William — Knowledge — History
2. History in literature
I. Title   II. Potter, Nick   III. Turner, John
IV. Series
822.3′3 PR3014
ISBN 0–333–42876–5

For
Rachel Phyllis Natasha Holderness
Fred and Vera Turner
Ninon, Joel and James Potter

Whatever happened to
All of the heroes,
All the Shakespearoes?
. . . No more heroes any more,
No more heroes any more . . .

(The Stranglers, 'No More Heroes')

Playes? Nay, what if I prooue Playes to be no extreame; but a rare exercise of vertue? First, for the subiect of them (for the most part) it is borrowed out of our English Chronicles, wherein our forefathers valiant acts (that haue line long buried in rustie brasse and worme-eaten books) are reuiued, and they themselues raised from the Graue of Obliuion, and brought to pleade their aged Honours in open presence: than which, what can be a sharper reproofe to these degenerate effeminate dayes of ours?

(Thomas Nashe, 'Pierce Penilesse his
Svpplication to the Divell')

Contents

Acknowledgements

This book is the work of three different people engaged in a common project, and the work has been collaborative throughout. Our greatest debt has thus been to each other; but, although in retrospect the beginnings of ideas and phrases have become lost, we do of course take individual responsibility for their final shape.

We wish to express particular thanks to the following, who have helped us either individually or collectively: Catherine Belsey, Tony Bennett, Gill Branston, Stuart Clark, Sam Dawson, Jonathan Dollimore, Brian Doyle, Sue Gagg, Ralph Griffiths, Terry Hawkes, David Hills, Russell Jackson, Arnold Kettle, Derek Longhurst, Graham Martin, Chris McCullough, Chris Powell, Glyn Pursglove, Neil Reeve, Peter Shoenberg, David Sims, Alan Sinfield, Jenny Taylor, the late Brian Way, Robert Weimann and Peter Widdowson.

Our thanks also to Louise Fleet for all her work in preparing the typescript.

G. H.
N. P.
J. T.

List of Texts

Part One   Theatres of History: Chronicle Plays

Andrew Gurr (ed.), *The New Cambridge Shakespeare: Richard II* (Cambridge University Press, 1984)

A. R. Humphreys (ed.), *The Arden Shakespeare: The First Part of King Henry IV* (Methuen, 1960)

A. R. Humphreys (ed.), *The Arden Shakespeare: The Second Part of King Henry IV* (Methuen, 1960)

Gary Taylor (ed.), *The Oxford Shakespeare: Henry V (Oxford University Press, 1982)*

Part Two   The Tragic Romances of Feudalism

Kenneth Muir (ed.), *The Arden Shakespeare: King Lear* (Methuen, 1972)

Kenneth Muir (ed.), *The Arden Shakespeare: Macbeth* (Methuen, 1962)

Part Three   'This is Venice'

John Russell Brown (ed.), *The Arden Shakespeare: The Merchant of Venice* (Methuen, 1959)

M. R. Ridley (ed.), *The Arden Shakespeare: Othello* (Methuen, 1962)

Introduction
John Turner

> *What might have been and what has been*
> *Point to one end, which is always present.*
> (T. S. Eliot, 'Burnt Norton'[1])

This book was conceived and written to explore our belief that Shakespeare's plays evince a serious interest in history. Each of the following discussions is an exercise in answer to the question, what do we see of the time and place in which the play is set? For none of the plays, except the specially commissioned *The Merry Wives of Windsor*, is set in or near contemporary London. The difference from Ben Jonson is extreme. Always in Shakespeare there is a historical or geographical distance, and commonly both together; and these distances become in performance a crucial aspect of the plays' dramatic meaning. The has-been or the might-have-been of the imagined play-world brings an enriched perspective upon the present to which it finally points us. Our interest, therefore, has been in the dramatization of history, in history as it is experienced in the theatre.

We have grouped the plays that we discuss by place or period rather than by genre (although the categories overlap) because we have wanted to emphasize the historical cast of Shakespeare's imagination. But of course the historical interest of the plays cannot be separated from the question of their genres. In performance, chronicle, comedy, romance and tragedy tend to re-create the real or imagined past (and therefore the present too) in characteristically different ways. Furthermore, study of the sources of each play shows not only changes of story and setting but also quite radical changes of genre. Therefore, although the plays are usually mixed in mode and resist simple categorization, we have always kept the question of genre in mind; and at appropriate moments we have inserted discussion of the categories that have most concerned us here (chronicle, romance and tragedy) as an essential element in our wish to understand their perception of, and intervention in, the historical process.

The plays depict something of the variety of the societies that

1

men and women have made for themselves; and in this way they
seem to us to partake in the early stages of that 'historical
revolution'[2] which characterized British intellectual life between
1580 and 1640. Mediaeval England, pre-Norman Scotland, republican Venice – each of these worlds is differently perceived, with its
own social formations, its own laws and institutions, its own
economic and military structures. Each society sustains its own
characteristic language, its own set of discourses and ideologies;
and thus, crucially, the great issues of morality and religion are
seen to lie within the historical process rather than above it. Man,
in making his own history, makes himself. The older mediaeval
conception, still residual in Shakespeare's England, that history
was a long and undifferentiated continuum exemplifying divine
providence and retribution seems simply irrelevant beside the
variety of worlds depicted in the plays. In Shakespeare we are
much closer to the temper of Italian humanism, of Machiavelli,
where history is rather the drama of human agency than divine.
The mediaeval morality play has been subsumed into that most
eclectic of forms, the Elizabethan and Jacobean drama, and in the
process it has become historicized.

It is not only history that interests Shakespeare, however; it is
also the nature of historical change – change resulting from the
struggle for power, commonly within the two great patriarchal
structures of family and state. Nor are the struggles which he
depicts accidental to the societies in which they occur; they are
inherent, structural. The plays focus upon those stress-points
(Brecht's *Bruchstellen*) where fracture is most likely to occur: for
example, upon the struggles for power and property between
aristocratic houses and monarchical states; upon the clashes
between military and civilian interests within the state; upon the
conflicts over succession and inheritance provoked by the law of
primogeniture. In play after play, conflict of interest, dramatized as
ideological contradiction or self-contradiction (or both), leads to
confrontation that threatens the *status quo* of family and state.
Traditionally, literary criticism has depicted the characteristic
pattern of Shakespearean drama in terms of the recovery of an
initially dislocated order. We argue on the contrary that the
characteristic pattern is one of transition – transition perceived as
historical necessity but complexly weighed in terms of its gains and
its losses, with the sense of loss always tending to predominate.
The question of genre matters here, of course: for whilst the

chronicles and tragedies create that sense of loss directly in their narrative line, the comedies and romances create it obliquely as their audience turns away from the conscious artifice and incompleteness of their closing social recomposition and negotiates the delicate transition from play-world to reality. You that way: we this way.[3] But in all the plays, whatever their genre, the imperfect cadences of their endings serve to create the imperfection of the world that has survived, and help us to articulate the sense of loss by which it may be judged.

The plays, that is to say, embody – and to a certain extent in performance they enact – an understanding of history that is at once materialist and dialectical. They depict history as a dynamic process driven by desires, ambitions and beliefs that operate so powerfully precisely because they spring from the deepest conflicts and contradictions of the societies in which they occur. We do not know what Shakespeare himself believed, but we claim this as the meaning of his plays, as he adventured upon them for the public stage. We shall return in our conclusion to this distinction between author and play. For the moment it is enough to suggest that what Raymond Williams has called the 'multivocal' and 'interactive'[4] nature of the dramatic form itself – its openness and interest in conflict, together with its grasp of the relationship between thought and circumstance – sharpened an interest in history; and that in turn a widespread curiosity in the histories of other times and places helped to extend the range of the dramatic form. Drama and history: these two recovered forms of Renaissance exploration co-operated to produce in Shakespearean drama what John Danby called 'literally a new organ of thought';[5] and so close was the co-operation between them that principles most commonly held by literary critics to be purely aesthetic, with an internal referentiality only (principles of contrast, balance, variety within unity and so on), are not finally separable from principles of historical inquiry into the has-been and the might-have-been of other societies.

The paradox of Renaissance exploration lies in its mixture of aggressive self-confidence, extending alike the empires of capital and curiosity, and its melancholy sense of rupture and loss; and this paradox is perfectly inscribed in the plays of Shakespeare. Successful as they were, they charted not only the passages that history had taken but also the passages it did not take. They gave voice also to that which had been lost, denied, defeated or

unrealized; and herein lies the peculiar value of their historical
sense, as it has interested us in this book.

Our title, *The Play of History*, epitomizes our attempt to mediate
between two critical methodologies, one traditional and one
modern, both with characteristic strengths but both of which seem
to us to have significantly misrepresented the value of the blend of
drama and history in the plays. The idea of the book was first born
out of our impatience at the traditional method of teaching
Shakespeare, still active if not still predominant in our schools,
colleges and universities, and perhaps deriving ultimately from the
providentialism of mediaeval history: the method which searches
the plays as fables containing universal truths that transcend the
conditions both of their own production and of our consumption.
The plays in this view illustrate what Wilson Knight has called 'the
religious content',[6] of all great art. The very largeness of such
claims, however, seems to us an impoverishment, dehistoricizing
the plays twice over, preventing our seeing them as Elizabethan
and Jacobean explorations of earlier times and other places; and
hence the emphasis on history in our title.

But as we went on we discovered also that we wanted to
distance ourselves to some degree from the 'new historicism' of
cultural materialism, a post-structuralist school of criticism similarly antagonistic to traditional methods and aiming instead 'to give
not so much new readings of Shakespeare's texts as a historical
relocation of them'.[7] The critics of this school argue that the
recovery of authorial meaning is impossible and, eschewing the
subjectivities of interpretative criticism, tend to treat the plays as
ventriloquisms of Elizabethan and Jacobean times, bearing witness
to contemporary political struggles which they are unable fully to
articulate because of their inevitable collusion with the dominant
ideology of their age. The job of the radical critic thus becomes to
give voice to all those who have challenged that dominant
ideology, in however incomplete or unconscious a way – exploited
colonial subjects, women, puritans, servants, masterless men –
until the necessary silences of the texts yield up their completed
histories of political repression. Readings are to be evaluated in
terms of their political tendency, and the text is to be strategically
mobilized to make it disclose the conflicts and the contradictions of
its history. As the strength of traditional criticism has lain in its

cultivation of subjectivity, the strength of this radical post-structuralism has lain in its disclosure of the unconscious or only partially understood presuppositions of both art and criticism. Our objection to it, however, is that, as with much 'vulgar Marxist' writing also, it tends too easily to collapse the cultural artefact into its economic base. In its impatience to enlist literary criticism under the banner of political engagement, it tends to disregard the degree of autonomy that a cultural artefact might achieve, as it struggles to make its own meanings amidst the complex currents of its times. So the historical perspectives of the plays are flattened into records of their own age, and their capacity still to generate subjective interpretation is sternly disregarded. It is in opposition to the suspicious rationalism of this criticism, its anxious determination not to be taken in by the text, its puritanical insistence upon direct political mobilization and its distaste for subjectivity that we have chosen to emphasize play in our title.

D. W. Winnicott, in his book *Playing and Reality*, inscribed a paradox at the heart of his account of the origins of play: 'the paradox, as when a baby creates an object but the object would not have been created as such if it had not already been there'.[8] The deployment of paradox here is a characteristic strategy to indicate both the rights and the limits of subjectivity whilst restraining the desire to draw the boundary between them – 'the line invisible/ That parts the image from reality', as Wordsworth put it.[9] For Winnicott the capacity to play happily was central to those symbolization processes whereby a baby begins to make acquaintance with the world and find that acquaintance creative and self-authenticating rather than compliant and dead; and yet still it is the otherness of the world that must be met. There is a similar paradox inscribed at the heart of literary studies, for here too a reader or spectator creates a work only because it is already there. Two things, that is, happen together in the course of reading or watching a play – two different things, which it is important to try to keep separate, even though the boundary-line is always lost between them: we re-create the work in our own language in order to claim acquaintance with it, to give it symbolic meaning in our own world, whilst at the same time we grapple with the language in which it was originally written in order to know it in its history. These two activities have tended in their extremes to produce what Brecht called empathic and critical approaches to literature, traditional criticism tending towards the former and post-structuralism towards the latter. But, as Brecht saw, both are necessary, each complementing the other; and indeed both activities are perhaps necessarily and ordinarily involved in the complex shuttling back and forth of the mind between self and other which constitutes the apparently simple act of understanding. We have argued here for both play and history, the former authenticating the latter, the latter disciplining the former; and we have tried in what follows to move discriminatingly between the two, the subjective appropriation of Shakespeare's plays to fashion our own symbols for present understanding and the objective attempt to see them in their own historical context.

To argue for the importance of a kind of play in literary criticism, of course, is not to argue for its innocence; for, as the disconcerting poetry of Blake's little chimney-sweep makes clear in *Songs of Innocence* ('if all do their duty, they need not fear harm'), even innocence is tarnished by experience. In the direction of its play a society reproduces itself. One glance at the variety of meanings given to 'play' in different languages at different periods – or indeed in any one society at any one period – is sufficient to show that we are not dealing with an objectively recognizable category of behaviour. [10] It is a concept which has signalled both approval and disapproval of a child's and of an adult's behaviour; it has had associations with ceremony and authority and also with mockery and debunking; it has invoked man's highest duties and his holidays from duty; it has spanned the whole spectrum of meanings from law to lawlessness and has sometimes enjoyed a privileged area apart from both; it has denoted both innocence and experience, licit and illicit behaviour in matters of adult sexuality; it has been used to describe the real and the false, the fictional and the merely fictitious; it has included and excluded ideas of sport, contest, even war; and it has been defined in terms both of chance and risk and of skill and mastery. But for us too the word holds promise of a world. We do not live under conditions of our own choosing and we need working hypotheses, based upon where we find ourselves, of the things we are to value.

The value of play was first upheld by the Romantic poets, and later theorized by object-relations psychoanalysis, in the search for the childhood roots of creative adult living, for an alternative life to that encouraged by an authoritarian culture interested only in compliance. Still today, this idea of play seems to us valuable in honouring the particular pleasure of literary studies, where the text invites our subjectivity in a special way and where critical understanding is authenticated by our response to that invitation. Especially is this true of Shakespearean drama, where subjective freedom of interpretation is inscribed so deeply into the text as part of its meaning. Such play is one of the things that we do and, doing, enjoy, and it seems therefore appropriate that the pleasure we take should be respected in the criticism we make. At a time when radical criticism has chiefly celebrated play in terms of the subversiveness of carnival, and deconstruction has dissipated the world into the play of signifiers, it seems right to emphasize the quiet advances to be won within the world by the play of literary study, whether singly or collaboratively undertaken, wherever its pleasures are to be found amidst the compliance demanded by our educational institutions. It has seemed, moreover, particularly right to do so in a decade that has seen all the play-areas of our society under constant threat.

For Shakespeare too the concept of 'play' was an important one; his theatre was built upon it, along one of the major fault-lines of his society. Leontes' words from *The Winter's Tale* suggest some of the ideological forces at work:

> Go, play, boy, play: thy mother plays, and I
> Play too; but so disgrac'd a part, whose issue
> Will hiss me to my grave: contempt and clamour
> Will be my knell. Go, play, boy, play.
> (I. ii.187–90)

Play may recapture the wise innocence of a prelapsarian Golden Age or it may be no more than childish folly to the jaundiced eyes of experience ('Go, play, boy, play'); it may be licensed pleasure or lawless licence with dangerous powers of subversion ('thy mother plays'); it may image a mind at home with its roles in the world or the utter dislocation of pretence and inauthenticity ('and I/Play too'). All these possibilities are acknowledged in the ironic bitterness of Leontes' words. The free play of his mind, we might say, drawing upon the normative sense of the word outlined above, is disturbed by the passionate irruption of jealousy: everything he has known – wisdom, morality, existence itself – is plunged into charade. Suddenly we lurch into that giddy feeling of infinite

recession so commonly experienced during the course of Shakespearean drama, as we find ourselves watching an acting character
acted by a character actor.... Our sense of dramatic illusion yields
to that sense of universal illusoriness for which the professional
actor has had so long to be a ritual scapegoat, with applause on the
stage and contempt in private life ('so disgrac'd a part').

Fair is foul, and foul is fair: Leontes' ambivalence about his wife
and child is expressed in a language that expresses a still deeper
ambivalence about play itself. For there is no normative understanding in Shakespeare whereby we may trace its value. His plays
are not moralities, for example; they do not point to the present
with an instructive finger. On the contrary, they make of the
theatre a place apart, a place of special licence, a haunt of
glamorous and often dangerous illusions whose value and relationship with reality is deeply problematical. What is the status of
an illusion? With what are we left when the revels are ended?
These questions are part of the meanings of the plays. If Milton
(and after him Wordsworth) is the poet in our history most
strikingly to exemplify a unified imagination, sure of itself, its
world, and the work to be done by art between them, Shakespeare
is the great poet of the imagination divided against itself; and in
this he was, in part at least, a product of the new commercial
theatre for which he wrote and in which his money was invested.
It is not that the value of play and theatre had been problematized
by puritan attack. It is rather that the Tudor state, attempting to
centralize and thus to secure its new authority, had uprooted
dramatic play from its previous homes in village, church and
manor and brought it to the metropolis, where, in the public
theatres, it had at once become susceptible to market pressures;
and hence the new self-consciousness about the value of play that
we find in Shakespearean drama, with its virtuosity of self-
confidence and curiosity shadowed always by a sense of rupture
and loss. The beauty of the plays is that – within the constraints of
censorship, in that licensed arena of special licence which was the
Globe – they enable us to imagine, as in the Histories and
Tragedies discussed below, the has-been and the might-have been
of a past in which, still today, we may see the impoverishment of
the present. But that sense of loss is not only enabling, it is
disabling too: for the imperfect cadences with which the plays all
end remind us too of the problem with which we have been
struggling here – the problem of how best to resist the supervision

of our play by the new alliance between state and capital that was being formed in Elizabethan and Jacobean England, and that Shakespeare explored in its most advanced contemporary state in the Venetian plays.

Part One
Theatres of History: Chronicle Plays

GRAHAM HOLDERNESS

1

Prologue: 'The Histories' and History

The question of genre seems unproblematical when applied to that group of Shakespeare's plays which dramatizes the course of English history from 1398 to 1485. Confidently grouped in chronological order and designated as 'histories' as early as the First Folio of 1623, they were evidently assimilated quite naturally to a non-dramatic category, that of historiography. Each play, bearing the title of a particular king, stands as the equivalent of a chapter of one of the Tudor chronicles; the whole series forming an integrated narrative of historical process. Unlike other genres such as comedy and tragedy, which have their origins in religious ritual, that of 'chronicle' produces a dramatic fiction directly based in the secularized representation of supposed historical fact. The mediating authority of the Tudor chronicles themselves links the plays indissolubly to the concrete history of the society they both address: so the two related terms 'English' and 'history' appear to define with sufficiently lucid certainty both the generic and the sociological categories to which these plays belong.

In terms of the historical and geographical criteria we have employed in this study, the term 'English' seems unexceptionably definitive. Linked with 'history', however, it becomes more problematical: how adequate a conception could an Elizabethan intellectual have had of the 'history' of the fifteenth century? In much traditional criticism the play of 'English history' is represented as little more than a patriotic rendering of certain commonplaces of Elizabethan ideology; and it is furthermore questionable, as I shall be arguing below, whether the 'new historicism' of Marxist/deconstructionist criticism has entirely succeeded in demolishing, or has to some degree merely translated, the 'old historicism' of Tillyard. If these terms are to be substantiated, it becomes necessary to engage more fully with the particular conceptions of fifteenth-century English society available

13

to, and within the intellectual and imaginative capacity of, a dramatist working in the 1590s.

For many years after the Second World War most readings of Shakespeare's chronicle plays took place within an ideological problematic established by critics such as E. M. W. Tillyard, G. Wilson Knight, Lily B. Campbell, and Derek Traversi,[1] who formulated, on the basis of a highly selective and politically tendentious reading of Elizabethan culture and society, a model of Renaissance ideology best exemplified by Tillyard's book *The Elizabethan World Picture* (1943). This ideology is said to have been centred on the concept of political 'order': Elizabethan intellectuals such as Shakespeare could not avoid thinking within the ideological framework prescribed by orthodox political, ethical and scientific ideas; they could not therefore help but believe 'order' to be a fundamental principle of the universe and an indispensable necessity in the state. Shakespeare's historical plays were for Tillyard straightforward articulations of this ideology of 'order':

> In his most violent representations of chaos Shakespeare never tries to persuade that it is the norm: however long and violent its sway, it is unnatural; and in the end order and the natural law will reassert themselves... it is not likely that anyone will question my conclusion that Shakespeare's Histories, with their constant pictures of disorder, cannot be understood without assuming a larger principle of order in the background..... In the total sequence of his plays dealing with the subject-matter of Halle he expressed successfully a universally-held and still comprehensible scheme of history: a scheme fundamentally religious, by which events evolve under a law of justice and under the ruling of God's providence and of which Elizabethan England was the acknowledged outcome.[2]

Reading *Richard II* within this problematic, Tillyard saw it as the inception of an integrated series of dramas illustrating the commonplaces of Tudor historical philosophy. Richard II was the last king to rule by direct undisputed hereditary right, and the England he ruled represents a culminating and final phase of mediaeval 'order'. Both hereditary continuity and providential order were broken by the usurpation of Henry IV, whose action and example substituted for the old organic polity a new *de facto* style of political leadership. The violation of social and natural order entailed in the deposition and murder of a king was subsequently avenged by divine providence in the form of a civil war and dynastic instability, which were finally resolved only by the beneficent accession of the Tudors.

It may perhaps seem an exaggeration to suggest that the critical orthodoxy of the 1940s can still impose its constraints on contemporary readings of Shakespeare's plays. Tillyard's work has been questioned and challenged on so many fronts that his 'Elizabethan World Picture' is easily visible now as the ideological fiction it always was: more intelligible as an intervention into the current cultural crisis of the Second World War than as an explanation of Renaissance culture and society.[3] Historical research, studies in historiography and cultural criticism alike have delivered us a much more complex picture of Renaissance society: as a turbulent and rapidly changing period in which competitions for power and legitimation created contradiction and dissonance throughout the cultural and ideological structure. We now recognize Renaissance historiography as more varied, more 'modern' and less constrained by government-imposed orthodoxy; and Shakespeare's history plays can now be perceived as locations of ideological, cultural and artistic contradiction. But, as Alan Sinfield and Jonathan Dollimore have demonstrated in a recent essay,[4] the metaphysic of 'order' which informed Tillyard's writing on the chronicle plays can still be seen to overshadow subsequent criticism, even criticism of an oppositional character. The problematic of 'order' (which Sinfield and Dollimore show to be derived from a long tradition of idealist philosophy) has proved harder to escape from than reductive and simplistic historical analyses and critical readings.

The most telling and comprehensive interrogation of this orthodoxy has emanated from the 'new historicism' of cultural materialist approaches to Shakespeare, which ruthlessly expose the idealism and ideological mystification of 'organic' theories, whether of text, individual or society. Where the 'old historicism' of Tillyard and others operated a transaction from text to history, imposing upon history the aesthetic patterns and coherences discoverable in literary works, the 'new historicism' works in the opposite direction, seeking to discern the 'real' of history through the ideological fabrications and aesthetic disjunctions of the plays themselves. The plays don't transmit a metaphysic of 'order', but construct an ideological coherence which can be interrogated to disclose the contradictions it contains; a Shakespeare play is fascinating precisely to the extent that it is implicated in and can be read to disclose both the struggles of its historical moment and their ideological representation. To see the play in such terms is not at all to conclude that it is merely a deluded and mystifying ideological fantasy.[5]

It seems to us unwise, however, completely to surrender, in the course of reading history through the texts, the genuine possibility that some kind of authorial 'mastery' shaped those texts, and shaped them deliberately to particular ends. The related critical problems of authorship and of intentionality render impossible any straightforward definition of what 'the author' 'meant': we can only speculate about the elusive, mysterious connections between William Shakespeare and the plays 'he' 'wrote'. Such speculation may be inevitable, pleasurable, even illuminating; but we are still left, in the end, with a bookful of plays and a handful of dust. The subject to which traditional interpretative criticism ascribes authorship is in fact 'Shakespeare', the *inferred* author; a volatile, flexible, changing construction, engendered, and constantly reborn and rewritten, by the plays.

What is certain is that in the public playhouses of Elizabethan London an overdetermined interaction of cultural forces (among which the writer was a decisive constituent element) combined to shape a number of dramatic texts which bestowed a complex unity on their fragmentary, heterogeneous and contradictory materials. That such interaction was an ideological operation goes without saying; and criticism – if it hopes to understand the historical nature of literature – must strive to deconstruct what has been so ordered. But these acts of unification can also now be seen to have expressed a historical consciousness (though not, certainly, that of an individual 'author'); a historical imagination which expressed a new and original grasp of the nature of history.[6]

The historical drama of the Renaissance straddled a cultural transition in which more recognisably 'modern' ways of understanding the past were born: in fact the emergence of that new historiography coincided with the demise of the historical drama.[7] But what evidence, what proofs can be offered of this proposed connection or analogy between historical dramas written in the years around the beginning of the seventeenth century and forms of historiography not properly established until after the Restoration? The chronicles of Halle and Holinshed, and other works of

Tudor historiography, can be established confidently as definite sources for the historical visions embodied in Shakespeare's plays: plays which occupy the same period of significant history mythologised by Halle, from the quarrel of Bolingbroke and Mowbray to the accession of Henry VII. Scholarship has demonstrated that these works were not as unitary or as orthodox as writers of the Tillyard school implied: they were rather compilations of heterogeneous sources, emanating from diverse perspectives within a period of great dynastic struggle and political change. Thus the chronicles themselves can be shown to have offered Elizabethan intellectuals both a global historical myth and a documentation of the contradictory materials that myth offered to contain and resolve: they were the source for different forms of historical and political knowledge. None the less, though we may challenge the Tillyardian orthodoxy by showing that both the Tudor chronicles and Shakespeare's historical plays formulate, within the framework of a historical myth, the materials necessary for its interrogation, we have only confirmed the dependence of the plays on 'official' Tudor historiography.

Further, a considerable body of work revising the 'old historicism' was initiated as early as the late 1950s, and has become widely accepted today: work which emphasizes the development within English Renaissance culture of Italian humanist methods of historical investigation, particularly the thinking of Machiavelli.[8] Italian humanism brought a more secular and sceptical spirit of inquiry to bear on historical issues: unlike mediaeval providentialism it supported a more rational and positivistic form of historiography. Ultimately, however, humanism was too exclusively concerned with history as a utilitarian political science, with the past as a repository of knowledge and experience applicable to the problems of modern Renaissance rulers, to appreciate fully the pastness of the past: humanist scholars were more aware of continuities than disjunctures between classical civilizations and the advanced European societies of their own day; more possessed by a vision of human permanence than alert to the possibilities of fundamental and irreversible historical change.

Mediaeval providentialism and Italian humanism, though apparently very different in their ideological perspectives, both tended to emphasize the unchanging and unchangeable in human history: mediaeval pessimism and humanist pragmatism shared common ideological ground. These currents of thought were undoubtedly the strongest influences on the thinking of Renaissance intellectuals applying themselves to historical speculation. It is all the more remarkable that we should find within Shakespeare's historical dramas, alongside echoes of Christian providentialism and Italian humanism, a grasp of history more akin to the new historiography of the seventeenth century than to either of those older perspectives. In all of Shakespeare's plays, as proposed in the Introduction, we find this grasp of the uniqueness and disparity of other societies, known to the imagination not through the continuity of a permanent and a universal human nature, but through distance and difference: historical disruptions of time, geographical divisions of space. Such a historical consciousness entered English historiography only gradually, initially through jurisprudential theory. In the writings of Sir Thomas Craig, Camden, Selden and Stowe, there slowly developed principles and methods of historical inquiry which eventually led to the great discovery of the Norman Conquest as a fundamental historical break in the continuum of English history. Within the past of England itself could be discovered an alien form of society: a unique and self-contained social formation, with its own institutions, its own peculiar economic and military systems, its own hierarchical social structure, its own individual codes of value and conventions of behaviour: feudalism. Imposed by force in the eleventh century, it could be seen to have undergone by the sixteenth fundamental historical change. This discovery marks the beginnings of modern historiography.[9] A contemporary awareness of it can be found, we are proposing, not only in the researches of Renaissance scholars and antiquarians, not only in formal historiography; but in the historical drama – written, self-evidently, in different circumstances and for a different medium, but embodying none the less a remarkably new understanding of history.[10]

Without wishing in any sense to confuse or identify the conservative old historicism with the radical new, we suggest that both tend equally to neglect the possibility that Shakespeare's plays may have represented such a historiographical initiative: since both are equally concerned to locate the plays into the cultural and ideological context of their own time. The Tillyard school insisted on representing the plays as expressions of an establishment ideology; the new historicism is concerned to identify the ideologies imperfectly mastered by the plays. If we grant the possibility that the plays may have achieved their own grasp of the past, both these accounts have to be qualified; and two dominant conceptions of the plays as history have to be re-examined: the view that they embody a transition from a mediaeval period understood to be stable, providentially protected and decorously chivalric to a world of crude *Realpolitik*; and the view that they construct from the raw materials of the past images of the contemporary, so that in them events and problems of the fifteenth century are addressed via the beliefs of the sixteenth.[11]

If our argument is accepted, it becomes possible to discover in the plays a clear, historically informed apprehension of the political struggles of later mediaeval society; in particular the long struggle between monarchy and nobility which developed out of the contradictory nature of the feudal order, and was arrested by the accession of the Tudors. These historical conflicts are inscribed into the language and structure of the plays in political, theatrical and cultural forms. Textual analysis of the chronicle plays in the light of Renaissance and modern historiography will show that in them the internal contradictions of a declining feudalism are represented both more clearly and more explicitly than is commonly recognized. It is often assumed that the dramatic structure of each play negotiates a transaction from crude, shapeless reality to the significant form of art; but, as we propose to demonstrate, the artistic shape of a Shakespeare play bears a range of specific historical significations inseparable from the particular qualities of its style and language. Finally, the plays depend on a recognition of the *political* meaning of cultural conflicts and competitions: differences of language and cultural code don't merely add to the rich variety and complexity of Shakespeare's myriad-minded art – they interact on the poetic and theatrical ground of a play's discourse to enact the antagonisms and *rapprochements* of historical contradiction.

2
Richard II

CHRONICLE AND PASTORAL

The term 'chronicle' itself, which supports our concept of a distinct *genre*, is much more difficult than it at first sight appears. The chronicle play as it developed in the later sixteenth century was a remarkably eclectic form, in practice rather unlike the stolid factual preoccupations of the Tudor historiographical narratives. The 'English history' plays which appeared on the public stages of Elizabethan London from the 1580s were as likely to be structured by comic or romance *genre* as by chronicle; as likely to contain Robin Hood, Maid Marian, Friar Tuck and Little John as the kings, queens and barons of real history; as likely to display the quixotic irresponsibility of a romance monarch wandering disguised through his kingdom as to depict the authenticated actions of a historical king caught in the toils of dynastic struggle and civil war.[12] Thus a historical play such as Marlowe's *Edward II* (1592) is notable for its very strict adherence to the matter of the chronicles: in all probability Marlowe consciously intended to insert some intellectual consistency into the eclectic variety of a popular genre. Shakespeare himself had already (before his own *Richard II*, and probably before Marlowe's play) gravitated towards this stricter historical form in his *Henry VI* and *Richard III* plays, though still maintaining generic freedom and the liberty of supplying invented incidents. But it was in *Richard II* (in my opinion influenced by *Edward II*) that Shakespeare chose to adopt a classically historical chronicle form, which draws all its characters, events and locations (with one significant exception) from works of literary historiography. As Shakespeare proceeded in the next play of the series to break this classical severity of structure and return to the flexible type of history play which can dispose its focus of interest across historical and fictional materials, the strict purity of *Richard II*'s chronicle form is evidently worth investigating.

The exception referred to above is the 'garden scene' (III. iv), a distinctive oasis of fictional material which introduces a generic inconsistency into an otherwise cohesive medium. Much criticism has assimilated the scene to the play's chronicle style by interpreting it as 'political allegory', an emblematic representation of the state that is represented naturalistically in the rest of the play.[13] The symbolic medium is introduced, according to traditional criticism, to point towards those metaphysical concepts of monarchy and the state conventionally regarded as Shakespeare's natural ideological context. Tillyard saw the gardener as a type of the ideal king, a legitimate monarch who rules his microcosmic kingdom correctly; and other critics have followed him to the same conclusion.[14] In these traditionalist accounts, religious overtones (the queen calls the gardener 'old Adam's likeness') are held to point to a theological vision of the state as a divinely ordained paradisal order violated by Richard's deposition, a 'Second Fall of Man'. According to this interpretation the garden scene is a kind of masque, in which a king, disguised as a gardener, discourses on the political and metaphysical dimensions of the state: the garden itself is nothing more than an emblematic location for a political discussion which has its real meaning only in the historical world of great events centred on court and king.

The editor of the Arden edition of *Richard II*, though reinforcing this conventional view, introduced another suggestion which potentially contradicts the traditionalist arguments: that the technique of the scene is pastoral, the gardeners 'humble people . . . who criticise the court and its great men in language and ideas drawn from their rural discipline'.[15] But, if the gardener is generically a gardener, can he also be a king? If the genre operative here is pastoral, can it simultaneously be chronicle? If the great are to be criticized by the humble, must there not be some fundamental distinction, some radical contradiction between the two worlds?

In fact, of course, these difficulties may amount to nothing: pastoral never was a genuinely simple or humble cultural form – it was rather a sophisticated medium produced by urban and courtly cultures to forge a purely imaginary and artificial connection between such a society and the experience, customs, culture and 'philosophy' of 'simple country folk'. 'Shakespeare . . . makes explicit what has always been clear about pastoral – that it is of the country but by and for the court or city.'[16] In political discourse pastoral could be employed specifically to elide the contradictions between monarch and subject, ruler and ruled:[17] when James I spoke of himself as a shepherd and his people as a flock, the very purpose of the discourse was to propose a particular political relationship, while simultaneously mystifying, in the identification of pastoral shepherd with seventeenth-century monarch, the contradictions between ruler and subject.[18]

The pastoral genre has, however, apparently from its inception, always contained two contradictory tendencies, exemplified by the relation between Virgil's *Eclogues* and his *Georgics*. There is on the one hand the sophisticated metropolitan pastoral designed to express emotions of nostalgia and longing ('Essentially the art of pastoral is the art of the backward glance', and Arcadia from its creation the product of wistful and melancholy longing'[19]) – for simplicity, innocence, pleasure. This form has no more than a tourist relationship with any actual country landscape, agricultural economy or rural populace, and is effectively a type of fantasy literature: 'The bucolic dream has no reality other than that of imagination and art.'[20] On the other hand (and this point seems largely ignored by historians and theorists of pastoral such as Poggioli), there is a kind of marginal opposition to the dominance of fantasy pastoral in the form of a literature which proposes a *real* preoccupation with country life, its economy, society and culture. At certain periods of cultural development (such as the later eighteenth and early nineteenth centuries) this tendency has arisen to eclipse the pastoral genre proper, and to insist that poetry about the country should be *about* the country, and not an artificial and escapist literary fantasy. Raymond Williams has called this tendency 'counter-pastoral'.[21]

The dominant Renaissance form was of course courtly pastoral, which appears in important and influential works such as Sidney's *Arcadia*, Spenser's *The Faerie Queene* and *The Shepheardes Calender*. In Sidney pastoral is mingled indiscriminately with chivalric romance; in Spenser it is employed in classical manner as a discourse for writing about the court. Shakespeare uses both pastoral and counter-pastoral differently, in more complex ways: and one of the areas he chose as a suitable ground for developing this generic strain was the English history play.[22] I propose to discuss *Richard II* as a contradictory fusion of chronicle and pastoral genres.

Despite the play's strict adherence to historically authenticated event and incident, it displays that mixture of representational and fantasy forms which seems central to the operations of the

Renaissance historical imagination. Even a writer with so 'modern' a historical consciousness as Samuel Daniel ('holding it an impiety, to violate that public testimony we now have, without more evident proof: or to introduce fictions of our own imagination'[23]) thought it appropriate to introduce so fictive a *genre* as pastoral into his narrative of Richard II's reign; and Daniel's poem was, I suspect, the source of Shakespeare's similar juxtaposition. What the two distinct discourses have in common is an abiding preoccupation with questions of justice: and in *Richard II* it is on grounds of justice that their *rapprochement* is joined.

SOURCES

Contemporary scholarly opinion can confidently assert that *Richard II* is based in a plurality of sources, and that there is little evidence of specific indebtedness to the most ideologically orthodox history, Halle's *Union of the Two Noble Houses of Lancaster and York.*[24] Shakespeare chose to open his play, it is true, at the same point as Halle, with the quarrel and abortive trial by combat of Bolingbroke and Mowbray; and Tillyard saw this as evidence of ideological complicity. Every historical narrative must begin somewhere, but history itself (once it begins to be understood in secular and evolutionary terms) is a process with no clearly definable inception: so every historical event, however decisive or transitional, must be rooted in pre-existent causes. To begin, as Halle begins, with an apparently stable monarchical authority confronted by a refractory nobility, is inevitably to propose or imply a historical model in which the legitimacy and power of the king are seen as unquestioned, and the factional carping of the barons perceived as unacceptable civil disobedience. The political framework thus established is a hierarchical paradigm of government: a king ruling by indisputable legitimate title and inherited sovereign right; a power-hungry nobility chafing under the constraints of intensifying subordination.

Yet the play itself does not take its own opening as a *terminus a quo*: on the contrary, the initial situation is rooted in precedent history, specifically in the imprisonment and alleged murder of the Duke of Gloucester. Throughout the drama we find a constant recursive movement, a series of references back to earlier historical events or periods. These are not simply exercises in nostalgic emotion or elegiac form: they are a recognition of history as a perpetual dialogue between present and past. Echoes of Gloucester's death are followed by Gaunt's and York's laments for the England of Edward III and the Black Prince (II. i), and other subsequent examples of aristocratic nostalgia for earlier days - a note sustained until Richard himself in Act III appropriates the elegiac mode and begins to eclipse all other perspectives on the past in the sun-like majesty of his myth of royal martyrdom.

The texts of Tudor historiography available to Shakespeare the dramatist–historian made abundantly clear that the quarrel of Bolingbroke and Mowbray was the *outcome* of a long political struggle as well as the precursor of dynastic collapse and civil war. In fact Shakespeare hardly needed to venture beyond the pages of Holinshed to find a detailed and impartial account of that political struggle, between a monarchy seeking to extend its powers into a new form of absolutism, and a nobility struggling to defend and preserve its privileged position within the feudal hierarchy. Later mediaeval history was evidently not an example of undisputed sovereignty challenged by baronial irresponsibility, but a competition for power between opposed, mutually exclusive and (given the context of a *feudal* society) *equally valid* forces within the ruling class.

Throughout Holinshed's narrative of the later years of Richard's reign, Shakespeare could have found a plain and unmistakable account of persistently continuous political conflict: the gradual encroachments of extending monarchical power and the increasing discontent of the aristocracy. There are scenes of open rebellion and armed conflict, executions of great magnates, the use of Parliament by the nobles to secure influence and power over and against the king. Moreover, Holinshed's narrative is particularly expressive of unresolved antagonism, since it draws itself on a variety of disparate sources, with scarcely any attempt to arbitrate between or reconcile them: pro-Ricardian French sources are juxtaposed with pro-Lancastrian versions of events.[25] Shakespeare's play not only reflects this conflict of sources but intensifies it: by, for example, foregrounding (from one of the French chronicles or perhaps from Daniel's *Civil Wars*[26]) the convention of Richard's 'lamentations'. The French historians gave Richard formal speeches of complaint, which formed the basis for the lyrical utterances of Shakespeare's king: embedded within the tough positivism of the Tudor historians, this elegiac note introduces a stylistic contradiction which articulates a political conflict. The consistent practice of these plays is to select and juxtapose source-material to produce such formal discordances, which in turn figure forth ideological contradictions.

This is perhaps an uncontentious assertion: we begin to make a larger and more original claim when we suggest that the plays embody such representations of conflict within a historically specific social formation. The ideological conflicts fought out within the plays are not between the abstractions of divine right and *Realpolitik*; or between the individualized stereotypes of a weak king and an ambitious subject; or between an idealized Middle Ages and a naturalistic present. They are specifically identified as those competitions for power between monarchy and aristocracy which modern historians recognize as characteristic of this transitional late-mediaeval reign. [27]

CHIVALRY AND TREASON

The initial dramatic crisis of *Richard II*, the event that precipitates a baronial rebellion, civil war, the deposition and murder of a king, is indisputably a mediaeval rather than a Renaissance custom: a process of law firmly attached to feudal society and to a constitutional structure quite unlike that of Shakespeare's England. 'No legal procedure was more closely connected with feudalism, or embodied its spirit more thoroughly, than the wager of battle.' [28] The practice of resolving a legal dispute by single combat (though it survived, outside the law, in the form of the convention of duelling, into the sixteenth century and beyond, and survives even into modern culture as a pervasive fictional archetype) belongs to the militaristic codes, conventions and institutions of a society in which the ruling class was organized as a military caste. Wager of battle provided formal procedures (conducted in the later fourteenth century in the Court of Chivalry) whereby an individual accusation or 'appeal' could be lodged against a defendant, who then had the obligation (if he denied the charge) to defend himself in armed combat against his accuser. [29] The institution was clearly of benefit to a hegemonic group such as the feudal aristocracy, which could validate itself culturally as well as politically by the very exercise of its professional skills; [30] and which, by shifting any civil or criminal problem to the ground of individual or family honour, could resist or negotiate claims and pressures from below and even from above in the feudal hierarchy. The institution declined as a consequence of various developments: Christianity, the ascension of economic power and political influence of a non-military class, the bourgeoisie, and the growing power of the monarchies; there is no recorded instance of it in England between 1571 and 1639.[31]

If we conclude that Shakespeare could have understood this judicial institution only from the limited perspective of a sixteenth-century intellectual steeped in the more mediaeval notions of his culture, and innocent of new currents of historiographical thought, then we can assume no particular grasp of the socio-historic specificity of the wager of battle in *Richard II*. And it is widely believed that Shakespeare applied to all his historical material the assumptions of his own contemporary legal and constitutional context: 'The concepts of law that define king and commonwealth in *Richard II* and guide the audience's assessment of Richard's reign are the same standards that many of Shakespeare's contemporaries used to assess their own monarch and society.'[32] This weighty and detailed argument by Donna B. Hamilton (which is typical of much contemporary assessment of the history plays, and represents essentially a continuation of the criticism of Tillyard and Lily B. Campbell) cites in evidence the authority of Sir Thomas Smith and Sir John Fortescue to prove that Shakespeare accepted the orthodox constitutional theory of his time, and hence believed that a monarch ruled by law and could not exempt himself from it: the king is, in Bracton's terms, *super homine* but *sub deo et sub lege*. Richard's failure as a king (which would presumably invite parallelism if a sixteenth-century monarch were to behave in a similar way) is to regard himself, and to hold himself, legally invulnerable and immune from prosecution.

This methodology offers little purchase on the issue of trial by battle, on which the play's whole action is based. Critics adhering to these principles have to regard the judicial combat as symptomatic of concealed conflicts and problems, rather than as in itself a site or discourse of such conflict.[33] For Hamilton, as for many other critics, the real issue is the king's guilty culpability over the murder of Thomas of Woodstock, Duke of Gloucester; and Bolingbroke's challenge is the only means by which a law-abiding subject can challenge the king's sovereign immunity. But the play nowhere definitively condemns Richard for the murder of Gloucester (though the Lancastrians certainly do) and Shakespeare's historical sources offered more than one account of that magnate's political career. The anonymous play *Thomas of Woodstock* (probably later in date than *Richard II*) drew on a tradition which characterized all the nobility, particularly the Lancastrians, as blunt and patriotic defenders of the free-born Englishman's liberties against royal tyranny. But thoroughly documented in other sources is the aggressive and ambitous role played by Gloucester in a long internecine struggle between nobility and monarch.[34] These rival historical traditions form a contradictory substructure for the play, and by articulating such differences the characters express their ideological conflicts. The Lancastrians constantly echo the *Woodstock* tradition – 'My brother Gloucester, plain well-meaning soul' (II. i.128); while Richard himself treats the Lancastrian dynasty as implacable enemies of his authority: 'As Herford's love, so his./As theirs, so mine, and all be as it is' (l.146).

If we assume, as Hamilton does, that the play presents the law as a monolithic national superstructure embodying the interests of all members of society, and guaranteeing rights and liberties to all - as Elizabethan common law purported to do – then the murder of Gloucester can confidently and unproblematically be evaluated as a criminal act, Richard condemned as unworthy of his high office, and Bolingbroke seen as constitutional defender of the subject's liberties and of contractual limited monarchy. But, if, on the other hand, we take the political context to be an infinitely more conflictive historical situation, in which disparate concepts of law are being mobilized into competition by antagonistic social groups – a society riven by the contradictory forces, centrifugal and centripetal, of a collapsing feudalism – then no simple evaluation of the king's legal and moral responsibilities will hold.

It is perhaps in the language and formalized structure of the play's dramatic presentation of these events that the historical meanings become clearly visible. Both are considerably intensified, even exaggerated, over the accounts in the sources; and the effective result is as completely mediaeval as could be imagined:

BOLINGBROKE.
    If guilty dread have left thee so much strength
    As to take up mine honour's pawn, then stoop.

By that and all the rites of knighthood else
Will I make good against thee, arm to arm,
What I have spoke, or thou canst worse devise.
MOWBRAY. . . .
I'll answer thee in any fair degree
Or chivalrous design of knightly trial;
And when I mount, alive may I not light
If I be traitor, or unjustly fight.

(I. i.73–83)

Throughout these scenes the number and frequency of technical terms drawn from the vocabulary of chivalry and the law of arms far exceed those to be found in the sources, and it seems probable that the author was frequenting some of the popular manuals of chivalry, or at least some mediaeval romance literature, as well as works of historiography. The procedures dramatized indicate a conscious authorial awareness of anachronism, the deliberate deployment of a specific mediaeval discourse, complete with unique conventions and specialist vocabulary, rather than a naïve and uncritical absorption of some mediaeval local colour.[35]

From where, in the play, does this chivalric discourse emanate? What social institution is the ground of this particular cultural growth? It is surprising to reflect how many critics have followed Tillyard in locating chivalric ritual in the political power and cultural hegemony of the king:[36] 'after the turbid confusions of the first scene, the ceremonial anonymity of the combatants is refreshing. Mutual recrimination gives way to formula, hysterical defiance to the incantations of the two heralds. . . .' The elaborate cultural 'order' of chivalry is identified with the ideal political 'order' of a providentially managed kingdom: the ceremonial formalities, stylized language and ritual conventions attributed to the king's penchant for ostentatious sovereignty. For Sanders, Richard's stopping of the combat is a betrayal of 'order': yet, viewed historically, a wager of battle between two great magnates is the last thing a fourteenth-century monarch with absolutist aspirations would wish to see. Technically the king's authority over the legal procedure is absolute: it is his prerogative to grant or deny combat, and his right to terminate the combat at his own inclination.[37] But the very nature of the feudal institution of judicial combat, if permitted to run its course, deprives the king of any real authority or control. The feudal law of arms enables the accuser, Bolingbroke, to shift the dispute from any judicial ground that we (or the Elizabethans) could regard as a proper legal process, to a primitive conflict of individual chivalric 'honours', a competition of martial skills. By granting the combat (as Froissart observed[38]) Richard devolves and transfers power from himself to his subjects; by arresting it, he reappropriates authority to the crown. The laws of chivalry were not an aspect or emanation of sovereign monarchy, but a code of values intrinsically and incurably antagonistic to the power of the crown:[39] by invoking that code Bolingbroke and Mowbray act out a political dispute that threatens to dispossess the king of any effective authority. Both combatants explicitly differentiate their position from royal protection or influence: Bolingbroke 'disclaim[s] the kindred of the king' (I. i.69) and Mowbray places his personal 'honour' higher than his loyalty to Richard (ll. 165–85); the two 'knights' meet on the common ground of a feudal ideology hostile to, rather than synonymous with, monarchical power: 'a common bond, called chivalry, uniting all who could aspire to ride to wars and tournaments'.[40]

In *Richard II* Bolingbroke appeals Mowbray of treason on the basis of charges derived from Holinshed: embezzlement, conspiracy and the procuring of Gloucester's death. It is generally agreed that the chief substance of Bolingbroke's charge is the murder of Gloucester, and that the thrust of his accusation is levelled against the king: the indictment of a royal favourite was a recognized strategy for undertaking a legally viable assault on the judicial immunity of the king. But can a king be accused, even indirectly, of 'treason'? Is not the very basis of the law of treason a legal protection of the king against those adjudged to be his enemies? In fact the concept of treason has a complex history, and was in English society (as it is in the play) the site of political contradiction and competing ideological appropriations. The term has two roots, one Germanic and the other Roman. The former derives from Germanic tribal custom and is strictly the notion of betrayal or 'faith-breach' (*Treubruch*) of an individual's loyalty to an individual superior. The latter derives from Republican Rome, and is in essence a prohibition against *laesa majestatis*, insult to those with public authority. In the former concept the crime is a personal betrayal; in the latter, an offence against the dignity of the state. By the fourteenth century in England the two concepts were incorporated into the law of treason (for instance, in the statute of 1352) as 'high' treason, against the king, and 'petty' treason, against a master by a servant or a husband by a wife. They coalesced into unity as the theocratic ambitions of later mediaeval kings moved towards policies of absolute monarchy; as king and state increasingly became indivisible. Under the despotism of the Tudor monarchs, any danger or even annoyance to the sovereign or the sovereign's dignity (which might include counsellors and lords of the realm) could be interpreted as treason: though of course it was unthinkable for any member of that state to allege 'treason' against the sovereign.[41]

The 'treasons' alleged by Bolingbroke against Mowbray include offences of *laesa majestatis* – betraying the king's trust, perhaps even (the charges are notoriously vague) 'accroaching the royal power' or 'encompassing the king's death' (i. i.87–108).[42] The third charge, however, falls outside such categories, if it is tacit common knowledge that the death of Gloucester was a secret execution ordered by the king. The offence is not one committed by a subject against the king's person, but an offence committed by the king against the majesty of the state, a corporate body which (in Bolingbroke's view) included great magnates such as Woodstock. Bolingbroke is not merely accusing Mowbray, on behalf of the king, of treason against a lord of the realm, since he implicates himself in the majesty of the state that has been affronted: Mowbray is a traitor 'to God in heaven, King Richard and *to me*' (emphasis added).

Bracton distinguished between the power of the king in an executive capacity (*gubernaculum*) where he could act freely and at will; and his authority in making and challenging the law (*jurisdictio*), where he must act in conjunction with his magnates. This implied that in some respects the monarchy was contractual in form; and the distinction gave rise in the thirteenth century to the notion of *corona*, the 'crown' which was the bond between magnates ('community of the realm') and king. The king could declare as treasonable any infringement of the rights and dignities of this collective 'crown'; but then the magnates themselves could claim that the king was not affording the crown adequate protection, or that a third party (one of the unfortunate upstart 'favourites') was violating the joint rights of king and barons (hence the ordinances of 1311 against Gaveston, and those of 1321 and 1326 against the de Spensers). In a kingdom such as England where Magna Carta maintained some feudal limitation over the monarchy – while elsewhere in Europe moves towards a more theocratic kingship were being made – it was more difficult for the concept of 'treason' to become definable simply as 'resistance to the king'. Feudal 'fealty' – a reciprocal, contractual relationship in which the king had obligations as well as rights – survived to offer a residual resistance to monarchs who sought a semi-divine status like that of the Roman emperors, requiring passive obedience from the subject.

Bolingbroke exploits the ambivalences of the concepts to imply that the murderer of Woodstock committed treachery not only as 'petty treason' of faith-breach against the duke (to which Mowbray, referring to a 'neglect' of his 'sworn duty', appears to admit), but as high treason against the ruling family or hegemonic fraction to which Bolingbroke himself belongs. Although the accusation is shaped within legal conventions presided over by an autocratic ruler (there is no possibility of open *diffidatio* or invoking the subject's right of resistance), the charge seems to invoke a contractual monarchy in which the magnates share power with the king and limit his prerogative. An offence against an individual or family within this class is an offence against the joint sovereignty of the crown. Bolingbroke even regards the legal responsibility for judging and punishing the crime as devolving on himself in person:

> he did plot the Duke of Gloucester's death. . . .
> . . .
> And consequently like a traitor coward
> Sluic'd out his innocent soul through streams of blood,
> Which blood, like sacrificing Abel's, cries . . .
> . . .
> To me for justice and rough chastisement. . . .
>
> (i. i.100–6)

Emerging into visibility here, through the ornate terminology of a proper legal accusation, are the more recognizably feudal motivations of individual honour, family dignity and the right of a subject to judge his king.

Those critics who see the culture and ideology of chivalry as an expression of 'kingship' must necessarily interpret Richard's stopping of the combat in i. iii as a denial of justice to the combatants; and others have followed in regarding the act as a reckless and foolish irresponsibility.[43] If it is recognized that judicial combat is represented in the play historically, as a remote and archaic legal process expressing and preserving the interests of the feudal aristocracy, and that the law of arms is not affirmed by the play as an appropriate means of securing justice, then Richard's action (whatever its ultimate consequences) can be seen as the affirmation of a politically expedient counter-policy, which insists on the absolute sovereignty of the king in matters of national security: 'Richard's sudden regaining of the initiative, and the submissions that follow it, can be seen as a ruler's stroke . . . .'[44] Trial by combat was universally condemned, as Andrew Gurr points out,[45] in the sixteenth century: its illegal descendant, the practice of duelling, was deplored and punished by law. Bacon argued that such individual conflicts led to family vendettas, and thence to social tumult and civil war. Even the popular manuals of chivalry, written in the thirteenth and fourteenth centuries, translated and published in the fifteenth, were touched with the more modern view: as Diane Bornstein has demonstrated, most of them condemn wager of battle as irrational, immoral and not to be permitted by a just ruler.[46]

The true conflict fought out at Coventry on St Lambert's Day is not, then, a trial of arms between Bolingbroke and Mowbray, but a trial of strength between two antagonistic ideologies, absolutist and feudal. Through the cultural conventions and legal procedures of chivalry, Bolingbroke challenges the power of the king; through a policy of monarchical absolutism Richard imposes his own royal prerogative on the quarrelling dukes. The immediate result is a temporary victory for the absolute king: longer-term results entail for Richard an absolute defeat. The ideology espoused by the nobles, archaic and primitive though it may be, is based on a contractual concept of monarchy: they seek, by the aggressive and militaristic methods appropriate to their class, to sustain or restore the feudal bond of fealty, a society of mutuality and reciprocal obligation between aristocracy and king. Richard's policy of royal absolutism, though capable of swift and irresistible executive power, isolates the king within his own realm, and thus undermines the collective basis of that power. As subsequent events in the play will serve to demonstrate, Divine Right of Kings is no substitute for effective political authority, which in turn depends, in this social formation, on the bonds of mutuality linking the ruling class as a 'community of the realm'.

PASTORAL AND POLITICS

Richard articulates his absolutist policy in a language of pastoral:

> For that our kingdom's earth should not be soiled
> With that dear blood which it hath fostered,
> And for our eyes do hate the dire aspect
> Of civil wounds ploughed up with neighbour's sword,
> And for we think the eagle-winged pride
> Of sky-aspiring and ambitious thoughts
> With rival-hating envy set on you
> To wake our peace, which in our country's cradle
> Draws the sweet infant breath of gentle sleep,
> Which so roused up with boisterous untuned drums,
> With harsh resounding trumpet's dreadful bray
> And grating shock of wrathful iron arms,
> Might from our quiet confines fright fair peace,
> And make us wade even in our kindred's blood,
> Therefore we banish you our territories.
> You, cousin Herford, upon pain of life,
> Till twice five summers have enriched our fields
> Shall not regret our fair dominions,
> But tread the stranger paths of banishment.
>
> (I. iii.125–43)

The king employs a medium of courtly pastoral to demonstrate and condemn the horrors of violence, defining them by constructing contradictory images of the violable and vulnerable. The discourse is both defensive and sanctifying: it privileges the values of peace and security, and demonizes the disorganizing militaristic feudalism (the 'grating shock of wrathful iron arms') that appears to threaten them. The very purity and simplicity of pastoral discourse confer on its pronouncements an apparent innocence of political motive and intention: mystifying and naturalizing certain kinds of power while invalidating others as alien and hostile.[47] Richard's former struggles against the magnates, his disposal of Woodstock, his stopping of the combat, his banishment of the protagonists, are recognized not as power but as a ratification of the natural. Even the act of banishment appears within this discourse not as an exercise of power, but as an appropriate exclusion of the putative source of violence from the domains of tranquillity.

Pastoral metaphor's stress on the deflection of external violence partially obscures the fact that what is being asserted here is *power*: yet the patent artificiality of the discourse renders it self-reflexive, and offers to both cast and audience a purchase on the politics thus ideologically mystified. Courtly pastoral is truly an *absolutist* discourse: it validates existing power as the natural; demonizes as violence whatever attacks existing power from without; and conceals any suggestion that the attribution and evaluation of violence might depend on its own exclusiveness and self-sufficiency. The purity and simplicity of pastoral values preclude any acknowledgement of reciprocal obligations or mutual inter-dependence: it is the product of an imperialist imagination. Above all it is a mechanism of cultural appropriation: the ambiguous royal plural establishes a claim to ownership and personal possession: 'our kingdom's earth' is to be defended against the hostility of the enemy within.

Bolingbroke is as quick to adopt the pastoral style as he had been to engage in chivalric discourse with Mowbray:

>   This must my comfort be:
> That sun that warms you here shall shine on me,
> And those his golden beams to you here lent
> Shall point on me and gild my banishment.
>
>   (ll.144–7)

The egalitarian universality of the sun's bounty is a familiar motif of pastoral romance, as is the embracing of exile as a welcome refuge from a corrupt or intolerable civilization.[48] Pastoral language has more than one dialect, and can be commandeered or appropriated for different purposes. Here Bolingbroke wrests the medium of courtly pastoral from the king, and, invoking some of its more democratic elements, shifts the competition between himself and his king to a more removed ground. At the same time he makes abundantly clear his determination to enter exile rather as the Lost Prince of romance than as a voluntary hermit or trainee rustic: the sun-image is both the universal source of life and a symbol of royal majesty; its beams are temporarily 'lent' to the king, but could perhaps be appropriated to 'gild' (i.e. to to confer royalty upon) Bolingbroke's banishment.

Then England's ground farewell, sweet soil adieu,
My mother and my nurse that bears me yet.
Where'er I wander, boast of this I can,
Though banished, yet a true born Englishman.

                                        (ll.305–8)

The pastoral of exile here puts itself into competition with the hegomonic pastoral discourse of the court: in a bare and unadorned language Bolingbroke claims an authentic heritage from England's maternal 'ground' and 'sweet soil'; and thereby establishes the perimeters within which the great contestation of power between king and nobility is to be enacted.

Just as Shakespeare found in the language of chivalry the grammar of historical conflict, he discovered in the genre of pastoral a range of dialects for articulating contests and competitions for authority, property and status.[49] Bolingbroke's return from banishment (III. i) is accompanied and justified by an invocation of aristocratic identity articulated in pastoral terms; the duke, now acting as dispenser rather than recipient of justice, charges Richard's 'favourites':

Myself, a prince by fortune of my birth,
Near to the king in blood and near in love
Till you did make him misinterpret me,
Have stooped my neck under your injuries
And sighed my English breath in foreign clouds,
Eating the bitter bread of banishment
Whilst you have fed upon my signories,
Disparked my parks and felled my forest woods,
From my own windows torn my household coat,
Razed out my imprese, leaving me no sign
Save men's opinions and my living blood
To show the world I am a gentleman.

                                        (III. i.16–27)

Couched in the formal strategy of baronial opposition, where responsibility for the mishandling of the crown is attributed to the 'evil counsellor' rather than the king himself, this speech defines Bolingbroke's status ambivalently as a personal prerogative ('a prince by fortune of my birth') and as validated by royal proximity of relationship ('near to the king in blood'). In earlier scenes both

Gaunt and York had voiced the self-division of men trapped in the double-bind of contradictory loyalties, to king and to kin (I. ii; I. iii.215–45; II. i.187–208); here Bolingbroke seeks to reconcile those obligations by consolidating a new nexus of power, formed by a restoration of the old cultural sovereignty linking crown with aristocracy. Poggioli defined pastoral as 'an aristocratic dream of personal justice', wherein justice operates not through a system of law but as a benefit graciously granted from on high and gratefully received from below. Sir Philip Sidney saw pastoral as an instrument of pity, the prime mover of personal justice; especially that based on the principle of *noblesse oblige*, which makes of justice not only an aristocratic obligation but also an aristocratic privilege.[50] Bolingbroke often speaks of the law, and invokes both legality and justice in his cause against the king; but the right to execute the favourites can derive only from a reconstructed system of law in which the 'gentleman' has powers comparable to those of the king. In this way Bolingbroke dispenses justice by personal authority in the manner of chivalric or pastoral romance.

Exile has not been for Bolingbroke a pastoral initiation into a simpler life, but a sour humiliation: 'the bitter bread of banishment' expresses the hurt pride of the abased aristocrat who has perforce 'stooped my neck under your injuries'. His return is signified by a symbolic act of cultural reappropriation, repossession of his rights of inheritance: he reclaims those lands, estates, properties and titles, the visible tokens of his 'gentlemanly' status, which have been expropriated by despotic injustice and transferred to the irresponsible opportunism of parasitic 'favourites'. The pastoral language of 'parks' and 'forest woods' is more than a strategy for reclaiming stolen property: it also defines a particular relationship between the individual and the 'land' (both private property and territory of the nation), which in turn affirms a claim to cultural authority, to be followed logically by a bid for political sovereignty. The question at issue is that unwittingly raised earlier by John of Gaunt – who owns 'this England'? Who has the best *de facto* claim on the property of the realm – the acknowledged ruler by hereditary right and dynastic primogeniture; or the aristocrat who proposes to unite crown and nobility in a restoration of the 'happy breed' of an earlier age?

Bolingbroke's feudal pastoral is juxtaposed closely with Richard's corresponding reclamation of England as the personal property of the king:

> I weep for joy
> To stand upon my kingdom once again.
> Dear earth, I do salute thee with my hand,
> Though rebels wound thee with their horses' hooves.
> As a long-parted mother with her child
> Plays fondly with her tears and smiles in meeting,
> So weeping, smiling, greet I thee, my earth,
> And do thee favours with my royal hands.
> Feed not thy sovereign's foe, my gentle earth,
> Nor with thy sweets comfort his ravenous sense
> But let thy spiders that suck up thy venom
> And heavy-gaited toads lie in their way,
> Doing annoyance to the treacherous feet
> Which with usurping steps do trample thee.
> Yield stinging nettles to mine enemies,
> And when they from thy bosom pluck a flower
> Guard it, I pray thee, with a lurking adder
> Whose double tongue may with a mortal touch
> Throw death upon thy sovereign's enemies.
>
> (III. ii.4–22)

The language of this speech echoes Richard's words in the stopping of the combat: the 'earth' of the kingdom is a pastoral *locus amoenus* invaded by alien and hostile violence; anthropomorphized again as a 'child', the earth of the realm is a site of violable innocence 'wounded' by the assaults of militaristic feudalism. There is, however, a great distance between the absolutist monarch who stood with his reluctant council to deliver sentence of banishment from 'our kingdom's earth'; and the strange, eccentric figure who caresses '*my* earth' with intimate maternal tenderness. Once more the king seeks to appropriate the realm by means of a pastoral fantasy: and elements of the pastoral landscape (the 'sweet' and 'gentle earth', of child-like innocence) are still there. But this is a perverted pastoral, invoking and conjuring the hidden evil in the idealized landscape: beneath the serenity of a flower-decorated 'bosom' lurk venomous spiders, adders, stinging nettles, heavy-gaited toads. Previously pastoral was used to mystify and naturalize the realities of power; now the user seeks to discover and extract power from the discourse itself: yet its very nature resists and denies the existence of power. The contradiction is illustrated by Richard's echo of ancient myth: 'these stones [shall/Prove armed soldiers'; but pastoral assures us that its innocent properties can never become instruments of violence or harm. The language Richard once used now begins to use him:[51] the effective power which supported and sustained that absolutist discourse has ebbed away, leaving an empty ideology beached on the shore of history. The primitive magic invoked by Richard's superstitious conjuration is the seed of the divine right of kings: the twin myths of omnipotent sacred majesty and of tragic royal martyrdom develop from these humble beginnings. The stinging nettle of perverted pastoral is to become in other hands the curse of providential punishment upon the Lancastrian kings and their Yorkist successors.

The garden scene draws together chronicle and pastoral, political conflict and landscape of husbandry. It also secures a contradictory *rapprochement* of pastoral and counter-pastoral forms, distinguishing their ideological tendencies and evaluating their respective contributions to the political action. For Richard's queen the garden is a symbolic paradise from which she and her husband are about to be expelled in a re-enactment of the original Fall; and in return for the gardener's communication she attempts to exercise the same primitive magic invoked by Richard, cursing the products of his husbandry:

> Gardener, for telling me these news of woe
> Pray God, the plants thou graft'st may never grow.
> (III. iv.100–1)

The gardener, however, is not an inhabitant of that courtly realm of pastoral fantasy in which the imperialist imagination holds unobstructed sway: his dialect is a counter-pastoral discourse which denies the efficacy of royal magic.

> Poor queen, so that thy state might be no worse
> I would my skill were subject to thy curse.
> (ll.102–3)

This is no landscape of pastoral *otium*: in this garden nothing grows unless it is planted, nothing flourishes unless it is tended; it is a world dependent on the exercise of the gardener's labour and skill.

At the beginning of the scene the queen predicts, on the assumption that she is entering a kind of courtly masque, that the gardeners will 'talk of state'. In fact the gardener talks directly about gardening: political analogies are restricted to suggestive metaphors, and it is the gardener's man who disentangles the threads of metaphor into simile, and explicitly draws the analogy between garden and state. In this way the scene resists incorporation into courtly pastoral, and establishes through the language of counter-pastoral an alternative model of the state: a 'commonwealth' in which a craftsman and his assistants[52] work together to restrain excessive growth and curb the spread of parasitic weeds. Although the language echoes ('sea-walled garden') John of Gaunt's elegiac lament for a lost England of feudal fealty, the gardener's vision is quite different from that realm of 'Christian service and true chivalry' (ii. i.54). The labourers of counter-pastoral comment scornfully though with compassion on the 'idle hours' of wasteful courtly play. Richard was not an effective gardener; Bolingbroke is:

> Oh what pity is it
> That he had not so trimmed and dressed his land
> As we this garden!
>
> (iii. iv.55–7)

> The weeds which his broad spreading leaves did shelter
> . . .
> Are plucked up root and all by Bullingbrook.
>
> (ll.50–2)

From the wisdom of his rural discipline the gardener draws metaphors of 'balance' to express the contractual nature of the political commonwealth:

> Their fortunes both are weighed.
> In your lord's scale is nothing but himself
> And some few vanities that make him light,
> But in the balance of great Bullingbrook
> Besides himself are all the English peers,
> And with that odds he weighs King Richard down.
>
> (ll.84–9)

Counter-pastoral expresses a melancholy but resigned secular understanding of political change. A king rules not by divine right but by hard work and a respect for the mutuality and reciprocal obligations of the 'commonwealth'. Pity is a luxury permissible to humankind but of no concern to nature or history.

In his long process of defeat Richard's imagination occupies what Poggioli called the 'pastoral of solitude', clearly distinguishable from the pastorals of friendship and of love. In Daniel's *Civil Wars* the king looks out from the window of his prison on a pastoral landscape:[53]

> O happie man, Saith hee, that I do see
> Grazing his cattel in those pleasant fieldes!
> O if he knew his good, how blessed hee
> That feeles not what affliction greatness yieldes ....

Like Henry VI, Richard finds his imagination possessed by the possibilities of escape, exile, pilgrimage, retreat to obscurity.[54] Finally, in the internal exile of his imprisonment, Richard establishes the ultimate sovereignty of the mind: like the man who loves islands, in D. H. Lawrence's story, he finds a space small enough to fill with his own personality. Solitary confinement is the culmination of absolute rule; the problems of mutuality and reciprocity no longer exist, as ruler and subjects merge into one solipsistic individual: 'A generation of still-breeding thoughts/And these same thoughts people this little world' (v. iv.8–9). Richard attempts to compare his prison to the world: but he succeeds only in talking about himself. The solipsistic fantasy of the imperialist imagination has finally conquered the world in the only way it can: by annihilating it, and occupying a vacuum of solitude in which the untrammelled ego can exercise uninhibited play. In the process of resisting and opposing the feudal forces of militaristic aggression and dynastic ambition, Richard has also excluded himself from the possibility for social contract offered by that social formation. Regarded from one point of view, that exclusion has all the melancholy lyricism of a personal tragedy; from another, it represents a dramatization of inevitable historical contradictions.

3
Henry IV, Parts 1 and 2

In *Richard II*, the Renaissance historical imagination exercised itself in two distinct and to some degree contradictory modes: one the familiar and easily recognizable discourse of 'chronicle drama', in which putatively 'real' historical events are enacted through a fundamentally mimetic and representational medium; the other a self-reflexive genre which contains, in its dialectic of pastoral and counter-pastoral, an active dialogue between 'realistic' and fantasy forms.[55] As we have demonstrated, the medium of chronicle represents its material in ways analogous to what we think of as legitimate historiography: replaying a vanished past in a dramatic discourse capable of clearly demarcating temporal and spatial distance. The deployment of pastoral genre is not, as has often been argued, an attempt to insert a dimension of the timeless into the turbulent flux of history; nor a medium for representing an essential human nature within a supposedly 'secondary' realm of political events; nor a discourse for validating the authenticity of private experience against the externality of public action.[56] Pastoral forms are employed in *Richard II* to articulate the political conflicts and ideological contestations of a real history.

The tension between representational and fantasy forms is developed in the next two plays of the tetralogy, *Henry IV, Parts 1 and 2*, to a much greater degree. This development is not so much, as we have seen, a strikingly innovative expansion of established forms as a reversion to older methods of dramatizing history founded by the comic and romance chronicle plays of the 1580s. The *Henry IV* plays and *Henry V* certainly maintain this new intellectual perspective on history, preserving and sustaining that remarkable theoretical grasp of historical distance so evident in *Richard II*; but, whereas in the initial drama of the tetralogy the vision of feudal society is a comparatively seamless totality, with only the stylized counter-pastoral of the gardeners to interrupt its historiographical cohesion, *Henry IV* expands the dramatic world to reincorporate the comic and romance genres and to embrace the linked but contradictory worlds of court and tavern, battlefield and highway.

PAST AND PRESENT

As acts of the historical imagination, the *Henry IV* plays offer a range of contrasts with *Richard II*: they are much less firmly attached to the solid *mimesis* of literary historiography, much less dependent on the chronicle sources; they display an infinitely greater liberty of invented incident, and focus intensively on a character – Falstaff – who can be tied to no recognizable historical provenance; and, although the plays are structurally framed by authentic historical events – the rebellion of the Percys and the battle of Shrewsbury, the Archbishop of York's revolt and the deception at Gaultree forest, the death of Henry IV and the accession of Henry V – the plays reveal far less particularity in the depiction and delineation of time and space, far less specificity of historical vision.

The principal effect of this expanded form for our purposes is its enlarged capacity for the juxtaposition of contradictions; and these are not just generic, the incongruities of main plot and sub-plot, or the indiscriminate 'mingling kings and clowns' complained of by Sir Philip Sidney, but an active historical juxtaposition and interrelating of the present with the past. Throughout *Richard II* the dramatic language is that of a reconstructed fifteenth century; in the·*Henry IV* plays current Elizabethan dialects, character-types, sociological phenomena rub shoulders with sharply delineated images of a feudal past. The abiding preoccupation of these plays is war: in *Richard II* war is primarily represented in its chivalric aspects; in the *Henry IV* plays topographical colour and detail are introduced belonging properly to Renaissance practices of warfare. Falstaff's exploitation of the recruiting-system represents a contemporary Elizabethan social abuse; while the duel of Hotspur and Hal derives from the feudal world of *Richard II*, takes place in a rarefied atmosphere of chivalric romance, and enacts the epic convention of a ritualized single combat on which the fate of the action depends.

When Sir Philip Sidney in the *Defence of Poesie* (1595) launched his famous protest against the Elizabethan public playhouse for its irresponsible transgressions of neo-classical decorum, he criticized its liberties with time and space as well as its violation of artistic rules and prescriptions:

For where the stage should always represent but one place, and the uttermost time presupposed in it should be, both by

Aristotle's precept and common reason, but one day, there is many days, and many places, inartificially imagined... you shall have Asia of the one side, and Afric of the other, and so many other under-kingdoms, that the player, when he cometh in, must ever begin by telling where he is, or else the tale will not be conceived... of time they are even more liberal: which, how absurd it is in sense, even sense may imagine, and art hath taught, and all ancient examples justified.[57]

Our preceding discussion of *Richard II* has demonstrated by reference to the play's language its capacity for enacting a genuinely historical vision of the past; but it is important to recall that any historiographical character we attribute to these plays must be of a kind that could have been enacted on the bare, unlocalized platform of the Elizabethan public theatre.

Modern theatrical methods of production depend extensively on techniques for specifying time and place by conventions of costume, setting, stage-design, lighting, music: Renaissance plays of English history are usually located by these methods into the historical period of their action. The Elizabethan public playhouse stage had no such resources: even so patently historical a history play as *Richard II* would have been performed in the customary contemporary costume, without scenery or historical props, on a bare stage whose absence of specific topical or spatial definition must have made 'historical drama' something very different from that to which we are accustomed. An analogy with our own 'modern dress' productions is misleading: contemporary dress for us signifies contemporary relevance, and is most often deployed to suggest that the plays have a continuous universality of application. A more suggestive comparison would be with the theatrical practice recommended by Brecht,[58] who urged that historical dramas should be located at least by costume and props into a dramatic universe of historical specificity, yet gave his characters an incongruously modern language to speak. Brecht's own plays would thus operate on a contradiction between linguistic modernity and theatrical distance. Though actors might visually mime a vanished place or time, the contemporaneity of their language would forbid any mimetic or representational illusion. By means of such incongruous juxtapositions, a play can be pointed at both the past and the present, the historic and the contemporary. In a Renaissance production of *Richard II* there would be an evident discontinuity between contemporary costume on a bare, un-localized stage, and the archaic poetic discourse of feudal chivalry. From this fertile space between present and past significations grow those pluralities of meaning we have identified as 'the play of history'. When the Earl of Essex's supporters asked the Lord Chamberlain's Men to perform *Richard II* on the eve of their abortive rebellion, their design was obviously to point the play's contemporary reference; but the play itself is so obviously concerned with events of the remote past that their object must have been to provoke the contemplation of a historical analogy rather than to treat the play as one of specifically current and topical association: to secure a knowledge of history through difference.[59]

NEW HISTORICISM FOR OLD

In Tillyard's seminal study, the *Henry IV* plays were constituted as a central component of the 'epic' of England: a broad and complex panorama of national life, unified and balanced into a coherent aesthetic 'order' mirroring the political order of the Elizabethan state. The central action of the plays is the education of a prince: the perfect English ruler, Henry V, is shown learning the wisdom of experience, undergoing trials of chivalry and morality, and achieving a perfect balance of character as a preliminary to establishing a perfectly balanced state. The plays are presented as operating between public and private dimensions, linking the formation of a perfect monarch to the unification of England as an ideal kingdom. Tillyard's study thus reproduces the plays as strategies of legitimation: cultural forms by means of which the dominant ideology of the Tudor state validated its moral and political power, through the voluntary intervention and commitment of a loyal and talented subject, Shakespeare.[60]

As we have indicated above, the ideological character of Tillyard's thesis has been thoroughly exposed and demystified, and a new historicism has offered to reconstitute the chronicle plays in different and politically oppositional ways. Leonard Tennenhouse[61] relates the chronicle plays of the 1590s to other genres such as the court masque, and finds in both a common ideological structure: the idealization of state authority. In Shakespeare's history plays, he argues, power is shown to descend not lineally, through blood and legal inheritance, but discontinuously, through power-struggles: political power is seen to depend not on *legitimacy* but on *legitimation*, on the capacity of the contender to seize and appropriate the signs of authority: 'Power is an inversion of legitimate authority which gains possession, as such, of the means of self-legitimation....'[62] Figures of carnival, forms of inversion and misrule, play an important role in these structures, since authority needs to define itself as order against oppositional energies that can be designated as 'disorder'. Henry V's misspent youth as the unruly Prince Hal bestows on him the oppositional character of a contender, a power of challenge to legitimacy; but the conflict enacted in the plays between authority and misrule serves to clarify rather than to interrogate the distinction between legitimate and illegitimate powers:

> The complete king was by birth entitled to the throne, but a youth misspent in low-life activities, at the same time, lends him the demonic features of the contender, a potential regicide, whose power has yet to be legitimized. The various conflicts comprising *Henry IV, Parts One and Two*, by virtue of resembling the vicissitudes of fate, in actuality cohere as a single strategy of idealization . . . the various confrontations between licit and illicit authority in the *Henriad* more firmly draw the distinction between aristocracy and populace even as they overturn this primary categorical distinction.[63]

The methods employed by old and new historicisms could hardly be more distinct: for Tillyard, order and misrule were simply real forces present in the moral and political world of Elizabethan England: Shakespeare's achievement was to designate and distinguish them as ethical categories, and to articulate a model of their appropriate relationship.[64] Tennenhouse regards the plays as constituent elements of a cultural formation in which state power was *producing* the images of its own legitimacy, and *provoking* the oppositional energies against which it could define its own licit authority; and the critic's own political evaluation of the plays is committed to an oppositional exposure of such strategies of legitimation. Old and new historicisms, despite their obvious antagonisms, appear to be in agreement that the capacity of the plays for historical signification derives exclusively from their function within Elizabethan culture and ideology; and that the relationship between dominant and subordinate ideologies within the plays is implicitly an orthodox or conservative one. Tennenhouse acknowledges, in a qualification unthinkable by Tillyard, that this view of the plays as a loyal expression of a dominant ideology is not the only possible interpretation: 'By examining how he includes recalcitrant cultural materials and dramatises their suppression under the pressure of official strategies of idealization, we could identify such a subversive Shakespeare.'[65] But the critic's concern with the general function of the plays within Tudor ideology here overrides his awareness of more radical potentialities.

The questionable premise at the heart of this argument is that the plays were in the Elizabethan theatre (and presumably still are in the available modern forms) capable of securing from their spectators a posture of ideological collusion: Tillyard would argue that the audiences were all instinctively loyal adorers of the Elizabethan state; Tennenhouse that the plays constituted the reception they required by involving the spectators in ritualized strategies of idealization where misrule could function only to validate rule.[66] If the plays are readdressed in terms of the two categories of our title – 'history' and 'play' – it can be shown that they were, and still are, fully capable of resisting such ideological containment and institutional closure.

IDEOLOGIES OF CHIVALRY

Richard II dramatized what could be described as a 'post-feudal' society in conflict, crisis and re-formation: the subsequent plays of the tetralogy enact that same rhythm of collapse and reconstruction. No 'new' society emerges from the demise of the Plantagenet monarchy: each re-formation inherits and preserves from the society it replaces similar historical conflicts and tensions, which then operate to evolve further forms of conflict and contestation. This remains true, as the subsequent chapter will show, even of Shakespeare's presentation of Henry V.

At the opening of *Henry IV, Part 1*, the king is presented with problems of internal strife, 'civil butchery'. Traditional accounts such as that of Tillyard suggest that the civil war originated with the deposition of Richard II;[67] but the plays identify and locate its provenance rather in the great structural conflict of post-feudal

society, the struggle between monarchy and aristocracy. Henry
hopes to restore feudal aggression to its ideal form, the crusade: to
draw contending factions and antagonistic parties into the 'mutual,
well-beseeming ranks' of a nobility united in (his father's words)
'Christian service and true chivalry' (*Richard II*, ii. i.54). But
chivalry, as the opening scene shows, is active nearer home than
the Holy Land, and the exercise of its values is provoking results
quite other than a unified national crusade. The Scottish resistance
to Henry's power is clearly a rebellion: but it is discussed by Henry
and his nobles as a chivalric competition, a sporting passage of
arms:

> WESTMORLAND. . . .
> On Holy-Rood day, the gallant Hotspur there,
> Young Harry Percy, and brave Archibald,
> That ever valiant and approved Scot,
> At Holmedon met, where they did spend
> A sad and bloody hour. . . .
> (*1 Henry IV*, i. i.53–7)

Chivalric virtues are possessed, shared, by treacherous rebel and
loyal retainer alike: and the king celebrates Hotspur, the chivalric
hero *par excellence*, in a language which subordinates political
values to heroic achievement:

> And is not this an honourable spoil?
> A gallant Prize?
> (ll.73–4)

Hotspur is here of course discharging his obligation of military
service as a loyal liege-man; but the king's praise of him, and
corresponding dispraise of his own son, are repeated later in the
play with specific reference to Percy's rebellion:

> For of no right, nor colour like to right,
> He doth fill fields with harness in the realm,
> Turns head against the lion's armed jaws,
> And being no more in debt to years than thou,
> Leads ancient lords and reverend bishops on
> To bloody battles and to bruising arms.
> (iii. ii.100–5)

Hotspur's deeds are celebrated here by the king in a heroic language which blurs and mystifies political realities: for these 'deeds' are after all not chivalric adventures to be validated by an ideology of feudal romance, but acts of resistance and aggression against the legitimate king. Henry's ideological confusion is accounted for in the same speech, where he draws symmetrical parallels between the prince and Richard II, Hotspur and his youthful self:

> As thou art to this hour was Richard then
> . . .
> And even as I was then is Percy now.
>
> (ll.94–6)

In terms of the feudal ideology which prompted Henry as Bolingbroke to resist and depose Richard II, Hotspur's 'military title capital' appears not merely as a heroic distinction of character, but as a qualification for sovereign authority:

> He hath more worthy interest to the state
> Than thou the shadow of succession.
>
> (ll.98–9)

Feudalism tends naturally (as in the German principalities) towards an elective form of monarchy, in which the ablest candidate is supported by the ruling nobility.[68] If the social contract between king and nobles is a *sine qua non* of stable political order, then this method of appointing a ruler provides a more effective guarantee of social cohesion than the dynastic principle of succession by primogeniture. Historically Henry did not claim the throne on an elective basis, invoking rather his descent from Edward III;[69] but the sponsorship and support of the nobility was the material basis of his claim. As a king pushed to power by the support of the nobility, Henry naturally regards a chivalric meritocracy as a valid institution; but, as a king seeking to establish the strength and legitimacy of his own dynasty, he recognizes such values as treachery and rebellion. In terms of the *feudal* dimension of his ideology he acknowledges Percy as a legitimate contender, and dismisses his own son's claims as negligible; in terms of his *monarchical* aspirations he must seek to crush Percy and validate lawful inheritance as a structural principle of the state.[70] Henry remains possessed and dominated by these contradictory ideologies: his consciousness fraught and divided between the monarchical and feudal perspectives which constituted the historical moment of his political career – the baronial challenge, the inversion of legitimate authority, the elevation of a leading opposition aristocrat to sovereign power.

'THE THEME OF HONOUR'S TONGUE'

The contender in question, Hotspur (Harry Percy), is perhaps Shakespeare's most memorable portrayal of the chivalric type. His heroic qualities are firmly established in the play's language – 'gallant', 'honourable', 'the theme of honour's tongue', 'sweet Fortune's minion and her pride' – before he actually appears; but this abstract paradigm of knightly virtues scarcely prepares us for the idiosyncratic earthiness and idiomatic satire of this 'northern youth' who has emerged as unofficial leader of the baronial opposition:

> HOTSPUR. My liege, I did deny no prisoners,
>   But I remember, when the fight was done,
>   When I was dry with rage, and extreme toil,
>   Breathless and faint, leaning upon my sword,
>   Came there a certain lord, neat and trimly dress'd,
>   Fresh as a bridegroom, and his chin new-reap'd
>   Show'd like a stubble-land at harvest-home.
>   He was perfumed like a milliner....
>   (*1 Henry IV*, I. iii.28–35)

Percy draws here on the *Woodstock* tradition of baronial 'plainness' to articulate a familiar antagonism between a provincial-gentry warrior-caste and a court-favoured, bureaucratic, non-military élite. We soon learn, however, that this style is a *persona*, and that Percy is by no means a simple representative of the *Woodstock* tradition – narrating the combat between Mortimer and Glendower, he abruptly shifts from 'plain' demotic satire to lofty heroic epic:

Three times they breath'd, and three times did they drink
Upon agreement of swift Severn's flood,
Who then affrighted with their bloody looks
Ran fearfully among the trembling reeds. . . .

(ll.101–4)

At this point the king is seeking to extract from his own
ideological confusions a firm distinction between 'valour' and
'treachery': Percy's retort is to insist on the self-evident pre-
eminence of heroic values. The colourful epic poem celebrating
Mortimer's bravery transcends in its heroic simplicity all considerations of complex political motive:

Never did bare and rotten policy
Colour her working with such deadly wounds. . . .

(ll.107–8)

The effect of dramatic contradiction is particularly sharp at this
point: for in a sense king and noble are speaking out of different
and antagonistic worlds of language. Hotspur's miniature heroic
poem is a stylized and self-reflexive discourse which offers to the
audience (whether we think of this as the on-stage audience of the
cast, or the audience of the theatre itself) for analysis as well as
appreciation: in other words, we know as we listen that the
meaning and value of such poetry rests in its narrative or theatrical
effectiveness rather than its correspondence with any 'objective'
reality; the auditors or spectators of *Beowulf* or *Star Wars* are not in a
position to question the 'truth' or 'authenticity' of the fiction they
are witnessing. The king speaks here out of a language-world of
stubborn facts and obdurate realities: either Mortimer did fight
with Glendower, or he didn't – no amount of stirring martial
rhetoric and vivid heroic colour can alter the fact. For Percy such
feats of arms belong to the world of heroic epic, not because they
are deeds of a nostalgically regretted bygone age, but because for
him true chivalric action occupies a transcendent realm of self-
validating virtues, quite independent of the tangled complexities of
politics. The king when confronted with such language uttered
from a posture of resistance is forced to deny its validity and to
subject it to evaluation by the criteria of political loyalty and civil
obedience; though his own position is contradictory, since he is
himself a creature of such heroic mythologizing –

WESTMORLAND. . . .
> The Earl of Hereford was reputed then
> In England the most valiant gentleman
> > (2 Henry IV, iv. i.131–2)

– and he remains consistently prone to judge political complexities in terms of the seductive rhetoric of heroic romance. Once
again representational and fantasy forms – this time 'history' and
'epic' – are incongruously juxtaposed to express the specific nature
of historical contradiction.

As we have seen, Hotspur can command more than one poetic
dialect: and in fact his plurality of utterances can exhibit ideological
contradictions analogous to those of the king. Engaged in con-
spiratorial plotting with the senior heads of his family, Northum-
berland and Worcester, Hotspur enters the language of history:

> Shall it for shame be spoken in these days,
> Or fill up chronicles in time to come,
> That men of your nobility and power
> Did gage them both in an unjust behalf
> (As both of you, God pardon it, have done)
> To put down Richard, that sweet lovely rose,
> And plant this thorn, this canker Bolingbroke?
> . . .
> No, yet time serves wherein you may redeem
> Your banished honours, and restore yourselves
> Into the good thoughts of the world again. . . .
> > (1 Henry IV, i. iii.168–80)

The issue of Richard's deposition is seen and judged here in terms
of political morality – the 'nobility' and 'power' of the aristocracy
regarded as synonymous with grave civic responsibilities. Questions of family dignity ('banished honours') are linked with
considerations of political justice ('an unjust behalf'), and the
reputation of the Percy family is evaluated in terms of historical
continuity ('fill up chronicles in time to come'). Prompted, however, by Worcester's Machiavellian temptations ('I'll read you
matter deep and dangerous'), Hotspur lapses into a disengaged
rhetoric of chivalric adventure, in which he himself becomes the
subject of his own epic poetry:

> By heaven, methinks it were an easy leap
> To pluck bright honour from the pale-fac'd moon,
> Or dive into the bottom of the deep
> Where fathom-line could never touch the ground
> And pluck up drowned honour by the locks
> So he that doth redeem her thence might wear
> Without corrival all her dignities . . . .
>
> (ll.199–205)

Political priorities and mundane practicalities are sheared away as Percy's imagination grasps at the transcendent illumination of chivalric honour: the elusive fantasy of self-validating virtue, the vivid romance of self-fulfilling action. This strategic rewriting of feudal ideology as chivalric romance certainly lends an attractive and luminous energy and vigour to the character of Hotspur; but the play never permits chivalric values themselves to become separated from their political basis in aristocratic disaffection and baronial resistance. Hotspur may present them as abstract qualities, but the historiographical vision of the drama always recognizes them as aspects of the ideological formation of a particular social class.

OPPOSITION AND TRANSFERENCE

The king plans his military campaign against the Percys in fundamentally pragmatic terms: the chivalric challenge of Hotspur remains to be taken up by the prince, previously a 'truant' to chivalry, who becomes at the battle of Shrewsbury a model of the feudal virtues, exercised now in defence of, rather than against, sovereign authority. The play is quite explicit in its presentation of this strategy of transference, by means of which the monarchy ritualistically appropriates feudal culture as it eclipses feudal power. From the outset Hal and Hotspur (both properly 'Henry') are regarded as doubles: the king half-wishes that his own son could be discovered a changeling, and Percy proved to be his legitimate heir. The prince exploits that parallelism to his own advantage by promising to exchange identities with Hotspur:

> For the time will come
> That I shall make this northern youth exchange
> His glorious deeds for my indignities . . .
> 　　　　　　　　　(*1 Henry IV*, III. ii.144–6)

In the famous passage in which Vernon describes the battle-array of the loyalist powers, chivalric splendour and heraldic colour have been appropriated to gild the Lancastrian cause:

> All furnish'd, all in arms;
> All plum'd like estridges that with the wind
> Bated, like eagles having lately bath'd,
> Glittering in golden coats like images,
> As full of spirit as the month of May,
> And gorgeous as the sun at midsummer;
> Wanton as youthful goats, wild as young bulls.
> I saw young Harry with his beaver on,
> His cushes on his thighs, gallantly arm'd,
> Rise from the ground like feather'd Mercury,
> And vaulted with such ease into his seat
> As if an angel dropp'd down from the clouds
> To turn and wind a fiery Pegasus,
> And witch the world with noble horsemanship.
> 　　　　　　　　　(IV. i.98–110)

Leonard Tennenhouse comments that here 'figures of carnival ultimately authorize the state as the state appears to take on the vigour of festival'.[71] Cultural forces that have hitherto acted oppositionally to invert and threaten constituted authority are here harnessed into the service of the crown: the energies of carnival and misrule, symbolized by the saturnalian images of May and midsummer, bulls and goats, become identified with the power of the state. In fact the process of transformation enacted here is a more complex one: as the forces of carnival are appropriated they are also transformed, and saturnalian vigour becomes chivalric romance: plebeian bulls and goats are subordinated to aristocratic estridges and eagles, or to the Pegasus of classical mythology; the unruly native energies of May and midsummer are disciplined to the abstract beauty of a 'feather'd Mercury' who exercises, with his 'noble horsemanship', the courteous skills of a chivalric education.

　　Tennenhouse is right to argue that it is very much in the interests

of this state to exploit (or even provoke) resistance from these
various oppositional forces, subversive carnival and feudal disaffection; since in the process of combating and defeating them the
state can appropriate their positive qualities and declare them its
own, just as the primitive tribesman wears the skin of a slaugh-
tered animal. But it should also be recognized that the self-reflexive
art of the play discloses and exhibits the mechanisms of this
process. As Hotspur dies he acknowledges the transference of
honours to his conquerer –

> I better brook the loss of brittle life
> Than those proud titles thou hast won of me...
> (v. iv.78–9)

– and the Prince's elaborate ritual of courtesy exercised towards
Hotspur's corpse explicitly dramatizes the temporary appropriation of chivalric values: the drama lays bare the device by which the
state has not only secured its defences against a dangerous enemy,
but also seized and appropriated that enemy's qualities in a gesture
of self-legitimation.

THE REALITIES OF POWER

The chivalric virtues are not then necessary constituent qualities of
a valid and effective sovereign authority: the plays' historiographical vision presents them rather as ideological constructions held by
a particular social group and available for manipulation by others
in the interests of political expediency. The Lancastrian monarchy
cannot, in fact, dispense entirely with chivalric 'honour' and the
feudal concept of justice, as the career of Henry V will be seen to
demonstrate; but they do not *need* these qualities in order to
exercise power. In *Henry IV, Part 2*, there are no heroic battles,
except in the burlesque form of the combats engaged in by Falstaff
with Pistol (ii. iv) and Sir John Colevile (iv. iii). In place of the
decorous heraldic challenges of *Richard II* and *Henry IV, Part 1*,
there is only the shabby deception and betrayal of the rebels at
Gaultree forest. It has frequently been argued that contemporary
Elizabethan views of warfare could accommodate themselves to
the necessity of duplicity and stratagem.[72] But this act of treachery,
juxtaposed between the chivalric dedication of Hotspur at Shrews-

bury and the stern but punctilious 'honour' of Henry V after
Agincourt, seems subversive of the values elsewhere invoked by
the monarchy in its own self-legitimation.

The conduct of the king's representatives at Gaultree is very
explicitly dramatized as a slippery Machiavellism: the Archbishop
of York's statement of rebel grievances is met with a series of
contradictory responses, including diplomatic concession,
generalized indictment of 'the times', and unqualified dismissal of
all dissident claims:

> WESTMORLAND. Whenever yet was your appeal denied?
> Wherein have you been galled by the king?
> . . .
> There is no need of any such redress
> Or if there were, it not belongs to you.
> . . .
> Construe the times to their necessities
> And you shall say indeed, it is the time
> And not the king, that doth you injuries.
> . . . it not appears to me
> . . .
> That you should have an inch of any ground
> To build a grief on.
> (2 Henry IV, IV. i.88–110)

This self-contradictory mixture of conciliation and denial constitutes a critical indictment of the loyalist cause. Shakespeare
enhances the severity of this sceptical interrogation by bringing
one of the king's sons, Prince John of Lancaster, into the
negotiations, where the sources make no mention of him – thus
specifying explicitly that it is the crown itself, acting through the
royal power invested in its representatives, that commits this act of
'faith-breach':

> HASTINGS. Hath the Prince John a full commission
> In very ample virtue of his father . . . ?
> (ll.162–3)

'I muse you make so slight a question', snaps Westmorland: and it
is Prince John who fraudulently agrees to consider the rebels'
grievances, and who offers them an illusory settlement sealed by
the word and oath of a prince:

LANCASTER. I like them all, and do allow them well
And swear here, by the honour of my blood
My father's purposes have been mistook
. . .
ARCHBISHOP. *I take your princely word for these redresses.*
LANCASTER. I give it you, and will maintain my word . . . .
(IV. ii.54–67; emphasis added)

The rebels' concern with social justice goes with an honest
trusting faith (qualified by Mowbray's scepticism, IV. i.189–96)
which, given the moral bankruptcy of the state, amounts to gullible
naïveté; and the state in turn is prepared to act with absolute
ruthlessness, to dispense with all ideological justifications and rule
by the exercise of strategic duplicity and naked power. Unable to
sustain the struggle to reconcile feudal with monarchical values,
Henry's own divided ideology breaks down; and splits, on the one
hand, into a weary resignation to political imperative, conceived as
irresistible 'necessity' (III. i.93–4); and on the other, into a pathetic
nostalgia for feudal order in his unrealizable dream of a crusade.
His psychological confusion of the geographical 'Jerusalem' –
which could be the location of Christian–chivalric prowess and
self-sacrifice – and the state apartment in Westminster where he is
destined to die (IV. v.235–40), articulates the irony and contradiction of his unhappy reign. Once again it falls to his son Henry to
devise a means of reconciling kingly power with the feudal
ideology of a strong, violent and inflammable aristocracy, and to
unite the divided 'community of the realm' on a foreign battlefield
of chivalric exploit and epic adventure.

THE HISTORICAL IMAGINATION

The assumption that Shakespeare, in company with other Renaissance dramatists and intellectuals, was capable of grasping and
possessing a clear and self-conscious imaginative conception of the
historical identity of a post-feudal society elicits from the chronicle
plays a set of readings different from either traditionalist or post-
structuralist critical practice. In much traditionalist criticism, questions of power are read in the light of moral absolutes, derived
from an imputed ideology of universal providential order; in much

cultural-materialist criticism, they are addressed as complex articulations of an implicit ideological orthodoxy. The historical approach we have outlined suggests that in these plays questions of political power are seen in the illumination of historical distance, and dramatized as elements of a historical process. As long as the plays are conceived as expositions or articulations of an ideology they remain *instruments* of that ideology: power-struggles are seen either as the operations of divine providence or as internally dissonant elements in a strategy of idealization. But if we locate those power-struggles within a specifically realized vision of a unique historical moment, in which historically constituted social groups and historically determined ideologies are shown contesting the grounds of political power, then they become objectively visible *as* power-struggles, and cease to function merely as strategies of legitimation for the Tudor regime. The historiographical vision of the plays creates within them an internal distantiation, which works to subvert and interrogate the rigid ideological problematic of Tudor political orthodoxy. 'The distance which separates the work from ideology embodies itself in the internal distance which, so to speak, separates the work from itself, forces it into a ceaseless difference and division of meanings.'[73]

This approach should be distinguished in two ways from a strong (and in its way admirable) current within traditionalist criticism – emanating from the 1950s, and associated with names such as A. P. Rossiter and Irving Ribner – which offered the first serious qualification to the rigidities of the Tillyard model.[74] Within such criticism a distinction is made between the crude simplicities of ideology and politics, and the freelance disengagement of the artistic sensibility: the supremely-gifted intelligence and sensitivity of a Shakespeare could never have been contained within any generally held world-view. We have not, for reasons suggested above, made the personal qualities of William Shakespeare our subject; and, with no disrespect to the writer's talents or powers, it seems safer to locate the drama's play of ideological contradictions in the heterogeneous and pluralistic field of discourse from which it emerged, rather than to infer superhuman potencies in an 'author' whose name may have been, for all we know, legion. Secondly, all criticism acknowledges, in one way or another, that the plays exhibit and contain contradictions: critical disagreement mobilizes around their origin and provenance, their function and significance, and their aesthetic and political effects. For traditional criticism the drama's containment of contradictions can represent a pre-foreclosed rehearsal of contemporary moral and political conflicts, or the distinctive capacity of the authorial genius to produce aesthetic order out of historical chaos. For post-structuralist criticism the plays reflect and express contradictions, but within a shaping activity which contributed to the formation of contemporary ideology in its global coherence. We argue that the plays do indeed articulate contemporary Elizabethan–Jacobean ideology; but in such a way as to render the operations of that ideology visible:

> What art makes us *see* . . . is the ideology from which it is born, in which it bathes, from which it detaches itself as art, and to which it *alludes* . . . makes us perceive (but not know) in some sense *from the inside* the very ideology in which it is held.[75]

IDEOLOGY AND PLAY

This interrogative disclosure of ideology is guaranteed by the *theatrical* nature of the plays as well as by their historiographical character; particularly if we are prepared to read their language within the grammar of the playhouses that produced them. It is evident from Sidney's critique, and from abundant evidence of other kinds, that the Elizabethan theatre conferred on historical drama an open-ended flexibility and freedom which was recognized as incompatible with the rigid discipline of neo-classical cultural theory. One aspect of this flexibility is that patterned juxtaposition of incongruous elements, 'kings and clowns', historiographical main plot and comic/romance/satirical sub-plot, which has always been recognized as characteristic of the theatrical imagination active in these plays. The relationship between the contradictory elements of such a heterogeneous and pluralistic structure has, however, been the subject of radical division and conflict of opinion. What position do Falstaff and his low-life companions occupy in the moral and political framework of the plays? Are they simply, as Tillyard and other traditionalist critics have argued, subversive elements over which the state must necessarily exercise a ruthless and uncompromising control? Or do they represent, as post-structuralist criticism holds, oppositional energies which paradoxically authorize the state as they challenge and are defeated by its power? It would probably be true to say that most criticism of *Henry IV* has engaged in a critical *processing* of the Falstaff elements to accommodate them into a stable and balanced artistic and political totality. This remains true even of that body of criticism which, drawing on anthropological theory, has attempted to locate Falstaff into popular Renaissance traditions of carnival and saturnalian misrule. C. L. Barber's fine study *Shakespeare's Festive Comedy* argues that Falstaff's function is saturnalian rather than subversive: that, as in the permitted carnival rituals of the ancient and mediaeval worlds, 'misrule' is a device which functions to consolidate 'rule'; but Barber admits that Falstaff represents a force *potentially* subversive, a 'dangerously self-sufficient everyday scepticism' which could conceivably threaten to fracture the allotted perimeters of licensed saturnalian revelry. None the less Barber sees the rejection as the inevitable outcome of the play's testing of Falstaff: 'The result of the trial is to make us see perfectly the necessity for the rejection of Falstaff as a man, as a favourite of the king, as a leader of an interest at court.'[76] A more recent anthropological study of *Henry IV, Part 1*, drawing on the work of René Girard, reaches the same conclusion: the play works in exactly the same way as primitive ritual, enacting a mythical encounter between the 'sacred' sacrificial violence of the state and the illegitimate 'profane' violence of its opponents:

> As the willing captive of drama's most private moments and thus the willing possessor of the secret thoughts and desires of characters in a play, the audience becomes, perforce, a collaborator in the action. That is, the mere fact of silent observation of a ceremony (social, religious, theatrical) compels one into a posture of collusion.[77]

An attitude of ceremonial 'collusion' is one of ideological complicity; and to this argument it is necessary to bring a reminder that the Elizabethan theatre was, of all cultural institutions, the least well-adapted to securing or guaranteeing such unproblematical reception. The theatres themselves provoked and promoted, and the plays themselves contain and transmit, the capacity to induce in an audience what S. L. Bethell called 'multi-consciousness', and what Robert Weimann defines as a 'two-eyed view'.[78] For every strategy of legitimation, the plays provide an alternative strategy of subversion; for every signal inviting the audience to accept the state's self-authorization and suppression of dissent, a contradictory signal encourages the spectator to interrogate the state's motives and purposes, and to 'collude' with its opponents. If we presuppose a theatre and a drama in which conditions of performance were such as constantly to reproduce pluralities of meaning, the effect of the plays is one of *contradiction* rather than *complexity*. Complexity is contradiction contained and positioned in a hierarchy of significance: the complex organic life of a cohesive totality, it enriches without subverting. Contradiction is produced when moral propositions and political ideologies are thrown into conflictive play in a cultural medium active in sustaining and preserving their difference, and as capable of disturbing, provoking and disorienting (Brecht's *Verfremdungseffekt*) as it is of reassuring, reconciling and consoling.[79]

The rejection of Falstaff at the close of *Henry IV, Part 2*, as the long-standing and unreconciled critical debate suggests, is an obvious location of such unmediated contradiction. Does Falstaff simply receive his just deserts, through the voluntary collusion of an audience which ideally would 'no more think of questioning and disapproving of that finale, than their ancestors would have thought of protesting against the vice being carried off to Hell at the end of the interlude'?[80] Or does a complicity in that rejection constitute, as Dipak Nandy has argued, a kind of 'treachery to ourselves', whereby we sacrifice both our admiration for Falstaff as a paradigmatic performer, and our respect for his dissenting satirical wisdom, in the interests of consolidating a narrow and intolerant state authority?[81] The play must and, as long as it remains current, probably always will provoke such contradictory responses, because it embodies the 'play' of an unresolved historical crisis enacted in a medium of interminably unresolved contradiction.

Richard II began with an open conflict between king and aristocracy, an overt contest between contradictory conceptions of law and justice. At the close of *Henry IV, Part 2*, the new king performs a ceremonial ritual of reconciliation (v. ii) in which he makes peace with his brothers as leaders of the loyal aristocracy, reuniting the divided 'community of the realm', and formally submits his power to the authority of the Lord Chief Justice. Such a strategy of appeasement would appear to constitute a final and effective resolution of historical and theatrical conflict. The price of this political settlement, the liquidation of feudal power and the suppression of Falstaff, may seem entirely appropriate and fair. But, since the practical authority of this 'new monarchy' is still *in in potentia*, the contradictions and the anxieties must remain: the end of *Henry IV, Part 2*, is a conclusion in which nothing is concluded, since it offers, in place of a final resolution, a trailer for a sequel, in which both the power and legitimacy of the new regime will be decisively tested:

LANCASTER: I will lay odds that, ere this year expire,
  We bear our civil swords and native fire
  As far as France. . . .

EPILOGUE. . . . our humble author will continue the story, with Sir John in it, and make you merry with fair Katharine of France; where, for anything I know, Falstaff shall die of a sweat, unless already a be killed with your hard opinions . . . .
                           (v. v.105–7; Epilogue, ll. 27–31)

The prospect of an uncertain and potentially problematical future (suggested by the paradoxical associations of 'civil swords', and the anticipated death of Falstaff) expands and complicates the narrative of an uncertain and contradictory past. As the play's unfinished closure turns the audience away from the remote regions of history to the near and familiar of the present, it is with an effect of uncompleted action: whether its focus is on the past or the present, on 1399 or 1599, on the completed struggles of post-feudal society or the tensions of contemporary Elizabethan England, the Renaissance historical imagination conceived of history as a continuity of unresolved contradiction.

4
Henry V

Criticism of *Henry V* offers a striking and unusually wide divergence of opinions: connected, at one level, with the controversial and historically relative character of the ideologies it addresses – patriotism, national unity, the justice of foreign conquest; but rooted, at another level, in the pluralistic discourse of the play itself. Critical responses to the play tended to be wholly positive or wholly negative until modern critics began to reconcile the contradictions into theories of balance, synthesis or dialectic. Accounts of the play would be either celebratory (patriotic, nationalistic, ringing with 'England's glory'); or denunciatory (pacifistic, anti-imperialist, hostile to the 'political' character of the Lancastrian kings). 'There is a noble patriotism in it', wrote the Tory Carlyle in 1841; 'Henry is rash, obstinate, proud, superstitious, seeking after vain renown and empty conquest', said the Liberal Charles Knight in 1849. Henry was to Yeats a 'vessel of clay' (1903); to Shaw 'an able young philistine' (1907); to Sidney Lee 'cast entirely in the heroic mould' (1908). To Una Ellis-Fermor he appeared as 'a monarch, modelled upon the greatest of the Tudors, Elizabeth herself'; to J. H. Walter 'a leader of supreme genius'; to Gerald Gould a 'perfect hypocrite', a man of 'unscrupulous brutality'.[82] The play evidently exists on a site of ideological contestation; and embodies within itself the peculiar coexistence of a brutal, reckless and hypocritically pious warlord with the hero of a patriotic tradition, the 'royal captain of a ruin'd band'.

There is a further dichotomy between these divergent perspectives, in that criticism favourable to Henry tends to locate its substantiating context in Elizabethan history and ideology, regarding him as a portrait of the prototypical Tudor monarch; while criticism hostile to his representation in the play tends to foreground particular contemporary contexts of reception, more or less explicitly articulating the critic's own ideological problematic. The former can span a wide range of critical approaches: the editor of the Arden edition, J. H. Walter, regarded Henry as Shakespeare's ideal king, conceived in terms of the humanistic political thought of the Renaissance; while Zdenek Stribrny, writing a Marxist analysis, none the less concurs with the substantive argument: 'he ... is the new national king, the herald of the Tudor monarchy, which is no longer a monarchy of the old type, but different and necessary'.[83] The latter tends to emerge from historical moments in which the political and military subjects of the play have been problematized by bitter experience: the first full-scale deployment of hostile arguments, by Gerald Gould, appeared in 1918. In the acrid smoke of these necessary controversies, it has been difficult to address with objective curiosity the particular historiographical character of *Henry V* and the nature of its theatrical realization. By examination of the sources, the play's theatrical devices and its treatment of history, it will be possible to demonstrate that *Henry V* is characterized by the same historical distancing and theatrical alienation we have found in earlier plays of the 'Henriad'.

HOLINSHED

One striking peculiarity of that chapter of Holinshed's *Chronicles of England, Scotland and Ireland* which deals with the reign of Henry V is its location: France. We might take this simply as an oddity immanent in the standard Tudor approach to historical writing: after all, Holinshed's chronicle is that of the 'Kings and Queenes of England, in their orderlie successions'. If the history of a country is defined primarily in terms of its monarch, then the king's activities will determine what is the nation's significant history. In the case of Henry V, the history of England ceases to concern England, and becomes an account of military campaigns in France. This temporary transference of a nation's history to a foreign ground was possible only within specific political conditions appertaining to a particular historical moment; and, if we start from the premise that these conditions may have been visible to the author of Shakespeare's plays, we shall recognize that the exporting of English history to France is dramatized in *Henry V* as part of the general historical process of post-feudal society as conceived by the Renaissance historical imagination.

We cannot assume, even in the case of Henry V, that Shakespeare was confronted with the simple task of articulating a unitary historiographical tradition, representing the king as the model of perfect kingship and the epic hero of a great national crisis. Holinshed's respect for Henry V is plain; but his narrative is hardly the sustained and uniform paean of sycophancy we are often led to expect from a propagandist for the Tudor dynasty. Shakespeare's preference for Holinshed rather than Halle as an immediate source may well be connected with the heterogeneity of Holinshed's material, the fact that it is far less firmly shaped and constricted by the 'Tudor myth', far more ready to deliver up those historiographical complexities, ambivalences and contradictions so useful for theatrical exploitation.[84] It is customary, in alluding to the sources of *Henry V*, to quote the famous passage from Holinshed's concluding tribute to the king:

> This Henrie was a king, of life without spot, a prince whome all men loved, and of none disdained, a capteine against whome fortune never frowned, nor mischance once spurned, whose people him so severe a justicer both loved and obeid (and so humane withall) that he left no offense unpunished, nor freendship unrewarded; a terrour to rebels, and suppressour of sedition, his vertues notable, his qualities most praiseworthie.[85]

A careful reader of Holinshed's narrative might well have peered around this abstract paradigm of kingly virtues, and taken note of more dubious details: such as a passage on the same page in which Henry, on his death-bed, protests the purity of his motives in conquering France (a passage not to be found in Halle):

> And herewith he protested unto them, that neither the ambitious desire to inlarge his dominions, neither to purchase vain renowme and worldlie fame, nor anie other consideration had moved him to take the warres in hand; but onelie that in prosecuting his iust title, he might in the end atteine to a perfect peace, and come to enjoy those peeces of his inheritance, which to him of right belonged: and that before the beginning of the same warres, he was fullie persuaded by men both wise and of great holinesse of life, that upon such intent he might and ought both begin the same warres, and follow them, till he had brought them to an end iustlie and rightlie, and that without all danger of Gods displeasure or perill of soul.

Holinshed bestows on the king his traditional honours: the virtuous prince, successful captain and equitable justicer. He also, with characteristic narrative fullness, dramatizes the dying king's conscience circling restlessly around the justice of his only achievement, the conquest of France. More confident in self-justification and self-exculpation than his father, his mind none the less broods, as Henry IV's had brooded, on the unresolved contradictions of legitimacy and power; and, as his father had longed for Jerusalem, Henry V speaks pathetically of his yearning for that 'perfect peace' which he had struggled to attain and establish by incessant war.

Although Exeter in Shakespeare's play asserts to the French king (II. iv.84ff.) that Henry's title to the throne of France has not been 'pick'd from the worm-holes of long-vanished days', it is abundantly apparent from the available sources that it was scarcely a self-evident claim, and it had certainly not been in the forefront of English policy since the reign of Edward III. Edward himself, despite his conquest of France, had not succeeded in his ambition of being crowned king at Paris; and most of the territories ceded to the English at the peace of Bretigny (1360) were liberated before his death, an event which drained the French war of most of its impetus. In 1396 Richard II married Isabella of France and arranged a twenty-eight year truce (though not a peace); and Henry IV made no move against France, being more concerned to placate French anger at the deposition of Richard.

In Holinshed the title to the throne of France is advanced, as it is in Shakespeare, through the 'sharp invention' of the clergy, who are threatened with a Commons bill urging that temporal lands 'devoutlie given, and disordinatlie spent by religious, and other spiritual persons, should be siezed into the king's hands'.[86] It is to deflect this bill that the clergy assert the king's claim to the French crown. The archbishop substantiates the claim by the pedantic and long-winded speech on the 'Salic law' which Shakespeare (I. ii.33–95) versified almost verbatim. That circumstance in itself is unusual enough to suggest an ironical intention: and in both contexts, Holinshed and Shakespeare, the archbishop's conclusion to an interminable and impenetrably obscure jumble of titles and hereditary principles is the obviously satirical 'as clear as is the summer's sun...'. Holinshed does not, it is true, at any point directly question the justice of Henry's claim, or probe the evident ambiguities that lie behind it: the fact that Henry's claim to the English throne was still a matter of dispute; and that, if anybody could claim the throne of France, it would be the descendants of Edward III's second son, the Mortimers. None the less the decision to invade France occurs, in Holinshed, not with a clear, agreed and self-evidently just claim, title or hereditary right; but with a deft piece of political manipulation on the part of the clergy, who would rather have the king ransack France than despoil their territories and possessions: 'Hereby the bill for dissolving of religious houses was cleerelie set aside, and nothing thought on but onelie the recovering of France, as the archbishop had mooved.' In Holinshed the king appears to be convinced by these manipulations: though his decision to invade France is certainly made with precipitation – he does not, for example, wait for a response from the French king to his demands. Shakespeare intensifies this sense of a ruthless determination by having the demand put with an army already in France, suggesting that Henry was predetermined to attack a foreign power and uses the Salic law merely as a pretext.

Holinshed's narrative of the French campaign itself combines the familiar celebration of English heroism and glorification of Henry's virtues, with clear-sighted, detailed and accurate accounts of military manoeuvres, sieges, sackings of towns. Furthermore, the historian's characteristic device of citing alternative sources ('diverse writers') enriches the medium of the narrative with a plurality of perspectives. He describes the taking of Harfleur as a successful military operation: 'The soldiers were ransomed, and the towne sacked, to the great gain of the Englishmen', [87] but then adds an alternative view, which stresses the human cost of military achievement:

> *Some writing of this* yeelding up of Harfleur, doo in like sort make mention of the distresses whereto the people, then expelled out of their habitations, were driven; insomuch as parents with their children, yoong maids and old folke went out of the towne gates with heavie hearts (God wot) as put to their present shifts to seeke them a new abode. [Emphasis added] [88]

The siege of 'Rone' (Rouen) is described from the English point of view, in terms of its strategic problems; but to this account is appended the pitiful details of a human tragedy:

> If I should rehearse (*according to the report of diverse writers*), how deerelie dogs, rats, mice and cats were sold within the towne,

and how greedilie they were eaten and devoured, and how the people dailie died for fault of food, and yoong infants laie sukking in the streets on their mothers breasts lieing dead, starved for hunger; the reader might lament their extreme miseries. [Emphasis added]

Prompted by Holinshed's rhetoric, the reader has no choice but to 'lament' the cost in human suffering of Henry's imperialistic adventure.

RIVAL TRADITIONS

Once again, Shakespeare need have looked no further than Holinshed for the basis of a pluralistic dramatic history. But beyond the works of formal literary historiography there were major generic inconsistencies within the legend of Henry V: in addition to the historico-hagiographical tradition of Henry as the ideal English monarch, there existed a popular comic-romance tradition celebrating the king's unruly youth as the 'madcap' Prince Hal. So sharp were the divergences of perspective between these contradictory reputations that a sudden road-to-Damascus conversion, from subversive contender to 'mirror of all Christian kings', became a necessary element of the mythology. Shakespeare's tetralogy, which combines both traditions, is flanked on the one hand by the pious prince and epic hero of Halle and the loyalist Lancastrian chroniclers; on the other by the rebellious 'roaring boy' of *The Famous Victories of Henry V*, the 'bully king' of Dekker's *The Shoemaker's Holiday*.[89] As we have observed in discussing *Henry IV*, these rival traditions can be understood, and certainly in some ways operated, as complementary opposites: the figure of the unruly prince humanizing the stern model of civic and military virtues; the power of the established king authorized by the distancing of his legitimacy from the libertarian wildness of his youth. But, as we have also demonstrated, in the theatrical and historiographical medium of this form of drama, contraries could be intensified into contradictions, and the serenely balanced totality of ideology fractured and resolved into its constituent disjunctures. In *The Famous Victories* the prince's engagement in immoral and criminal activities is entirely consistent with a character of blasphemous lawlessness. In the 'Henriad', Prince Hal declares at the very outset (*1 Henry IV*, I. ii.190–212) that his purposes are legitimate and opportunist, so that he appears, in his slumming expeditions and carnivals of misrule, much more explicitly an *agent provocateur*, fostering the very disorder from which he will ultimately and formally dissociate himself. In *Henry V*, despite the whipping-out of the offending Adam, the contrary traditions are still operative; but, as Anne Barton has shown, they exist in unreconciled contradiction rather than co-operative conjuncture. Henry's attempt in Act IV to transgress, with the aid of disguise, the gulf between king and subject (see below, pp. 77–9) is actually balked by the obdurate resistance of the social hierarchy, the inflexible contingencies of the political situation.[90]

FORMAL AND POLITICAL UNITY

Critics writing on *Henry V*, from Tillyardian to Marxist, have insisted on the play's 'complex unity'.[91] There is clearly a link between the critical ascription (and the attendant valuation) of aesthetic unity in the drama and the fable of political unity ostensibly achieved within its action. Henry V, according to historical legend, unified the nation; Shakespeare reflected and endorsed that triumph by creating a drama of exemplary aesthetic unity; which in turn reflected the social and ideological unity of the Elizabethan state:

> It is possible that the insistent emphasis on unity in 1. 2.180–213, with illustrations drawn from music, bees, archery, sundials, the confluence of roads and streams, is ... a reflection of Shakespeare's concern with unity of action in the structure of the play.[92]

That 'insistent emphasis', and all the allusions quoted to the symbolism of unity, belong in fact to the speech of one character, author of the 'sharp invention', the Archbishop of Canterbury. Canterbury's speech about the commonwealth of the bees (I. ii.183–220) has naturally been seized on by those concerned to fit the play into the frame of the 'Elizabethan World Picture'. It describes an ideal commonwealth, stratified into diverse functions, ruled by a principle of order – a 'rule in nature'. In the beehive all activities are co-ordinated to one common purpose: the ordered state. Through the perspective of the beehive we receive an image of the human hierarchy – king, magistrates, merchants, soldiers, tradesmen, labourers – going about its everyday business. But what is the exact nature of the analogy with the human affairs of the 'peopled kingdom'? And what has all this to do with war or with France? The archbishop's moralizing foregrounds the value of obedience; but obedience is hardly at issue here – no one has disobeyed, no one indeed has issued any instructions; and Canterbury's sermon doesn't have the kind of oblique focus that Ulysses' speech on 'degree' has in *Troilus and Cressida*. The metaphor of the beehive appears to be a means towards imaginative comprehension of the political and moral structure of the commonwealth; but, as Canterbury's rhetoric slides further away from the human community into the symbolic universe of the beehive, the concrete object of comparison becomes increasingly remote. The metaphor is rather a way of absenting the actual commonwealth and excluding it from debate:

> I this infer:
> That many things, having full reference
> To one consent, may work contrariously.
> As many arrows loosed several ways
> Fly to one mark, as many ways meet in one town,
> As many fresh streams meet in one salt sea,
> As many lines close in the dial's centre,
> So many a thousand actions, once afoot
> End in one purpose, and be all well borne
> Without defect. Therefore to France, my liege.
>
> (i. ii.204–13)

The literal meaning of this is that France can be safely invaded if the state co-operates in a harmonious unity of action. At a deeper level, perhaps, Canterbury has a more elusive meaning: both the crown and the church have achieved what they want here, and the diverse interests of church and state have combined to 'one consent'. By this time we have forgotten, if we ever knew, what the 'one purpose' was: an ideal commonwealth? a rule in nature? obedience? None of these, in fact; but 'France'. France – war with France – has now become the symbol for the unity of the English commonwealth; the integrity of the state is evaluated in terms of united assent to the king's purpose, which is war. War with France thus becomes a touchstone of English order.[93]

IDEOLOGY AND DISSENT

Henry IV described his own reign 'but as a scene/Acting that argument' of civil war. His son is determined to resolve those disharmonies in foreign conquest.[94] The act of transferring England's history to France is a means of absenting the English commonwealth from itself, and staging its self-evaluation in the distanced arena of a foreign quarrel. The play reveals that Henry's policy is a suspension, not a solution, of those problems: his ambition is to suppress and then bury them beneath the glorious monument of an Agincourt. The only other domestic task that faces him is that of ostentatiously extirpating the remaining forces of dissent within England itself.

Halle and Holinshed both relate that the treachery of the conspirators Cambridge, Scrope and Grey came to light on the night before Henry's departure for Calais. Shakespeare begins his scene (II. ii) by suggesting that their treachery is clear and open long before this moment:

> BEDFORD. Fore God, his grace is bold to trust these traitors.
> EXETER. They shall be apprehended by and by.
>
> (II. ii.1–2)

The treachery of the conspirators consists, according to Exeter, simply of the intention to murder Henry for a foreign purse: a contract killing suborned by France. Henry, obviously well-informed of these developments, tricks the conspirators into signing their own death-warrants. They confess that their motive was assassination for gain; but one of them, Richard, Earl of Cambridge, hints at a deeper motive:

> For me the gold of France did not seduce,
> Although I did admit it as a motive
> The sooner to effect what I intended.
>
> (ll.151–3)

The three men arraigned here as traitors – Richard Plantagenet, Henry Scrope and Sir Thomas Grey – actually represent, as Shakespeare well knew, the cause of the deposed Richard II: the surviving elements of that Ricardian faction which continued to operate as a dissenting opposition to the Lancastrian regime, which formed the Yorkist power in the Wars of the Roses, and which succeeded in murdering Henry's son and putting three kings – Edward IV, Edward V and Richard III – on the throne of England. Holinshed, Halle and Daniel all make these points explicitly; and Shakespeare himself had made a retrospective reference to this conspiracy in Henry VI, Part 1 (II. v.82–91).

It is important to consider why this rival claim to the throne (of particular importance in the context of a foreign war undertaken by a king with strong reasons for eclipsing the dubiousness of his *own* domestic claim) should be so obviously suppressed, appearing only in those elusive, obscure words of the Earl of Cambridge. Holinshed follows Halle closely in relating this event:

> This doone, the king thought that suerlie all treason and conspiracie had beene utterlie extinct: not suspecting the fire which was newlie kindled, and ceassed not to increase, till at length it burst out into such a flame, that catching the beames of his house and familie, his line and stocke was clean consumed to ashes. Diverse write that Richard Earle of Cambridge did not conspire with the lord Scroope and Thomas Grey for the murdering of king Henry to please the French king withall, but onelie to the intent to exalt to the crowne his brother-in-law Edmund Earle of March as heir to Lionel Duke of Clarence. . . . Therefore destitute of comfort and in despair of his life to save his children he feined that tale, desiring rather to save his succession than himselfe, which he did in deed; for his sonne Richard Duke of York openlie claimed the crown, and Edward his sonne both claimed it and gained it, as after it shall appeare. Which if King Henry had at this time either doubted, or foreseen, had never beene like to have come to passe, as Halle saith.[95]

Daniel further intensifies the irony and complexity of this historical situation: Henry's 'unsuspicious magnanimity' didn't foresee the subsequent dynastic struggles:

> Or else, how easie had it been to thee
> All the pretendant race t'have laid full low?[96]

Daniel then characteristically expands this generalization by observing that such an enterprise as rooting out the rival line would in practice have been far from easy, and fraught with contradictions:

> Such wrongs are held meet to be done
> And often for the state thought requisite:
> As, when the public good depends thereon,
> When great injustice is esteemed great right:
> But yet, what good with doing ill is won?
> Who hath of blood made such a benefit,
> As hath not fear'd, more after than before,
> And made his peace the less, his plague the more?

The historians were particularly impressed with the *impossibility* of extirpating conflict in such a historical moment, and concerned to foreground the contradictions underlying Henry's apparently totalitarian rule. In Shakespeare Henry has evidently succeeded in narrowing all political problems of the realm to a single focus, and in subjecting all questions of loyalty and opposition to the single criterion of the Anglo-French conflict. If Englishmen are not wholeheartedly with Henry, they can be so for only one reason – complicity with France. The king has secured such complete ideological control over his society that the rival claim to the throne, and all its attendant historical contradictions, evaporate. The Earl of Cambridge is silent about his dynastic motives so as to cover for his family; but his reply appears to comply with Henry's hegemonic ideology. In fact, of course, this appearance of a state completely purged of all internal opposition, all dissent suppressed and complete loyalty guaranteed, is an illusion: but an illusion to be cultivated by a king determined to make his mark in history as the perfect ruler of a perfected kingdom.[97]

THE CHORUS AND EPIC THEATRE

The play's representation of the possibilities for unity in history is thus double-edged, discontinuous and contradictory. No success ful resolution of historical contradictions is dramatized in the play; and, if we turn our attention to the theatrical qualities of *Henry V*, we shall find that the imaginative unification and aesthetic closure regarded as indispensable to a successful work of art are in fact breached by an internal dialectic, which interrogates the ideology of national unity and demonstrates the distance between artistic resolution and political pacification. The primary instrument of this

method is the device of the Chorus, employed in this play with a
uniquely systematic comprehensiveness. William Hazlitt was the
first critic to recognize the link between this innovative theatrical
method and the historiographical character of the play: like the
Chorus, his argument dwells on the distance between theatrical
representation and historical actuality, and foregrounds the possibility of contradiction between them.

> Henry V, it is true, was a hero, a king of England, and the
> conqueror of the king of France. Yet we feel little love or
> admiration for him. He was a hero, that is, he was ready to
> sacrifice his own life for the pleasure of destroying thousands of
> other lives; he was a king of England, but not a constitutional
> one, and we only like kings according to the law; lastly, he was a
> conqueror of the French king, and for this we dislike him less
> than if he had conquered the French people. How do we like him
> then? We like him in the play. There he is a very amiable
> monster, a very splendid pageant. As we like to gaze at a
> panther or a young lion in their cages at the Tower, and catch a
> pleasing horror from their glistening eyes, their velvet paws,
> their dreadless roar, so we take a very romantic, patriotic and
> poetical delight in the boasts and feats of our younger Harry, as
> they appear on the stage and are confined to lines of ten
> syllables; where no blood follows the stroke that wounds our
> ears, where no harvest bends beneath horses' hooves, no city
> flames, no little child is butchered, no dead men's bodies found
> piled in heaps and festering the next morning – in the or-
> chestra![98]

This foregrounding of dramatic conventions and theatrical experience – 'as they appear on the stage and are confined to lines of ten
syllables' – acts on the spectator like the bars on a wild beast's cage,
transforming the nature of his experience: converting fear to
pleasurable wonder, hatred to admiration and excitement. Hazlitt
takes it for granted that a modern audience could not admire this
kind of king or this kind of play in terms of any current public
morality: the audience's pleasure is therefore independent of moral
sentiment. He is not speaking, though, about a suspension of
moral judgement in the liberating fantasy of the theatrical experience, as his metaphor of the caged animal makes clear: we don't
forget how dangerous a caged panther really is; nor do we forget

(the play prevents it) that this king is, by post-Civil War standards, a reckless warlord, the son of a usurper, and a brutal imperialistic conqueror. We don't forget, while watching the play, that somewhere else a harvest is trampled, a city burns, a little child is butchered. It is precisely because we know the reality and power of these things that we watch them being trapped in theatrical conventions, confined to the medium of art, with such fascination, horror and delight. The king may be, in Hazlitt's excellent phrase, an 'amiable monster', but a monster he remains.

The bars on a wild beast's cage are evident tokens of its confinement and of our safety; we see them, and we see it through them. Dramatic conventions are not, as a general rule, so overtly displayed and laid bare: but in *Henry V* they are as visible as those cage-bars. The Chorus continually exhorts the audience to supply, by a sustained imaginative participation, the topographical colour and realistic detail necessary to provide the drama with a historical location:

> Can this cock-pit hold
> The vasty fields of France? Or may we cram
> Within this wooden O the very casques
> That did affright the air at Agincourt? ...
> . . .
> ... let us, ciphers to this great accompt,
> On your imaginary forces work.
> Suppose within the girdle of these walls
> Are now confin'd two mighty monarchies
> . . .
> Piece out our imperfections with your thoughts ....
> (Prologue, ll.11–23)

And these directives have usually been accepted at face value, as defensive, apologetic and ashamed of the Elizabethan theatre's poverty of resources. *Henry V*, it has often been suggested, is truly an epic rather than a dramatic play, and the Chorus can only lament, from the bare boards of an unworthy scaffold, the absence of space, pictorial decor and narrative scope proper to the epic form.[99] More recent criticism has taken a more positive view of the device, seeing it as a strength rather than a weakness of the Elizabethan playhouse, in its capacity to provoke active imaginative involvement from the spectator. Gary Taylor writes, the great speeches of the Chorus – like those of Henry – consist largely of excitations to extraordinary effort ('Work, work your thoughts!'), combined with narratives of great geographical, temporal and emotional sweep. . . . Such narratives are no more 'undramatic' than Clytemnestra's great description of the beacons which brought her news of the fall of Troy: instead, like the imperatives to imaginative effort, they directly convey a sense of the packed energy and strength of purpose which overcomes the inertias of time and space. Shakespeare makes the energies of audience and cast express and suggest the magnitude of an historical achievement . . . . [100]

In fact the chorus achieves quite the opposite effect: rather than using the platform of the stage to adumbrate a historical actuality, it calls the attention of the audience away from the dimension of history to a focus on the physical conditions of the theatre itself, foregrounding the artifice of the drama's construction. The 'vile and ragged foils' which would normally be acceptable to the audience as signifiers of the broadswords of Agincourt, become visible as theatrical props; the 'wooden O' which could readily, by means of the conventions contracted between actors and audience, be imagined as the space of a historic battle, resolves instead into the space of a theatre. If the play is 'epic', it is so not in the Homeric but in the Brechtian sense: it does not seek to absorb the spectator completely into a self-sufficient dramatic experience, in which he/ she is lost in an intense empathic identification with the triumphs and sufferings of the epic hero, but rather seeks to cultivate in the spectator, by the use of 'alienating' dramatic devices, an attitude of critical detachment and objective curiosity. Of course both modes of attention are involved, as they are in Brecht's own plays: but the excitement of empathy takes place within a context of heightened and stimulated critical awareness. Just as there is no effective affirmation of the possibilities for political unity in the state, there is no seamless and self-contained aesthetic unity of the dramatic structure: each reinforces in the other an effect of discontinuity and contradiction.

CHORUS AND ACTION

The most 'epic' of the choruses is that opening Act IV. In a
typically paradoxical conjuncture, a vivid poetry of action is used
to describe a moment of *in*activity – the tense stillness of the long
night before Agincourt, the vague sounds and flickering lights of
military preparation. In another subtle image for the nature of the
drama, the Chorus sites itself in an imaginary no-man's-land, an
empty space about to be filled with the drama of history. From that
perspective the Chorus distinguishes, in traditional fashion, between the 'confident and over-lusty French' and the 'low-rated
English', who wait in melancholy dejection 'like sacrifices' for the
apparently inevitable defeat. Against this sombre background the
figure of Henry appears in the full splendour of a heroic myth:

> O, now, who will behold
> The royal captain of this ruin'd band
> Walking from watch to watch, from tent to tent,
> Let him cry, 'Praise and glory on his head!'
> For forth he goes and visits all his host,
> Bids them good-morrow with a modest smile,
> And calls them brothers, friends and countrymen.
> Upon his royal face there is no note
> How dread an army hath enrounded him;
> Nor doth he dedicate one jot of colour
> Unto the weary and all-watched night;
> But freshly looks and overbears attaint
> With cheerful semblance and sweet majesty;
> That every wretch, pining and pale before,
> Beholding him, plucks comfort from his looks.
> A largess universal like the sun
> His liberal eye doth give to every one,
> Thawing cold fear, that mean and gentle all,
> Behold, as may unworthiness define,
> A little touch of Harry in the night.

> (IV, Chorus, ll.28–47)

The proffered image is, of course, irresistible: it is impossible *not*
to admire courage in the face of desperate odds, the gaiety and
insouciance of a truly brave leader, the sense of fraternity and a
common bond with the common soldiers; above all the *equality* of

Henry's leadership, the generosity of feeling extended to 'mean and gentle all'. Richard II sought to define 'majesty' exclusively in terms of the king's person; for Henry it is a quality that can be shared and experienced by every participant in the battle. Beyond the battlefield itself, if Henry's political ambitions can be realized, the majesty earned by the heroic 'ruin'd band' is to be transferred, to the corporate body of the English nation.

The action of Act IV, far from sustaining or substantiating this impressive prologue, subjects the heroic vision of Henry and his army to an intensive interrogation. Act IV is a sustained development, facilitated by the dramatic device of the king's disguise, of the themes of equality and national unity propounded by the Chorus. In appearing as a common man, Henry is able both to enact the ideology of egalitarian majesty *and* to disclose the distance between these pretensions and the real inflexibility of social relations in the army and the nation the king is attempting, in his own body and in his dual role as captain and king, to identify.

Equality is first invoked in a comic way by Pistol's question to the disguised king:

> Art thou officer?
> Or art thou base, common and popular?
> (IV. i.38–9)

Pistol's ornate compliments to the (apparently absent) king recall, inevitably, Falstaff; the phrase 'imp of fame' was used by Pistol in the very moment of Falstaff's rejection (2 *Henry* IV, v. v.42). This blunt, soldierly king will have no truck, perhaps, with flattery and compliment, susceptibility to which was the characteristic vice (in the Lancastrians' eyes) of Richard II. On the other hand, the echo of Falstaff's rejection here[101] specifies the limited nature of Henry's egalitarianism: the comic, subversive characters are kept firmly at a distance by political shrewdness and frigid, ascetic self-control. Pistol is a particularly dangerous character in this respect, since his actions and his language so persistently and precisely parallel those of the king. Pistol and Nym brawl over the hostess (II. i) as Henry and the French king fight over Katharine; Pistol accompanies the army to France 'to suck, the very blood to suck' – an image which comments on the main action by its combination of suggestions: parasitism, to live by blood-letting, the claim of 'blood' which supports the whole bloody enterprise. He extracts a rich ransom from a French soldier by violent threatening, the method Henry uses to win Harfleur; and his ludicrous rhetoric parodies too accurately Henry's militaristic speechifying, his Marlovian megalomania Henry's insatiable ambition.

The theme of equality is then developed fully in Henry's conversation with the three soldiers Bates, Court and Williams. From the security of his disguise, Henry asserts the essential humanity of the king's person: 'I think the king is but a man'. Bates's cold truth, however, penetrates the armour of the king's disguise: *this* is how an ordinary man, who is not a member of any chivalric or aristocratic elite, feels on the night before a battle:

> BATES. He may show what outward courage he will, but I believe, as cold a night as 'tis, he could wish himself in Thames up to the neck. And so I would he were, and I by him, at all adventures, so we were quit here.
>
> KING. By my troth, I will speak my conscience of the king. I think he would not wish himself anywhere but where he is.
>
> BATES. Then I would he were here alone. So should he be sure to be ransomed, and a many poor men's lives saved.
>
> (IV. i.110–18)

Bates's interrogation of Henry's purposes and of the whole expedition offers to the audience an alternative position of intelligibility: in which it becomes possible to question the moral justice of the king's quarrel, the political value of military success; and even to glimpse in embryo a democratic pacifism affirming that kings should fight their own battles rather than involve their peoples in bloody war. Bates argues that the king's quarrel is so entirely the king's responsibility that the soldiers who die in it are absolved of their guilt: 'If his cause be wrong, our obedience to the king wipes the crime of it out of us' (ll.126–8). Henry vigorously denies this suggestion, characteristically exculpating himself of moral responsibilities which are clearly his. His arguments may be theologically convincing, but they certainly don't convince Williams, who continues to refuse Henry's egalitarian ideology of a nation organically bound into cohesive unity by a national quarrel with a foreign enemy; and who evidently recognizes the argument as a displacement of the problem, from the hierarchical realm of history to the levelling kingdom of death. When Williams' insistence on the essential *in*equality of king and common man becomes unanswerable, Henry finds himself pushed into a different kind of quarrel – the very kind he has no wish to see: a civil conflict between Englishmen, an internecine opposition between subject and king.

After the departure of the soldiers, Henry is able to relapse in soliloquy into his true royal identity, and to disclose his real ideology. Kingship is a heavy responsibility, accompanied by external signs of rank and power, unreal compensations for the 'hard condition' of greatness. By contrast the king's subjects, signified throughout by terms of aristocratic contempt – 'fool . . . wretched slave . . . peasant' (ll.255–72) – live in bestial contentment. This paternalistic diatribe against the common people is a response to the uncomfortable common wisdom of the soldiers: against which Henry defends himself by identifying it as ignorant prejudice rooted in the 'gross brain' of the contemptible 'peasant'. The soldiers themselves are hardly, in practice, immune from similar anxieties; and they scarcely benefit from the king's 'peace'.

NATIONALISM AND CHIVALRY

Henry's egalitarianism seems to represent, in the theatre at least, an effective challenge to the pre-eminently feudal ideology of war still dominant in the French camp. The French think only of the exploits and honour of their nobility, and regard their common soldiers as 'superfluous lackeys' (IV. ii.26). Henry seeks to unite his nation by incorporating his common soldiers into the majesty of the realm: the earnest democratic heroism of his language differs strikingly from the chivalric vaunting of the French nobles. And yet, what is the ground of this national unity?

> We few, we happy few, we band of brothers.
> For he today that sheds his blood with me
> Shall be my brother; be he ne'er so vile
> This day shall gentle his condition.
>
> (IV. iii.60–4)

The victors of Agincourt are to belong, not to a united nation, but to a crack military elite: the dissolution of hierarchy is envisaged

only within the embattled ranks of an army, the ideal commonwealth invoked by a universalization of the heroic language of
chivalry. This is a reconstruction of feudal ideology, not a genuine
nationalism; the only ground for this unity of the English nation is
the field of battle. 'England' is defined simply in terms of this army:
the 'few', the 'band of brothers' whose occupation is to fight and
kill. England is united only ideologically, in a spurious cohesion
achieved by the channelling of feudal action into foreign war. The
Welsh, Scottish and Irish officers obviously symbolize some
political act of union: but they are professional fighting men, who
talk only of war; they can hardly be held to represent a united
kingdom. The theatre is the ideal medium for the representation of
such an image of union, since a small group of characters can
symbolize a nation as well as they can symbolize an army. But a
theatre which draws attention to the ideological character of its
own dramatic strategies can disclose the ideological character of
the social reconciliations it enacts. While the spectator can be
excited by the fighting camaraderie of this heroic body of men, the
play insistently reminds him that such camaraderie of the battlefield can signify the unity of a nation only in a limited, temporary
and essentially unreal sense.

It is a nation, for one thing, composed entirely of men. There are
only three women in the play: Mistress Quickly, now Pistol's loyal
wife; the French Queen, a diplomatic extension of her husband;
and Katharine the French princess. Katharine's function is that of
an object of value in a political strategy: her father offers her to
Henry as a placatory ransom before the siege of Harfleur (III,
Chorus, ll.29–30). Henry himself makes a display of wooing her
with soldierly bluntness; but he regards her crudely as an object of
his ambitions, and his language continually identifies her with the
treaties, territories and titles that are his supreme preoccupation
(v. ii.95–7, 168–70, 305–7). It is particularly appropriate that the
self-reflexive medium of the Elizabethan drama should have been
employed to interrogate this militaristic and patriarchal ideology,
since Elizabethan dramatic convention excluded women from the
stage as firmly as they are excluded from Henry's chivalric 'band of
brothers'.

Even within the strategic cohesion of the military unity, Henry's
ideology is still too firmly attached to the values of the feudal
aristocracy to become a genuine national sovereignty. The slaughter of the French prisoners, which aroused some conflicting

sentiments in Holinshed's narrative, is presented in *Henry V* with
all the ambivalence of theatrical and historical contradiction.
Gower and Fluellen (IV. vii) assume that the massacre is a reprisal
for the killing of the boys guarding the English luggage train. In
fact, we know from the previous scene, Henry knew nothing of
this when he gave the order: a command which seems rather to
arise out of Exeter's romantic and sentimental account of the
deaths of York and Suffolk. The chivalric language of *Richard II* and
Henry IV, Part 1, returns with vehemence as two noble warriors,
dying in their own noble blood, seal a final knightly *Blutbrüders-
chaft*: 'brave soldier ... honour-owing wounds ... The noble Earl
... in this glorious and well-foughten field/We kept together in our
chivalry ... with blood he seal'd/A testament of noble-ending love'
(IV. vi.7–27).

Henry's response of intense personal grievance and swift
ruthless reprisal manifest him to be, not a consummate military
strategist, but an incurable adherent of feudal and chivalric
values. In performance IV. vi was obviously designed to end on a
note of grim parody: the Quarto text keeps Pistol present throughout this scene, permitting him as the royal train departs to advance
and deliver to the audience a suitably bloodthirsty 'Coup' la gorge'.
Opportunistic criminal and chivalric prince are brought close
together in a gesture of identification omitted by almost all editors
as a piece of irrelevant 'stage business'.[102] When Henry reads the
list of those killed on the English side he names only those with
titles, from duke to esquire. The list of dead contains 'none else of
name'; though it might have contained, among those nameless
common soldiers, Henry's companions of the previous night,
Bates and Court, whose names he never sought to know.

Recent criticism of *Henry V*, though conscious of its potentiality
for producing pluralities of meaning, and aware also of its strongly
negative and satirical dimension, none the less insists on retaining
the option for a positive view of its heroic ideology. Norman
Rabkin refers to Henry's language of chivalry, camaraderie and
national unity as 'stunning rhetoric', which 'almost literally moves
us'.[103] The persuasive effect of this rhetoric is not, apparently,
dispelled by the hearer's awareness of it as rhetoric: Rabkin quotes
Michael Goldman –

We are thrilled because he is brilliantly meeting a political

challenge that has been spelled out for us ... it is a moment
when he must respond to the unspoken needs of his men, and
we respond to his success as we do when a political leader we
admire makes a great campaign speech: we love him for his
effectiveness.

This argument assumes a degree of prior commitment, a
predisposition to empathy: what would the listener's response be
if he were a member of another party? What loyalty hears as
eloquence, criticism perceives as rhetoric; and, though critical
consciousness of rhetoric is not incompatible with a responsive
excitement, a rhetoric which declares itself – especially where
fundamental ideological differences are possible – cannot guarantee its persuasive effect on the listener: as anyone whose nation has
recently been involved in war will readily acknowledge. Shakespeare's dramaturgy in *Henry V* is like that of Brecht: it promotes
admiration, yet places obstacles in the path of spontaneous
identification; it induces empathy *and* objectivity, but not in a
mutually cancelling relationship, since the objectivity is a way of
self-consciously perceiving the empathy. The spectator thinks
feelingly, and feels with thought.

> Epic theatre ... derives a lively and productive consciousness
> from the fact that it is theatre ... elements of reality ... are not
> brought closer to the spectator but distanced from him. When he
> recognizes them as real conditions it is not, as in naturalistic
> theatre, with complacency, but with astonishment.... In one
> who is astonished, interest is born.[104]

The interest born from Shakespeare's drama is rooted equally in
self-conscious historiography and self-reflexive dramaturgy: in that
dialectical *rapprochement* of chronicle and theatre we have designated the 'play of history'.

Part Two
The Tragic Romances of Feudalism

JOHN TURNER

5

Prologue: From Chronicle History to Tragic Romance

Although Shakespeare's interest in the poetry of feudalism waned after the completion of the second tetralogy, it revived with the accession of James; and now his chosen dramatic form was that of tragic romance. The chronicle histories had explored the ideology of feudalism within the context of the mediaeval struggle for power between king and aristocracy; but it had never become dominant in the plays because Shakespeare had never imagined a society existing solely within the single state of a feudal formation. Hence our description of the world of the Histories as 'post-feudal'. With *King Lear* and *Macbeth*, however, this changes. Here we find the poetry of feudalism as it might once have been lived. There is a new inwardness to the poetry here, a new metaphoric richness which is Shakespeare's attempt to re-create the totalized world-view implicit in the concept of the feudal bond.

The sovereign reason for Shakespeare's revival of interest in feudalism was the language in which the new king liked to see himself. For again and again James had urged upon his subjects the nature of the bond that should bind them together: 'as yee owe to me subiection and obedience: So my Soueraigntie obligeth mee to yeeld to you loue, gouernment and protection'.[1] These last are the responsibilities of power that a tyrant neglects; and, because Lear and Macbeth similarly neglect them and come to unhappy ends, the plays have often been seen – surely inadequately – as 'courtly compliment'[2] to James and 'expedient affirmation'[3] of the rights that he claimed. Yet in fact James's understanding of the nature of his own power, schooled in the feudal constitution of Scotland and flattered by personal dreams of absolutism, had already provoked great hostility in England, as Shakespeare certainly knew. James had spelled out his ideas at length in *The Trew Law of Free Monarchies*, with its finely inappropriate subtitle *The Reciprock and Mvtvall Dvetie betwixt a Free King, and his Naturall Subjects*:

85

the whole subiects being but his vassals, and from him holding all their lands as their ouer-lord, who according to good seruices done vnto him, chaungeth their holdings from tacke to few, from ward to blanch, erecteth new Baronies, and vniteth olde, without aduice or authoritie of either Parliament or any other subalterin iudiciall seate.[4]

These absolutist claims had not been tempered when James addressed his English parliaments, and it is not surprising that they brought him into collision with those members of the bourgeoisie, gentry and aristocracy whose interests were protected by the customs of common law and parliamentary prerogative. It was a collision which could not but draw attention to the cultural differences between the two kingdoms that James was trying to unite, the fact that (in Perry Anderson's words) 'two radically distinct polities were now combined under the same ruling house'.[5] It had been the clash between *droit écrit* and *coutume* in France that had prompted the researches of legal scholars into the origins of feudal law;[6] it was to be the clash between Irish and English law that would prompt the researches of Sir John Davies;[7] and it is my argument here that it was the clash between James's essentially mediaeval Scottish thought and that of the English constitutionalists that prompted Shakespeare's own particular kind of research and led him to explore the imaginative potential of the language used by James – an oddly inappropriate, old-fashioned rhetoric it must have seemed too, belonging to another time and place, intended to promote an absolute monarchical power which had in fact already been long retrenched in England by the Commons.

King Lear and *Macbeth*, that is, are plays about national origins, written in an age when 'discussion of political origins played a crucial and distinctive role in the political thought'.[8] They are plays recognizably about the prehistory of their Jacobean present, about that early feudal world whose ideology and social formations were still residually present in Jacobean Britain. This category of 'early feudal' is, of course, mine not Shakespeare's; for, despite the impressive scholarly achievements of sixteenth-century continental jurisprudence,[9] the category of feudalism does not seem to have been known in Britain in 1605. The only exception to this that I know is to be found – in Latin – in Sir Thomas Craig's *Jus Feudale*, a work born out of study on the continent, devoted to an analysis of

Scottish law and published with a dedication to James in 1603. I use the term 'feudal', therefore, not in its technical legal sense but with a broader application to describe a society bonded together in a pyramid of personal reciprocity of duties and rights; and I call the worlds of these two plays 'early feudal' not to make a clear distinction between them and the world which Shakespeare himself inhabited but rather to suggest their relationship to it within a changing continuity. It is a relationship rather like that between the Western film and contemporary North American society. Shakespeare has imagined worlds of kings and barons, without legal, ecclesiastical or parliamentary structures, without merchants, artisans or labourers – without all those classes of people whom he imagined for the chronicle histories or the Venetian plays. For he is not now experimenting with chronicle history. Drawing still upon chronicle history but treating it with a new freedom that in itself constitutes part of his meaning, he is writing tragic romance. Reworking powerful familiar tales of national origins, he is exploring the might-have-been of historical fact, the imaginative potential of language still residually alive, in order to bring fresh light to bear upon the present.

For the plays are Shakespeare's elegiac response to what Keith Thomas has called the sense of 'the decay of the old social bonds',[10] in a new age which Robert Burton was to describe thus: 'Our *summum bonum* is commodity, and the goddess we adore *Dea Moneta*, Queen Money.'[11] Of the men of this new age Burton wrote, 'no charity, love, friendship, fear of God, alliance, affinity, consanguinity, Christianity, can contain them, but if they be anyways offended, or that string of commodity be touched, they fall foul'.[12] *King Lear* and *Macbeth* explore earlier, seemingly more generous cultures in the idealized poetry of their ideology; but they explore them too in the fallibility of their material praxis, tracing the inner contradictions that led to their passing-away. Moreover, they re-enact this historical failure as theatrical experience, so that their audience might live through it during the course of each performance and turn away at the end into a world which seems to be continuous with that of the play's last scene. The plays, we might say, *produce* the contemporary world in the tragic loss and the subsequent anti-climax of their conclusions. They are in this much more than kingly compliments; in their complex seeing, in the interplay which they make possible between past and present, they do much more than flatter James. They are tragic elegies for worlds that never were, but their romance never loses its hold upon the real; in their exploration of the might-have-been of feudalism, they provide an idealized vision of property, community and power which, despite the inevitable collapse of the social formation that sustained it, continues still today to hold a mirror up to the denatured world that has succeeded it.

6

King Lear

In what time and place did Shakespeare set *King Lear*? The question, despite its seeming innocence, has provoked quite incompatible replies. Hazlitt thought the play set in 'barbarous times, in which alone the tragic ground-work of the story could be laid';[13] and most critics today, mindful of its uncertain gods and savage men, would acknowledge a measure of truth in the claim that Shakespeare imagined a pre-Christian Britain for *King Lear*. Alternatively, however, the play is held to be set in a Christian mediaeval England, even to show (in Danby's words) 'the feudal state in decomposition'[14] before the competition of emergent capitalism; and again most critics, mindful of its Christian imagery and gracious heroine, would agree that Shakespeare gave to his story a more recent setting than he found in his chronicle sources. How is the play to be produced? Bearskins or armour? The apparent incompatibility of these two readings, both equally justifiable and equally controvertible from the various texts of the play,[15] has given rise to those uneasy charges of anachronism that have always hovered around *King Lear* with peculiar persistence. Tolstoy put it most directly: 'The action of *King Lear* takes place 800 years B. C., and yet the characters are placed in conditions possible only in the Middle Ages . . . .'[16] Dr Johnson had been able to excuse this same incongruity between 'the barbarity and ignorance of the age to which this story is referred' and 'the idea of times more civilized, and of life regulated by softer manners' only by citing Shakespeare's general habit of anachronism: 'he commonly neglects and confounds the characters of ages, by mingling customs ancient and modern, English and foreign'.[17] Yet, as we have just seen in our study of the second tetralogy, Shakespeare could be historically precise when he wanted to be; and it will no longer do, we believe, to appeal to the 'illogical syncretism'[18] which he is supposed to have shared with his age to answer the questions that surround the setting of *King Lear*.

What, then, was Shakespeare up to? For clearly it is a matter of design that, as Rosalie Colie puts it, the play's action should be so 'mysteriously sited both in time and in place'.[19] W. W. Greg had already observed in 1940 that Dover was 'the only place mentioned in *King Lear* as connected with the action',[20] and guessed that such deliberate vagueness was Shakespeare's attempt not to impede the rapidity of his plot with the material particularities of time and distance. Earlier still, Bradley had lamented Shakespeare's indefiniteness but had been more than compensated by the universality which consequently he believed inherent in each incident of the play: 'This world, we are told, is called Britain; but we should no more look for it in an atlas than for the place, called Caucasus, where Prometheus was chained by Strength and Force and comforted by the daughters of Ocean....'[21]

And here is yet a third answer to our opening question, seemingly transcending the contradictions between the other two: the arena of *King Lear* is the no-time and no-place of myth. Yet this account too will not quite do; for, although the business of the play *is* with myth, we are led so close to Dover cliff that we know the myth as one of our own national past. It is here that I want to begin my own answer to the question of the play's time and place – firstly with those myths of national origin which were so important in Elizabethan and Jacobean times and from which discussion of the play should never (it seems to me) be divorced, and secondly with those strategies of romance by which the ideological power of such myths was commonly reinforced.

KING LEAR, CHRONICLE, MYTH AND ROMANCE

In 1926, in his essay 'Myth in Primitive Psychology', Malinowski made an important distinction between myth and chronicle: whereas chronicle, he argued, was concerned with the past in its pastness, myth was concerned with the past in its abiding presence. Myth, he said, 'is not merely a story told but a reality lived ... a retrospective, ever-present, live actuality'.[22] Three functions of myth in primitive society particularly preoccupied him. First, he said, it serves to provide a community with a sense of its communal identity through time. 'It fulfills a function *sui generis* closely connected with the nature of tradition, and the continuity of culture, with the relation between age and youth, and with the human attitude towards the past' (p. 146). Second, it helps to provide that community with its imagery of good and evil:

it expresses, enhances, and codifies belief; it safeguards and enforces morality; it vouches for the efficiency of ritual and contains practical rules for the guidance of man. Myth is thus a vital ingredient of human civilization; it is not an idle tale, but a hard-worked active force; it is not an intellectual explanation or an artistic imagery, but a pragmatic charter of primitive faith and moral wisdom.   (p. 101)

Third, it is particularly active in areas of community life 'where there is a sociological strain, such as in matters of great difference in rank and power, matters of precedence and subordination, and unquestionably where profound historical changes have taken place' (p. 126). The difference from chronicle is clear: myth is not a record of the past but a justification of the present, serving 'to glorify a certain group, or to justify an anomalous status' (p. 125).

The category of myth that concerns us here, of course, is what Malinowski calls the myth of origin, characteristically describing a primal catastrophic dispersal and a subsequent heroic colonization of new terrain. By mediaeval times it had become customary for European chroniclers to trace their various national descents back to the dispersal of the Trojan princes after the fall of Troy; and English chroniclers too, following Geoffrey of Monmouth, had commonly claimed descent from Brutus, the alleged descendant of Aeneas.[23] So it is that we find in Holinshed the tale of how Brutus' companion Corineus succeeded in the conquest of what was to become Britain by overthrowing the gigantic aboriginal inhabitant, Gogmagog, in a heroic wrestling-match. King Lear was the tenth in the line of nineteen rulers that made up the dynasty of Brutus; and this story thus belongs to the earliest and most violent days of British history, a history filled with tales of partition, civil war and reunification until the dynasty's final disintegration under Gorboduc.

The tales themselves sustained varying degrees of interpretation, from the almost mythic bareness of parts of Holinshed to the overmoralized sentimentality of so much of A Mirror for Magistrates. But to the political moralist who wished to uphold the Tudor state, and to the Tudor monarchs themselves, who seized upon these histories and popularized them (long after such myths of national origin had become discredited amongst continental historians), they were made to illustrate the necessity both for political unity under a single sovereign head and for orderly succession under the law of primogeniture. In particular, they provided Awful Warnings of the devastation caused when these principles were disobeyed. *Gorboduc* draws the orthodox political moral:

> Within one land, one single rule is best:
> Divided reigns do make divided hearts;
> But peace preserves the country and the prince.[24]

The tales, however, were intended not only to guide conduct but also to legitimize power. Genealogies were constructed to derive the Tudor dynasty directly out of the line of Brutus, and ancient prophecies were interpreted to show each Tudor monarch as a second Brutus, come to reunite for ever the divided kingdoms of England, Wales and Ireland. The black holes in time were to be occluded, the dangerous discontinuities of history papered over with myths that would confirm authority and marginalize the claims of political opposition. Many believed these myths as history, some thought them false, whilst others, such as Spenser with his antiquarian interests, found them of poetic value for their power to weave together the past, present and future in a celebration of national prestige:

> For the Methode of a Poet historical is not such, as of an Historiographer. For an Historiographer discourseth of affayres orderly as they were donne, accounting as well the times as the actions, but a Poet thrusteth into the middest, even where it most concerneth him, and there recoursing to the thinges forepaste, and diuining of thinges to come, maketh a pleasing Analysis of all.[25]

In the words of Lévi-Strauss, 'what gives the myth an operational value is that the specific pattern described is timeless; it explains the present and the past as well as the future';[26] and he goes on to say what we have already seen in the history plays, that political ideology has largely assumed the function of myth in Western civilization. But the business of *King Lear* is not with the politics of myth-making but with the materials of the myth of national origin, with those same materials that Spenser had had Prince Arthur read in the House of Temperance towards the end of book II of *The Faerie Queene*. 'The famous auncestries/Of my most dreaded Soueraigne', he called them in compliment to Elizabeth, in order to claim those tales of 'infinite remembrance'[27] as part of the prehistory of the present. Brutus, Arthur and Elizabeth were all woven together into a seamless tapestry depicting what is indeed (in Malinowski's terms) the *mythical charter* of the Tudor pacification, designed to unify the nation in time and place, instruct it in political obedience and ease its areas of sociological strain.

Nor was James slow to take up and encourage this Tudor history for his own ends. When in 1604 he had himself proclaimed the King of Great Britain, he was deliberately encouraging the reintroduction of an antiquarian geographical term – *Britain* (falsely derived from Brutus) – in his attempt to establish 'one single rule' in Scotland and England and a happy ending to centuries of hostility; and by the autumn of 1605 he was celebrated publicly in London, in the Lord Mayor's show, as the second Brutus who, fulfilling Merlin's ancient prophecy, would reunite what the original Brutus had put asunder. That this was his dearest ambition, he had long since admitted in *Basilikon Doron*, advising his son in the event of his becoming king over Scotland, England and Ireland.

> And in case it please God to prouide you to all these three Kingdomes, make your eldest sonne *Isaac*, leauing him all your kingdomes; and prouide the rest with priuate possessions: Otherwayes by deuiding your kingdomes, yee shall leaue the seed of diuision and discord among your posteritie; as befell to this Ile, by the diuision and assignement thereof, to the three sonnes of *Brutus*, *Locrine*, *Albanact* and *Camber*.[28]

It is clear, therefore, that when Shakespeare chose around 1605 to write *King Lear*, no doubt with a court performance in mind, he was drawing upon a highly topical and politically sensitive area of national history. Indeed, if we remember Glynne Wickham's words, the story of Lear had a particularly significant relationship to James himself: 'when *King Lear* was written, James was himself possessed of three children; the Duke of Cornwall, the Duke of Albany and Princess Elizabeth'.[29] So what, then, was Shakespeare up to?

In his conclusion to 'Myth in Primitive Psychology', Malinowski draws attention to the development of specifically literary forms out of the cultural praxis of myth. 'Myth contains germs of the future epic, romance, and tragedy. . . . Myths of love and of death, stories of the loss of immortality, of the passing of the Golden Age, and of the banishment from Paradise, myths of incest and of sorcery play with the very elements which enter into the artistic forms of tragedy, of lyric, and of romantic narrative' (pp. 143–4). Gillian Beer has noted how 'romance tends to use and re-use well-known stories whose familiarity reassures',[30] so that each new start is also a recapitulation. This ritual element in romance, binding past and present together, springs out of a central preoccupation which it shares with the related genre of the fairy-tale and which both share with myth: a preoccupation with areas of sociological strain, with those fault-lines of a society along which its most devastating fractures threaten always to recur. Myth, romance and fairy-tale have taken the most dangerous of experiences to their heart. In fairy-tale (and this accounts for the vigorous survival of the genre today in its current forms) those experiences are commonly centred in the family; in romance they may be more widely located – between friends or lovers, for instance, or even between fellow citizens of a shared culture. But the family remains in both the most frequent area of preoccupation; and we must remember of course that in Elizabethan and Jacobean England the family, undergoing a period of crisis that provoked a widespread reinforcement of patriarchal authority,[31] was the central unit and the type of all political organization. In these dangerous areas the business of romance and fairy-tale is most commonly with happy endings. They are fictions that men and women tell themselves in confirmation of their faith that the injustices of real life will not destroy their faith in Justice or jeopardize their sense of the worth of survival. Romance, that is, maps the world along the contours of our idealism; and, if its nostalgia or occasional tragedy should signal contradictions imperfectly resolved, its chief aim is nevertheless (like myth) to provide hope, to smooth over the discontinuities of the past and to ease the sociological strains of the present.

Since the publication of Maynard Mack's *'King Lear' in our Time*, the romance elements in *King Lear* have been very widely discussed. For Shakespeare took much of his main plot from *The True Chronicle Historie of King Leir*, which is in fact gentle pastoral romance rather than chronicle history, and to this he brought a tragic sub-plot out of Sidney's aristocratic pastoral romance,

Arcadia: there can be no doubt that he was consciously dealing with what Mack called 'the heady brew of romance'.[32] Indeed, the main plot from its very start establishes associations with romance that shape our deepest hopes. We are influenced, consciously or unconsciously, by tales such as 'Cinderella', which tells of parental injustice, of 'the agonies of sibling rivalry, of wishes coming true, of the humble being elevated, of true merit being recognized even when hidden under rags, of virtue rewarded and evil punished'.[33] We are influenced by tales in which pride goes before a fall – tales of 'the Abasement of the Proud King' such as that of Nebuchadnezzar:

> they shall drive thee from men, and thy dwelling shall be with the beasts of the field, and they shall make thee to eat grass as oxen, and they shall wet thee with the dew of heaven....
>
> Wherefore, O king, let my counsel be acceptable unto thee, and break off thy sins by righteousness, and thine iniquities by shewing mercy to the poor; if it may be a lengthening of thy tranquillity.[34]

Kent's story too is traditional romance, worked up out of the undisguised figure of the good counsellor in the source play: for in Shakespeare we see a loyal courtier, banished for honest speaking, enter his master's service in disguise, quarrel with the servants of his master's enemies, and at the last reveal himself in the hope of a final reconciliation. The sub-plot too is typical romance: the good brother disinherited through the stratagem of a forged letter and obliged to disguise himself as a beggar until the time is ripe to return to single combat and the offer of kingship. Even the most extreme of Shakespeare's stage-events – Lear's crown of weeds, or Gloucester's leap at Dover – suggest the customary materials of comedy and romance. Indeed, the whole structure of the play itself, with the movement of its sympathetic characters away from the corrupt centres of power to the houseless nature of its middle acts, is built upon what Michael Long has called 'classic festive-comic lines'.[35] It has now become commonplace to consider *King Lear* alongside *As You Like It*; and the comparison has particular point if it serves to remind us of the way that the play (unlike any other Shakespearean tragedy) leads us, even when we know it well, to ache after that happy ending implicit in its ancient story-lines.[36]

To speak more closely, *King Lear* is a study in complementary relationships of authority and service;[37] and our response to the central focus of the Lear–Cordelia relationship is shaped precisely by two complementary traditions of romance, each of which is used by Shakespeare elsewhere and which might surely seem sufficient together to bring the play home to a final reconciliation. There is the romance of the ruler whose education is completed by exposure to feel as his subjects feel (utilized most obviously by Shakespeare in *Measure for Measure*, in both parts of *Henry IV* and in *Henry V*). Such romance shows how, through the ruler's *incorporation* of his subjects' experience, a community may be reconstituted under the protection of sympathetic authority. In the words that Daniel used to praise the sympathetic rule of James, 'the Prince himselfe now heares, sees, knows'.[38] Then there is the complementary romance of the subject, in which a dependant's patience is rewarded after long abuse (as Hermione is rewarded in *The Winter's Tale*). Here too the community is re-established, this time in the security brought by undeviating service. The conjunction of these two complementary traditions in *King Lear* creates the expectation that the ruler and the subject together will be brought to recognize both their common humanity and their different, but reciprocal, social responsibilities; the dangers that lurk within all authority–service relationships will thus be defused and society re-established in the ideal self-image of its own dominant ideology. Especially does this seem likely when we perceive the overall structure of the play to be one of pastoral romance. For in romance the oppositional proves beneficent, and regeneration is by that which is contrary: the injustice of society is healed by the ideal equity of nature, the proud king restored by confrontation with houseless poverty, and lowly virtue brought into its full inheritance by the persecution of powerful vice. Such indeed seems the certain direction of the play, as Lear meets Cordelia in the wilds behind Dover at the end of Act IV.

But Maynard Mack's description of *King Lear* as 'the greatest anti-pastoral ever penned'[39] suggests the nature of the shocks that Act v has in store for us. For this is a play in which the oppositional does not bring regeneration; instead, it breaks out in open contradiction that leads to terminal collapse. Shockingly, the tragedy negates all our expectations, even at the simplest level of the narrative; for this is the first version of the story in which Cordelia does not win a military victory over her sisters and reinstate her father on the throne. Dr Johnson was right, after all, to be horrified; for the play maps reality along the contours of a terrible disillusion and leaves us darkling indeed. So deliberate is Shakespeare's design to shock that Gary Taylor's guess seems very plausible: that the play in Quarto was entitled 'True Chronicle Historie', rather than 'Tragedie' as it became in the Folio, precisely to delude its first audiences into expecting the happy ending of its chief source.[40]

Our disillusion at the narrative outcome is also a betrayal of our expectation of romance; for *King Lear* presents the ideal pacifications of romance in a much more chilling perspective. To borrow a fine phrase from Shelley, all those 'beautiful idealisms of moral excellence'[41] which effect the reconciliatory rituals of romance are here seen to be ineffective when faced with the powerful social contradictions which it is commonly their business to reconcile. The play explores in particular, perhaps, the contrary truths to everything that Spenser had celebrated in book II of *The Faerie Queene*, where temperance had overcome the temptations of anger and lust and had sealed up the discontinuities of history in a timeless iconography of goodness. Here in *King Lear* temperance succumbs to anger and lust,[42] and a rift is opened up in history. The poet, using to the full that special licence not granted to the historiographer, has brought forward by nine generations the extinction of Brutus' line; and in so doing he has brought into play that violence and destructiveness which constantly attend upon social contradiction.

King Lear has been called 'a courtly compliment'[43] to King James; it has been considered an Awful Warning to his people and parliament in their resistance to the union of Scotland with England;[44] it may even be considered an Awful Warning to James himself;[45] and no doubt it will yield such meanings. But they are not spelled out for us; *King Lear* is remarkable precisely for its freedom from the kind of framework that we find in *Gorboduc*, where all things are made to spell out the credenda and agenda of political orthodoxy. We are left at the end not with dogma but with dead loss. The effect is similar to that which Fulke Greville believed was aimed at in classical tragedy: 'to exemplifie the disastrous miseries of mans life, where Order, Lawes, Doctrine, and Authority are unable to protect Innocency from the exorbitant wickednesse of power, and so out of that melancholike Vision, stir horrour, or murmur against Divine Providence'.[46]

Yet this is not ancient tragedy but tragedy of his own national history that Shakespeare has written. He has assimilated pagan to Christian and barbaric to mediaeval in order to re-create a Tudor myth of national origin; but he has done so, once again, only to betray expectation. For *King Lear* subverts not only romance but also the mythical charter of its own country. It tells not of a civilization won for the present with heroic difficulty in the past, but of a civilization lost with anguish for all time – a loss which was absolute but is still present with us, informing our understanding of the disastrous miseries, the injustices and the violence which still succeeds, in our lesser world, upon the breakdown of social reciprocity.

IMAGES OF GOODNESS: CORDELIA AND KENT

The question of reciprocity, of course, is crucial. When Lear enters at the end of the play with Cordelia dead in his arms, he is desperately searching for expression that will do justice to the enormity of the sense of injustice that he feels:

> Howl, howl, howl! O! You are men of stones:
> Had I your tongues and eyes, I'd use them so
> That heaven's vault should crack.
>
> (v. iii.256–8)

These words, in which we hear grief modulating into rage, are deeply typical of a recurrent pattern in the play. 'By none/Am I enough beloved', lamented Wordsworth's Matthew by the fountain.[47] *King Lear* depicts a world in which no one can say *enough*, in which neither grief nor rage is satisfied; and in consequence the individual mind is driven to the uttermost extremes of fantasy to conjure up its happiness. Hence in part the play's exploration of the transformational devices of romance. But Lear's cry here, of course, would also transform the world: he would howl until the heaven's vault crack. We cannot tell what mixture of grief or rage is in his voice, whether he aims perhaps at the world's regeneration, or more simply at its destruction, in the cracking of divine remorselessness. It might be either, for pity and anger, sorrow and

rage are the antithetical feelings in *King Lear* through which men
and women try to make the justice that they cannot find. Yet it is
all to no avail: the power of Lear's words can, in their expression,
effect no more than a moment's brief transformation of a reality
whose loveless injustice persists. The long clear light of romance
that illuminates reality throughout *The Faerie Queene* has been
diffracted; in Donne's words, 'The sun is spent, and now his
flasks/Send forth light squibs, no constant rays.'[48]

It is the presence of Cordelia and Kent in the play's opening
scene that calls attention to the importance of reciprocity – and also
to its dependence upon a common language. For one brief moment
in that scene, despite the pressure they are under, they still have
access to a language in which they believe they may speak both
what they feel and what they ought to say. For one brief moment,
then never again, the possibilities of courtesy and honesty appear
to coincide – though even here, ominously, Cordelia has already
been driven to say in an aside that she would rather 'love, and be
silent'. Her difficulties are obvious:

> I love your Majesty
> According to my bond; no more nor less.
> . . .
> You have begot me, bred me, lov'd me: I
> Return those duties back as are right fit,
> Obey you, love you, and most honour you.
> Why have my sisters husbands, if they say
> They love you all?
>
> (I. i.91–9)

It is hard to say what mixture of angry defiance and riddling satire
colours the love in her voice as she struggles under her father's
usurpation of language and ceremony; and certainly her spirited
arithmetical talk of dividing her love is not a happy solution. Kent
too has to struggle:

> Royal Lear,
> Whom I have ever honour'd as my King,
> Lov'd as my father, as my master follow'd,
> As my great patron thought on in my prayers, –
>
> (ll.138–41)

Then, two lines later, he is driven into unmannerly plainness. It seems, therefore, that hitherto both Cordelia and Kent have been able to accommodate an ideal conception of their relationship with Lear within the real court world, but that now it has become impossible. They can no longer speak courteously what they feel; and, in destroying that middle ground upon which the reciprocities of conversation rest, Lear is effectively already banishing them from their society.

When Cordelia tells her father that she loves him according to her *bond* – 'no more nor less' – she is using the word that declares her faith in the ideal charter of that society. For Shakespeare has imagined the world of his play much more precisely than it is imagined in any of his sources; he has given it a feudal structure and language in which his audience could recognize the prehistory of their own Jacobean present. Cordelia's *bond* is the feudal equivalent of the Roman *pietas*, a matter of neither spontaneous feeling nor legal duty but an alloy the stronger for being compounded of both; and it is the word in which all the themes of the play briefly meet. Nature and society, affection and duty, prudence and love, religion, custom, value, law and the sense of justice: all these are composed in Cordelia's attempt to recall her father and king to her own ideal conception of the responsibilities of his authority. She is declaring that love is defined by its limits, that these limits are determined by the customary proprieties of their society, and that without such limits love becomes tyrannical and extreme. She is declaring that a woman is more than a chattel, a subject more than a slave.

But the ideal which Cordelia and Kent serve is contradicted by the real. The self-constituted ritual in which Lear engages his court in the opening scene of the play should not be seen simply as a love-test; it is an improvised perversion of the feudal ceremony of commendation, when a subject openly declared his loyalty to the king, and the king in return granted him his particular charters. Lear's irresponsible vanity thus does not only strike at the heart of his favourite daughter: it also strikes at the heart of the relationship between love and property which is, ideally, the cornerstone of the feudal system and which all its ceremonies of allegiance are designed to reinforce – and in so doing it draws out that system's latent contradictions into open conflict. No longer after Lear's act can a corrupt system of patronage and flattery idealize itself as a system of loving mutual service. Power is released from the imaginative discipline of sympathy and service, and runs at once to extremes; and, indeed, the rapidity of the political degeneration after Lear's abdication suggests how deeply rooted that tendency already was, both within the royal family and amongst the military powers of the great aristocratic houses.

Critics of *King Lear*, particularly since Danby, have fallen into a habit of interpreting the play in terms of a clash between feudal and bourgeois ideologies, with Shakespeare's sympathies firmly centred upon the feudal. 'As Nature goes dead, community becomes competition', wrote Danby concisely; the 'benevolent thesis' of feudalism succumbs before 'the new age of scientific inquiry and industrial development, of bureaucratic organization and social regimentation'[49] which is somehow represented by Edmund in the play. James Kavanagh similarly writes of the destruction wrought by 'an individualist ideology that lives the world as a field of calculation, self-gratification and perverse desire' upon 'the hierarchical ideology of fealty, faith and restraint, which lives the world as a field of reciprocal obligation'.[50] It has become the orthodox reading of our time: that 'the old, patriarchal society has been stripped by the new men, the new, hard materialists'.[51] Yet it is surely unlikely that two king's daughters and one illegitimate nobleman's son, all of whom are killed, should have been chosen by Shakespeare to express an emergent bourgeois ideology: rather, the true subject of *King Lear*, it seems to me, is not an old order succumbing to a new but an old order succumbing to its own internal contradictions. The king is unequal to the great demands made of him; the aristocracy cannot harmonize its interests; and the family, the social unit through which political power is both secured and delegated, is nowhere able to ensure its orderly survival. We may think Lear unwise to have divided his kingdom until we remember the results of Gloucester's exclusive favouring of legitimacy and primogeniture. The society fractures along its own fault-lines; and it is of no avail to blame the coarse imaginative self-will of Lear and Gloucester, since that self-will itself is a consequence of the political structure they wish to preserve.

Cordelia is disinherited and Kent banished, but Shakespeare saves them both from the prospect of immediate desolation by dramatic devices characteristic of romance: he finds a husband for the one and a disguise for the other. These are, of course, more than mere devices; they are ways of exploring those strategies by which, in fact and fantasy, men and women sustain themselves in their struggle against injustice. Cordelia makes it known to her suitors that she was disinherited 'for want of that for which I am richer' (I. i.229), and the French king finds himself strangely drawn to this 'unpriz'd precious maid' (l.258) whose virtue has made her despised and rejected of men:

> Fairest Cordelia, that art most rich, being poor;
> Most choice, forsaken; and most lov'd, despis'd!
> (I. i.249–50)

These paradoxical figures of speech, so typical of the inversions found throughout the play, suggest the idealization of which the characters will now stand in need if, deprived of their common language, they are to accommodate themselves to the increasing restrictions of the real. 'Hath not God chosen the poor of this world rich in faith, and heirs of the kingdom which he hath promised to them that love him?' (James 2:5): such idealization, of course, is a familiar consolation for suffering in fairy-tale and romance, myth and religion alike. It holds out the possibility of carrying on, even of starting afresh; and, as Cordelia leaves, her romantic marriage seems to be offering her just such an opportunity of a fresh start. 'Thou losest here, a better where to find' (I. i.260), says France. But *King Lear* does not follow its sources to France, and there will be no fresh start elsewhere; fortified by her idealization and the power that her marriage gives her, Cordelia will return to the struggle.

Kent will not even leave. When courtesy and plainness fail, his first impulse – like Cordelia's – is towards a transcendental idealism that inverts the world before him. 'Freedom lives hence, and banishment is here' (l.180), he says. Then, in the new perspective which displacement brings, he hits upon the romantic device of disguise that enables him too (as Cordelia's marriage enables her) to continue to serve.

> If thou canst serve where thou dost stand condemn'd,
> So may it come, thy master, whom thou lov'st,
> Shall find thee full of labours.
> (I. iv.5–7)

This self-disguise enacts a widespread fantasy of neglected servants – and more particularly of unacknowledged lovers (the 'servant' such as Viola in *Twelfth Night*, for instance) – to win regard by anonymous attentions. The intolerable fact of real neglect and contempt becomes in imagination the ideal opportunity for patience; and Kent, serving incognito, will abase himself that what he really is may finally be gloriously recognized and the ideal relationship between authority and service re-established.

Barish and Waingrow, comparing Kent with the servile Oswald, describe him as 'the quintessence of the good servant and the touchstone for service throughout the play';[52] and of course Cordelia's loyal, self-sacrificial attention to her father's business[53] is everywhere commended. But we need to characterize this goodness, this service; we need to see it in the context of the play's romantic structures. For the compassion that Kent and Cordelia come to feel for Lear, on the dispersal of whatever anger and indignation they may have felt at first, belongs to an idealistic transformation of reality of which the most striking aspect is the idealization of the person of the king himself. Kent in the storm speaks of 'the old kind King' (III. i.28) and Cordelia at Dover of her 'dear father' (IV. iv.23) – words that bear eloquent testimony to their capacity for pity but that also have a curious insufficiency about them. For pity is not enough. Kent and Cordelia, in fact, exhibit a familiar response to threat: they turn back towards an ideal internal object, split off (in part at least) from any real object in the external world. That ideal object is, of course, the sovereign whom they had once seen in Lear and whom now, in Lear's dereliction, they cannot relinquish; and hence the strange incommensurateness of their pity to the man before us on stage, the strange disjunction between the pitiable figure they describe and the tragic figure we see.

The point is, such idealization subtly inhibits the very reciprocities it aims at – something seen most poignantly in the delicate incongruities of the so-called 'recognition scene' (IV. vii). This scene has been persistently sentimentalized by critics who share the romantic illusions of Cordelia and Kent; but the truth is, however, that the scene is not altogether one of recognition. Cordelia (like Kent) addresses Lear with tender courtesy as king, and then she kneels before him. It is hard to imagine a more moving act of forgiveness, a more generous gesture towards restitution; for she offers him her vision of his ideal sovereign self.

Yet her terms of address send Lear down at once grotesquely on
his knees – dazedly, it seems, half afraid of mockery, half fancying
her an angel. The father kneels to the daughter, the king to the
subject. The moment is profoundly moving in the depth and value
of the feelings and recognitions involved; but – equally important –
it is also exquisitely embarrassing in the disjunction between those
feelings and recognitions. Lear will hear no talk of kingship. The
plain language of his self-description, flickering between shame,
wonder, self-pity and humility, coupled with the courtliness of his
address to Cordelia, enacts perfectly his intuition that value lies
most in the inversion of all that formerly had been. Such is *his*
idealization. Father and daughter, even at this most moving
moment of their love, are feeling different things: Cordelia (as in
romance) would turn the broken man before her back into the king
her father, whilst he (also as in romance) would be reborn as a new
man and no king. Shakespeare tempts us with the poignant
awakening of romance expectation, only to frustrate us with
languages and feelings that do not quite enmesh; and so it goes on
to the end. 'Shall we not see these daughters and these sisters?'
(v. iii.7), urges Cordelia with tough determination to out-frown
misfortune.

> No, no, no, no! Come, let's away to prison;
> We two alone will sing like birds i' th'cage:
> When thou dost ask me blessing, I'll kneel down,
> And ask of thee forgiveness....
>
> (v. iii.8–11)

The king runs into prison (under arrest as he is), imagining with
his daughter to transform it into a kind of hermit's cell, where the
painful mysteries of life will be revealed and loss be hallowed into
sacrifice. This fantasy of power and omniscience is opposite to that
in which initially he mapped out the division of his kingdom; and it
is hauntingly beautiful. Yet it is far indeed from that full restoration
for which Cordelia and Kent had longed, and his daughter can do
more than look at him, weep, love and once again be silent.

Silent tears are the last that we see of Cordelia until Lear enters
carrying her dead body and demanding that men should howl
aloud their cry for justice; and these tears, as she watches the
extraordinary behaviour of her sovereign father, seem to express at
the last her own paradoxical recognition of how little her pity and

her service have achieved and yet how little anything else in the world is worth. There are no words left for her; the language and iconography by which she has lived her life have disintegrated with the disintegration of the society which sustained them, and she seems finally to have become aware of the great distance between herself and her father, between her own lonely images of goodness and the outer world in which they have failed to find accommodation. The fragmentation already begun in the play's opening scene is here completed with the marginalization of those virtues in which a feudal society had seen its best self. That society has now succumbed to its own inner contradictions; and in Cordelia's lament before her frenzied father, as in Lear's lament at her death, we see emblems of how the feudal pieties of pity, love and service, idealized as they have become, can do no more than contemplate the unjust world which they have been compelled to vacate. For certainly they are powerless to change it.

'Is this the promis'd end?' (v. iii.262), asks Kent. 'Or image of that horror?' adds Edgar with a flicker of his characteristic impulse to qualify. Questions proliferate at the end of the play, searching the seemingly inscrutable *whys* of injustice. 'Why should a dog, a horse, a rat, have life,/And thou no breath at all?' (ll.305–6). These are questions asked both *within* the play by its characters and *of* the play by its audience: for the play's theatrical self-consciousness, here as it concludes its business with the mythical charter of its country, involves the past inescapably in the present. It both recalls and keeps alive the tragic awareness that, in a society where the reciprocities of authority and service have broken down, there *are* no answers to such questions, either in the promised ends of religion or romance. The tableau of that curiously inverted *pietà*, as – shockingly – the father enters with his dead daughter in his arms, undoes not only the audience's faith in its own society and its own history but also every romance and myth by which it has tried to maintain that faith, including (most disturbingly) the Christian one. The gods have not thrown incense upon sacrifice, the girl who went about her father's business will come no more to redeem nature from the general curse which twain have brought her to. Neither faith nor works of any kind can achieve that. For the consolations of metaphysics and art, like those attendant upon everyday goodness, are shown in this play to be ineffective without the primary reciprocities of social justice – and these reciprocities have long since vanished, both from the world of *King*

Lear and from its playhouse, it seems. Their loss, moreover, is absolute; and, significantly, it is the loyal imagination of Kent that is stretched to pronounce the extraordinary epitaph upon the man who for so long, against so many odds, survived their loss: 'He but usurp'd his life' (l.316). Lear usurped his life when he began to live it for himself alone; and in so doing he entailed upon Kent, as upon Cordelia, a paradoxical idealization of the concept of service to compensate for its scant success in reality. Finally now, Kent is prepared to live out this paradox to its furthest extreme: he will obey the supposed summons of the master who could scarcely recognize him, in order to serve him in death.[54] This final paradox emphasizes both the persistence of the human need for reciprocity and the fact of its irretrievable breakdown in the prehistory of the present – a contradiction central to the world of *King Lear*, and inscribed by Shakespeare into this redrafted mythical charter of his country so that his audience might know not only the past but its own time too by the idealized attenuation, the marginalization, of what yet remain its dearest images of goodness.

IMAGES OF EVIL: GONERIL, REGAN AND EDMUND

There is another way to seek reciprocity and justice, not through pity and service but through contempt and tyranny; for in this way too the master is confirmed in the ideal self-image of his own authority. This is a strategy, however, rendered unstable by its basis in denial and contradiction: it denies the subjective need for love out of which it grows, and it pursues relationship by denying the objective reality of other people. Its cause, nevertheless, is real enough – the unappeasable hunger originating in unacceptable injustice. At the root of it all in the patriarchal society of *King Lear* is the figure of the father. For the envies of sibling rivalry, seemingly so central to the play, resolve, as Bettelheim noted in his discussion of 'Cinderella', into a still more primary experience of injustice: 'Despite the name "sibling rivalry", this miserable passion has only incidentally to do with a child's actual brothers and sisters. The real source of it is the child's feelings about his parents.'[55] The 'villains' of the piece – Goneril, Regan and Edmund – have been brought by paternal injustice to despise the most central relationship of their society, the filial bond; and now their every thought and deed is an act of revenge upon it.

The play opens as their revenge begins, and it traces their fierce demolition of all the pieties upon which their civilization depends, in order that they themselves might stand freely forth amidst its ruins. Yet there is a deep, potentially suicidal contradiction at the heart of this strategy: they would empty authority of all its true worth in order to assume authority themselves. Some words of Janine Chasseguet-Smirgel, describing the fundamental unproductiveness of perversion, suggest themselves here: 'The pervert is trying to free himself from the paternal universe and the constraints of the law. He wants to create a new kind of reality and to dethrone God the Father.'[56] For Goneril, Regan and Edmund *are* perverse. However much they might idealize their 'independent intellect',[57] the fearlessness of their prudential self-interest or the talismanic objects of their desires, they cannot create a new, satisfactory kind of reality. Their oppositional energies, even as they destroy the middle ground upon which both the reciprocities of *pietas* and the negotiations of prudence depend, fall into that instability and inconsolability which Masud Khan has identified as the hallmark of perversion.[58] Edmund's 'no less than all' (III. iii.24) becomes the precise antithesis in the play to Cordelia's 'no more nor less'. The tragedy of the 'villains', therefore, is one of unsuccessful liberation, of oppositional energies so far marginalized by the experience of social injustice that they fall into perversion; and it is their peculiar distinction that, drawing out the contradictions of the old to its destruction, they yet create nothing new.

We sense at once what is to come from the sisters when they are left alone at the end of the opening scene: they are to be tempted with appalled fascination towards the limitlessly receding horizons of their own desires. Despite the rationalizations of self-interest which they offer, they are in fact seduced by the perverse pleasures that lie on the other side of prohibition – pleasures that lead by inner necessity to the murder of the one and the suicide of the other. The secret heart of these pleasures is envy. Melanie Klein has identified an important psychic opposition between envy and gratitude which is useful to us here: envy is passionate to spoil or to destroy the good object for its tantalizing insufficiency, whilst gratitude is affectionately appreciative of its independent existence in all its imperfections.[59] Cordelia, we remember, could still imagine the reciprocity of gratitude; but Goneril and Regan in the perverseness of their envy become compulsively committed to desecrate the image of their father, who has made their present lives so unendurable to all of them. In this situation Cordelia had returned to the past for images of hope, but her sisters are driven to hunger for future satisfactions; and hence, of course, their incapacity for gratitude. 'Ingratitude, thou marble-hearted fiend' (I. iv.257) cries Lear, denied the sympathy he feels his due: 'Monster Ingratitude!' (I. v.37). But Goneril and Regan know where to lay the blame – 'he always lov'd our sister most' (I. i.288–9) – and now the whirligig of time brings in his revenges. The rage with which they seethe ('By day and night, he wrongs me', snaps Goneril at I. iii.4) becomes free to express itself; and the vindictive game by which they strip Lear of his retinue exemplifies, as do the bright ideas that are enacted upon the bound body of Gloucester, the obscene daring of their inventiveness. For they too must transform the world, make it conform to their own idea: all other ways of seeing must be put out.

Edmund proves to be the third person who turns the envy at the heart of the sisters' collusion into a fiercely competitive jealousy – for such is the ironically shrunken conclusion to all the limitless possibilities that had opened out before them. Like a talisman, Edmund comes to emblematize all the idealized male glamour inspired and betrayed by their father, whilst each sister represents to the other all that is most hateful in herself. Goneril's words in fear of Regan say it all:

> But being widow, and my Gloucester with her,
> May all the building in my fancy pluck
> Upon my hateful life.
>
> (IV. ii.84–6)

Her sense of the hatefulness of her life is not only proleptic, however; for her life is hateful to her *now*, in *both* senses of the word – odious to her because filled with hatred, from which the sole possession of Edmund's love seems the only chance to redeem her. Yet, as Lear is cheated of Cordelia by death, so is she of Edmund; and hence her outraged cry that he is not vanquished, only 'cozen'd and beguil'd (v. iii.153). It is a perfect symmetry of felt injustice: like her father she would howl against the injustice of it all, and like her father too she has good cause. The building of her fantasy *has* been plucked down upon her, and – after one last idealization that shows her to be her father's daughter still ('the laws are mine, not thine' – 1.157) – her confession and suicide pronounce the last judgement on her life. For she has created nothing new; her oppositional energies have been marginalized and corrupted by the injustices of the system she has opposed, wasted amongst the destructive perversities of hate and envy. Even her hostility to the 'paternal universe' proves unproductive in the end, as she turns to find in Edmund the man to whom 'a woman's services are due' (IV. ii.27).

It is Edmund, in fact, who most exhilaratingly sets out to create 'a new kind of reality and to dethrone God the Father'. He is the true opposite to Cordelia in the play, and his opening words (aside, like hers, addressed directly to the audience) challenge all the distinctions that she had tried to organize in her understanding of bond – nature and society, affection and duty, prudence and love, religion, custom, value, law and the sense of justice:

> Thou, Nature, art my goddess; to thy law
> My services are bound. Wherefore should I
> Stand in the plague of custom . . . ?
>
> (I. ii.1–3)

These are the pleasures of sacrilege: it is wholly characteristic that Edmund's adventure in morality should both begin and end in a sporting challenge, initially of the gods and finally of his elder brother. For, in a fine phrase of Conrad's, he has 'an adventurer's easy morality which takes count of personal risk in the ethical appraising of his action'.[60] He is tempted to dare, to gamble hugely upon the nature of reality with his life as the stake. 'Now, gods, stand up for bastards!' (1.22): such a challenge, dethroning the gods, dispossessing his brother and finally destroying his father, gives him the sentiment of being and the hope of reward that he cannot find in the pieties of love or service. For, of course, as a younger brother labouring under the double burden of illegitimacy and parental disregard, he has no place in his world. He has been done a bitter injustice and his response is correspondingly vindictive: to turn against the male figures and the patriarchal customs that have marginalized him, to deify the immoral fecundity of his absent mother and to bind himself to 'the lusty stealth of nature' (1.11) whose desire has the force of law. His father had boasted that there was 'good sport at his making' (I. i.22); and it is precisely this sense of sport that Edmund revisits upon him. It is indeed, as

Marilyn French has observed, 'a savage imitation';[61] for the very nature of such children seems to be revenge.

We should perhaps best understand Edmund's ideology, opposing nature to society and thereby turning Cordelia's vision upside-down, as a perverse parody of the pastoral fantasy that shapes our romance expectations of the play – the fantasy that the injustices of civilization may be repaired by invoking the ideal equity of nature. It is perverse because grounded in envy, because (to quote Chasseguet-Smirgel again) 'this reversal of a system of values is only the first stage in an operation whose end is the destruction of all values'.[62] But in its perverseness it serves as a grim reminder of the ineffectuality of romance to bring about the redistributions of wealth and power that matter. There is indeed an appeal open to society from nature, to the centre from the margins, to the wealthy and powerful from the poor and impotent. There is indeed justice in Edmund's demand, and truth in his perception of what he must do to get it; and it is his thoroughness that finally, by the assassination of Cordelia, prevents the play from yielding the consolations of romance. The oppositional is not to be always so easily integrated as pastoral suggests.

It is fascinating to see what Shakespeare has made of the traditional romantic pattern of the rise, fall and death-bed conversion of the villain – for Edmund, dying after defeat at the hands of his brother, determines to do good and, if possible, avert Cordelia's death. Yet nothing could be further from the easy certitudes and naïve moral reparations of romance. Edmund is not converted, and he does not repent. His intention is quite precise: 'some good I mean to do/Despite of mine own nature' (v. iii.242–3). It seems that his one good act will be done to spite himself and the world he has built in the image of his own conception. 'Yet Edmund was belov'd' (l.238) – the deaths of Goneril and Regan, following hard upon Edgar's narrative of care for his dying father, complete the change begun in Edmund by his defeat and imminent death. Yet, as he contemplates the perverse reciprocities of that unholy *ménage à trois*, all three marrying in an instant, how shall we gauge the tones of self-lacerating irony and awakened gratitude in his voice? His admission of a lifelong hunger for love and approval is an important insight into the origins of his own nature; his sense that 'the wheel is come full circle' (v. iii.173) confesses some kind of justice in his death; but the bitterness in his voice reminds us too that he had good cause to hunger for love and for justice. It is consciously an incomplete reparation that he attempts. His death does not integrate him into a reconstituted community, as we might have expected; the injustices of history are not so simply to be set to rights.

By this bitter resistance to the compositions of pastoral and romance, Edmund has helped to draw out the contradictions within the ruling class of Lear's Britain and destroy it. The middle ground upon which love and prudence might have met has been usurped by the fathers; the children's compensatory – even heroic – idealizations of self-sacrificial goodness or self-seeking evil have been extinguished; and the loss is absolute. Furthermore, Edmund – the Bastard, the Unwanted, the Marginalized – emblematizes all the injustices of the history that we have inherited out of Lear's Britain. He does not bear them away as a scapegoat might; even in his death, he brings them into play. Similarly, the sisters – the Wicked Sisters, the Ugly Sisters – emblematize all the envious malice still at the heart of family life. Shakespeare leaves his Jacobean audience (and ourselves too, at our greater distance) to know the lesser world of the present in the shadow of this prehistory of injustice and, most important of all, to know it by the *ambivalence* with which we participate in its theatrical representation. For, if we see the beauty of Cordelia's goodness, we also see the glamour of Edmund and the sisters. The great hierarchy of authority and service that had ideally constituted the reciprocities of feudal society can no longer be invoked by the end of the play; the apparent coherence of both its social forms and its moral language has been destroyed, and nothing is left in its place. Simply, Shakespeare has turned his historical and romance materials upside-down: the heroic past out of which Tudor and Stuart moralists drew their mythical charter yields in *King Lear* an understanding of the present as a time and place of abiding injustice, where morality remains problematical and reciprocity incomplete.

CONCLUSION: 'WHEREFORE TO DOVER?'

Lear and Gloucester, like Edmund (and perhaps like all three sisters too), die with love upon their lips – love which symbolizes all the glory that their lives are capable of, and yet which cannot be won into the continuity of relationship. They glimpse the light in the moment of its fading. Gloucester's flawed heart, we are told, unable to support further conflict, ' 'twixt two extremes of passion, joy and grief,/Burst smilingly' (v. iii.197–8); and, after that great tragic arraignment of the *whys* of an inscrutable providence, Lear's heart does the same: 'Look on her, look, her lips,/Look there, look there!' (ll.309–10). Are we in the presence of illusion or illumination? of loss or enrichment? of desolation or redemption? These questions have gathered around the end of *King Lear* with particular persistence; and rightly so. It is the insistence upon the one or the other by way of an answer that is mistaken – for it is our doubt that matters, not our capacity to still it. The concern of the play is amongst those difficulties that beset judgement in a flawed society where authority has broken down; and hence the importance of mixed feelings as a mode of understanding. Wordsworth, meditating upon a similar social situation with Shakespearean tragedy very much in mind, described this sense of intellectual and moral perplexity strikingly well:

> So meet extremes in this mysterious world,
> And opposites thus melt into each other.[63]

It is not simply that the world falls, as Cordelia had perhaps foreseen, into extremes of more or less, but that these extremes themselves run into one another. James I described this, if anything more strikingly still than Wordsworth, in *Basilikon Doron* when he came to gloss the Aristotelian notion of virtue as a golden mean between extremities: 'the two extremities themselues, although they seeme contrarie, yet growing to the height, runne euer both in one: For *in infinitis omnia concurrunt.*'[64] The justice which it is the business of pastoral romance to recover has become problematized; and we have been brought, as Hamlet by the ghost, to 'a more removèd ground' (i. iv.61) which offers only troubling and ambiguous perspectives. Illusion or illumination? desolation or redemption? even, comedy or tragedy? The *grotesqueness* which Wilson Knight identified in the play, perplexing our responses to the sufferings and deaths of Lear and Gloucester (and of Edmund and the sisters too), is a meeting in 'new sublime incongruity'[65] (which is *not* tragi-comedy) of the extremes of comedy and tragedy. The play's grotesqueness is its mode of re-creating the political fragmentation of Lear's Britain, and thus of establishing the living connexion between the present and its imagined prehistory.

There have been many attempts to find consolation in *King Lear*, by rewriting its ending, by finding redemptive power in Cordelia's virtues or, more recently (and characteristically of our time, perhaps), by focusing upon 'the quiet, unrecognized will to decency that exists in every people, every nation'.[66] But even this sense of decency becomes grotesque in the play. A people, a nation, must really constitute a society if its acts of decency are to be free from the taint of absurdity: such absurdity, for instance, as attaches to Edgar's disguised assistance of his father, where – 'O fault!' (v. iii.191) – prudence and service prove to be so catastrophically at odds. As Danby put it, summarizing his understanding of the play, 'the good man needs a community of goodness';[67] and it is just the possibility of such a community of goodness that tantalizingly fails to survive in the contradictory world of *King Lear*.

'Give me the map there' (I. i.36): Lear begins as though he *were* Britain (as France is France, perhaps), possessing absolute authority over all the loves of men, all the powers and properties of nature and all the uncertainties of time. But, as we have seen, his absoluteness only serves to draw out the contradictions within the ruling classes of his kingdom; and then the grotesque ministrations of the Fool and Poor Tom initiate him further still into the contradictions of the rest of his country, where authority has also failed to serve. The Fool belabours him with a fantastic iconography of folly – of horses drawn by carts, of asses borne by men, of fathers beaten by daughters – whilst Poor Tom wields a more fantastic iconography still: of unrelenting persecution by grotesque fiends in punishment for sin. These intensifying accusations of folly and religious guilt, dissociated as they are from compassion, bring Lear to the point of breakdown, and he succumbs to the storm of madness that breaks over him – a storm that is both within and without him. For there *is* one special sense in which the king *is* the kingdom, in that his relationship with the external other is also relationship internalized: and so here, conducted by two suffering subjects who have also become *alter egos*, Lear is initiated into the counter-world which his injustice has created, both for himself and for others, both subjectively within the mind and objectively upon the heath.

The king meets the Bedlam beggar in the wilds of Nature: if the business of romance and pastoral is with regeneration through that which is contrary, we might now expect the rebirth of both king and kingdom. But there is to be no fresh start for this fragmented world, where contraries melt into each other and become irrecoverable for the recomposition of social order. Lear pities or he curses; he prays for houseless poverty or calls down punishment on his daughters; he tears off his clothes to become 'the thing itself' (III. iv.104) or he crowns himself with weeds; he is now a king, now a satirist turning his kingdom upside-down, now a plain man disclaiming it. Illusion and illumination flicker across his mind so fleetingly that we cannot speak of his coming to the truth through madness; for it is the very condition of his insanity that he cannot integrate the various idealizations of goodness and evil that flit before him. If we think of the king as a mirror, we surely see no consolation through the distorting fragments into which Lear's mind has shivered; and neither does Gloucester offer a better hope, drifting grotesquely between patience and despair as he blindly waits upon the chance of war. For theology, moral law, social custom, human feeling itself have all been drained of the coherence which only shared convention can give. Perhaps it is Burke, his imagination deeply shaped by Shakespeare, who in his *Reflections on the Revolution in France* most deeply appreciated the tragedy of total social disintegration depicted in *King Lear*. 'Society is indeed a contract', he wrote, but not merely the business contract that the radicals described. 'It is a partnership in all science; a partnership in all art; a partnership in every virtue, and in all perfection'; and when that partnership is destroyed, he went on, 'the law is broken, nature is disobeyed, and the rebellious are outlawed, cast forth, and exiled, from this world of reason, and order, and peace, and virtue, and fruitful penitence, into the antagonist world of madness, discord, vice, confusion, and unavailing sorrow'.[68] Freedom lives hence, and banishment is here – such is the grotesque fate of Lear's Britain, as it falls into the confusion caused by its own injustices.

But every end is a beginning, of course, and Edgar is the young man at the end of the play who has to try to start afresh. He seems at first sight to be the typical hero of romance, the quester who will rediscover the community of goodness. For all his strategies of survival succeed: a long series of disguises enables him to avoid persecution, to help his father and finally – as the nameless knight of chivalry – to defeat his treacherous half-brother and resume his rightful place in the world. The *true* romance hero, by resourcefulness of body and mind, takes on the enemy and by defeating him defines the future categories of good and evil for his community; and Edgar accordingly responds to persecution by a compulsive determination to know the worst that his community is capable of, to bear in his own person the marks of its uttermost in poverty, contempt and degradation. He determines 'to take the basest and most poorest shape/That ever penury, in contempt of man,/ Brought near to beast' (II. iii.7–9). It is not just a question of disguise. His Poor Tom, after all, is a remarkable performance, and like all remarkable performances it is an exploration. He needs, like Lear himself on the heath, to test himself against the worst, to incorporate it, in order to find confidence for the future. But such is the confusion of Lear's Britain that Edgar cannot discover the worst. 'Who is't can say "I am at the worst"?' (IV. i.25), he asks, and the question reveals once again the recurrent pattern of the play – that the contrary cannot be incorporated (or even identified, it seems), the regenerations of romance cannot occur. The paths of injustice do not lead to justice; and, when Edgar insists at the last that 'the Gods are just' (v. iii.169), the deaths of Lear and Cordelia prove him wrong. He is both brave and kind, certainly, but the improvisations of his rather pharisaical moral earnestness reveal an abiding confusion in him, caused by the moral disorientation of his country; and finally he is compelled to admit the exhaustion of all his attempts to measure the things that he has seen: 'we that are young/Shall never see so much, nor live so long'. The world itself has aged, it seems, and the romance hero confesses the failure of his quest to bring new life to his kingdom.

'It was solemn, and a little ridiculous, too, as they always are, those struggles of an individual trying to save from the fire his idea of what his moral identity should be.'[69] Marlow's words, ironic and sympathetic in their comment upon Lord Jim, suggest the mixture of emotions with which we watch not only Edgar but all the characters in King Lear, as they attempt in their various ways to restructure the world so as to save something of what they value from the fire. To read well The Faerie Queene would have meant, for Spenser, to carry its organizing distinctions of goodness and evil into our furthermost understandings of each area of our community life and thus to work in hope for its regeneration. But here in the problematical moral world of King Lear our hope is betrayed, and we are drawn instead to watch – with something between ironic wonder and tragic pity – the extraordinary lengths to which men and women must go to keep alive their private sense of justice in the absence of a just community. The play traces the capacity to idealise to its extremes; and in so doing it shows that the satisfactions which might derive from community can find no surrogate in the grotesque tortuosities of the individual fantasy.

Burke was in no doubt: 'society is indeed a contract', he wrote. James I, however, would have dissented, for he argued in *The Trew Law of Free Monarchies* that, if contract were the appropriate word to describe the relationship between subject and king (which he denied), it was a contract of a very special nature – a contract of which, he said, 'God is doubtles the only Iudge'.[70] But what was 'doubtles' to James was by no means so clear to many of his subjects, including many clergymen, lawyers and parliamentarians who insisted that the king's power could not go unchallenged in the great issues of church government, common law and popular sovereignty. When Shakespeare came to write *King Lear*, therefore, the question of contract was politically very sensitive, especially with regard to the difficulties that James was having in imposing his absolutist claim upon recalcitrant parliaments; and the play, although not mentioning 'contract' directly in its political sense, nevertheless shows itself deeply concerned with what C. H. McIlwain has called 'the one feature of the feudal relation that is conspicuous by its absence in James's politics'[71] – namely, the idea of reciprocity. McIlwain continues,

> Of the reciprocal duties of *dominus* and *homo* so prominent in the mediaeval conception of English kingship there remains not a trace: it has been replaced entirely by the Roman conception of a king *legibus solutus*, placed at a distance so immeasurably above his *subditi* that he can in no way be bound by earthly law to the performance of any duties to them. The relation of his subjects to him, on the other hand, must consist *entirely* of duties, and duties to which no limits can be put.

King Lear traces a society where the reciprocal relationship between authority and service has broken down, where desire can no longer say *enough* and flies instead to the limitless extremes of *no less than all*, and where in consequence the vulnerable customs and institutions of that society are destroyed. A world collapses beyond repair; the ideal possibilities of feudal reciprocity, moving as they are, lose touch with material reality and are lost for ever. This play is surely much more than 'a courtly compliment' to the king who was trying to unite England and Scotland, a cautionary tale to the people who were resisting him. It *may* indeed be seen in this way, for it has the openness characteristic of myth (and it had to pass the censor); but such readings seem to me to constrict its openness, reaffirming the very relationship between authority and service which the play dissolves and attempting to sanitize the contaminating impact of a history which the play shows to be disintegrated beyond the reach of bond or contract.

Holinshed tells how Corineus, the companion of Brutus in his invasion of what became Britain, wrestled with one of its original gigantic inhabitants, Gogmagog, and threw him over a cliff by Dover – 'by reason whereof the place was named long after, *The fall or leape of Gogmagog*, but afterward it was called *The fall of Douer*'.[72] *King Lear*, most especially at the moment of Gloucester's attempted suicide, turns upside-down that traditional epic picture of a founding act of violence in which the aboriginal enemy is finally overthrown and civilization established for all future time. Shakespeare has brought all his cast back to what Malinowski called their sacred 'spot of origins',[73] back to Dover, the 'very verge' (II. iv.144) of their confine, and there they meet with despair, madness, disillusion and death. They can neither overthrow nor incorporate that which is contrary. Shockingly, the play reinterprets the mythical charter of its country, assimilating the recent feudal past with romance flexibility to the stories of its first beginnings. It depicts the history of its nation as nightmare, the doom of its Jacobean present inscribed inescapably in the social formation of its determinant prehistory – a prehistory when the complementary opposites of authority and service, nature and society, goodness and evil first began to melt mystifyingly into one another, and the possibilities for a community of goodness faded for ever into an inscrutable world charted only by its injustices. *King Lear*, that is to say, does not only imagine the past: it *brings it into play*, with a power that romance cannot integrate, cautionary tales cannot discipline and catharsis cannot palliate. The play is *dangerous* (a question I shall return to after my discussion of *Macbeth*): it *initiates* its audience into the injustice, confusion and violence of the past which become in performance the injustice, confusion and violence of the present. The disabling contradictions of the world that it imagines, and the grotesque counter-cries of the unslaked imagination for justice, become in the theatre the twin poles upon which the smaller world of the present turns – still today, a wheel of fire that our tears scald.

7

Macbeth

Macbeth is perhaps still most commonly considered as a fable
teaching universal truth. We go to it to elucidate psychological
conflicts between the creative and the destructive, moral conflicts
between the good and the evil, metaphysical conflicts between the
sacred and the unholy. Nor does the play disappoint us, for to
consider it as a fable is genuinely to respond to something in both
its structure and its poetic power. If it shares with *King Lear* the
excitement of the sacrilegious, it has in addition a rich and
memorable poetry of the sacramental; and it is this strongly
antithetical structure, so reminiscent of the morality tradition, that
gives the play its air of universality, its capacity to tempt us to
forget that the morality by which we judge the products of history
is itself a product of that same history. All too often critics of
Macbeth have been tempted to discard its Scottish setting as
superficial trappings, distracting us from the inner body of truth
which should be our real concern. The play, we are told,
penetrates 'to the lower levels of the self, for which social, religious
and political life provides only an outward garment'.[74] 'It is not
"about Scotland" as *Coriolanus* is about Rome or *Othello* about
Venice';[75] and our duty therefore is to discern 'the moral meaning
of this stage narrative abstracted from the annals of Scottish
history'.[76] Even Tillyard, who seems at first to argue that the play *is*
about Scotland and should be considered 'the epilogue' of the
English Histories, proves in the end to mean no more than that
'"Scotland"' (his inverted commas make the point for him) is, like
England, important only in so far as it exemplifies the universal
laws of God's providence operating through nature and human
conscience.[77] It is an argument as inadequate to the historical
imagination at work in *Macbeth* as it was inadequate to the History
Plays.

Those critics who have found the play seriously interested in
Scotland have generally found it so in compliment to King James.
Macbeth is a fable written to keep a drowsy king awake;[78] its aim is
to promote political obedience and to marginalize opposition, to

celebrate the beginnings of the union between England and Scotland, and to glorify the ancestries of the new king in such a way as to seal up the awkward disjunction of his accession. Yet such a reading, although occasionally expressed with that easy cynicism which sees all human achievement as the fruit of self-interest, is usually felt to be inadequate to the tragic power of the play. H. N. Paul's *The Royal Play of 'Macbeth'* is the classic exposition of the play as kingly compliment; and yet he sees that 'in *Macbeth*, as in the other great tragedies, the noble man who has fallen becomes at the end an object of pity and not of hatred'.[79] Muriel Bradbrook too, in her essay 'The Sources of *Macbeth'*, saw that the '*political* highlights' of the play, especially those dealing with the success of that 'canny young man' Malcolm, produced scenes 'the least tragic in tone' in the whole play.[80] Critics who have appreciated the serious historical concern of the play, that is, have also noted a certain discrepancy between their rival senses of the play as compliment and the play as tragedy.

My purpose here is to trace back this discrepancy to its origins in two rival Scottish traditions of interpreting relations with England, the unionist and the nationalist; each was known to Shakespeare, each seems to have been responsible for certain changes that he made in his source material, and they have been brought together deliberately in *Macbeth* in order to problematize our understanding of historical progress by the theatrical experience of tragedy. For *Macbeth is* a play about Scotland, seized at a crucial moment of transition in its history – transition from cultural independence of England to an increasingly close relationship with it, of which the recent coronation of James had marked the latest stage. Yet Shakespeare has not written a chronicle history of that transition; his interest is not in the has-been but in the might-have-been of history. Like *King Lear*, *Macbeth* is a tragic romance, exploring the language, metaphor and myth of a society which we are encouraged to identify as the prehistory of the present. What might it have been like? What have we gained, and what have we lost? The romance possibilities of Scottish feudalism centre upon the figure of Duncan, and we shall see that the antithetical structure of the society that Shakespeare has imagined for Duncan lies at the heart of his inquiry into these possibilities. For the morality play has entered history, and the exploration of the seemingly universal truths of fable in fact resolves itself into an exploration of the kind of society that might sustain such fable.

SCOTLAND: UNIONISM AND NATIONALISM, THE RIVAL TRADITIONS

James was in no doubt about the benefits that union would bring, and he urged his 1607 parliament towards its completion in the vexed questions of citizenship, legislation, commerce and national defence. Union would perfect the historical process that had begun with 'seuen little Kingdomes, besides Wales', and ensure peace, prosperity, prestige and – interestingly, in the light of *Macbeth* – power enough for the people 'to defend themselues from all outward inuasions, and their head and gouernour thereby enabled to redeeme them from forreine assaults, and punish priuate transgressions within'.[81] So the king's power too would be enhanced and consolidated – against, for example, such feuding aristocracy as he had met in Scotland, whom quarrel led 'to bang it out brauely, hee and all his kinne, against him and all his'.[82] Addressing his first parliament, James invoked in metaphor the integration he hoped to bring about in reality:

> What God hath conioyned then, let no man separate. I am the Husband, and all the whole Isle is my lawfull Wife; I am the Head, and it is my Body; I am the Shepherd, and it is my flocke: I hope therefore no man will be so vnreasonable as to thinke that I that am a Christian King vnder the Gospel, should be a Polygamist and husband to two wiues; that I being the Head, should haue a diuided and monstrous Body; or that being the Shepheard to so faire a Flocke (whose fold hath no wall to hedge it but the foure Seas) should haue my Flocke parted in two.[83]

This flight of poetic fancy must have seemed empty rhetoric to many of James's listeners.

When he came to write *Macbeth*, however, perhaps with a court performance in mind, Shakespeare made a number of adaptations to his source material in Holinshed which suggest a desire to compliment the shepherd and celebrate the unity of his flocks. These adaptations are well-known and I need only select and summarize here. In the pageant wrung from the weird sisters, there is personal compliment to the king upon the long lineal descent from which he derived his right to both English and Scottish thrones; and the play is careful to preserve all James's alleged ancestors – Duncan, Malcolm, Banquo, Fleance and Old Siward – free from moral fault. Duncan in particular is changed from the negligently gentle ruler of Holinshed, whilst his murder is planned by Macbeth only with Lady Macbeth and not in conspiracy with those 'trustie friends, amongst whome Banquho was the chiefest',[84] as the chronicles tell. There is political compliment too to James upon his unionist aspirations, seen in many small changes that ignore the military, political and cultural differences between England and Scotland that Holinshed describes. England, for instance, no longer helps Sweno's invasions. Instead, we see two sister nations acting in increasingly close co-operation; and all these changes serve one common dramatic purpose in the play – to isolate Macbeth in what A. P. Rossiter calls 'the *wilfulness* of the murder'.[85]

Other changes serve the same effect: the suppression of any possibility that Macbeth might have a legitimate tanistic claim upon the succession which Duncan usurps for his own descendants in proclaiming Malcolm Duke of Cumberland; the omission of the ten prosperous years of Macbeth's reign; and the suggestion that his final overthrow was the consequence less of civil war than of the invisible slipping-away of the thanes and the gentle rendering of Dunsinane. Some of Shakespeare's most memorable dramatic inventions similarly isolate Macbeth in the horror of his deed: his hallucination of the dagger, his direct involvement in the assassination, his bloody hands, his hallucination of Banquo's ghost at the banquet. Only Lady Macbeth (almost wholly Shakespeare's invention out of hints of an ambitious or a taunting wife) shares Macbeth's knowledge at the start of the play, and we quickly see that this shared knowledge will separate rather than unite them.

So, on the face of it, we have a play of sound political tendency, marginalizing opposition and celebrating the restoration of a rightful monarchy. It is surely a play that would please a king who had just survived the treachery of equivocating subjects in the Gunpowder Plot.

> My Thanes and kinsmen,
> Henceforth be Earls; the first that ever Scotland
> In such an honour nam'd.
>
> (v. ix.28–30)

These words indicate the carefulness of Shakespeare's choice of historical period – the period when reconciliation between two warring nations first seemed possible, under the guidance of James's own canny young ancestor, Malcolm.

But fair is foul, and foul is fair. The reconciliation at the end of *Macbeth*, foreshadowing the wider reconciliation to which James was committed, embodies more than one view of the changing historical relationship between the two countries. For the nationalist tradition in Scottish historiography argued that the *rapprochement* of the two nations at the time of Malcolm Canmore marked the end of the Scottish independence of language, manners and culture that had sustained a genuine heroic age. Hector Boece had argued this case clearly in *The Description of Scotland*, which Holinshed prefaced to his own chronicles; and the emphasis is crucial for *Macbeth*.

In processe of time therefore, and chéeflie about the daies of Malcolme Cammor, our maners began greatlie to change and alter. For when our neighbors the Britons began, after they were subdued by the Romans, to wax idle and slouthfull, and therevpon driuen out of their countrie into Wales by their enimies the Saxons, we began to haue aliance (by proximitie of the Romans) with Englishmen, speciallie after the subuersion of the Picts, and through our dailie trades and conuersation with them, to learne also their maners, and therewithall their language, as I haue said alreadie. Heereby shortlie after it came also to passe, that the temperance and vertue of our ancestors grew to be iudged worthie of small estimation amongst vs, notwithstanding that a certeine idle desire of our former renowme did still remaine within vs.

Furthermore as men not walking in the right path, we began to follow also the vaine shadow of the Germane honor and titles of nobilitie, and boasting of the same after the English maner, it fell out yer long, that wheras he in times past was accompted onlie honorable, which excelled other men not in riches and possessions, but in prowesse and manhood, now he would be taken most glorious that went loaden with most titles, wherof it came to passe, that some were named dukes, some earles, some lords, some barons, in which vaine puffes they fixed all their felicitie. Before time the noble men of Scotland were of one condition, & called by the name of Thanes, so much in Latine as

Quaestores regij, gatherers of the kings duties, in English: and this denomination was given vnto them after ther desert and merit.[86]

Here is a very different picture of the civilized peace and commercial prosperity that James believed would flow from the union of two sister nations. Boece praises instead the temperance in food, drink, dress and domestic comfort that had once enabled a proud small nation to maintain its independence of the larger military powers around it. He celebrates a spartan manhood, fit, severe in punishment, generous in peace but supporting their leaders in war with a fierce loyalty that never stooped to treachery. Nor were the women less rigorous, fighting alongside the men in war, and in peace taking 'intollerable paines'[87] to rear and suckle their own children to preserve the honour of their family line. Holinshed echoes Boece:

> Through this their sober fare, with the exercising of their bodies herewith in continuall trauell, they grew more strong and greater of bodie, than their ofspring are found to be in these daies: for they were more in resemblance like vnto giants than vnto men of our time, with great and huge bodies, mightie armes and lims, pressing vpon their enimies like vnto fierce lions, bearing downe all before them, without dread of anie danger, for that they excéeded all human strength and power.[88]

All this has been lost, Boece laments, through avarice, luxury, 'continuall trade of merchandize and hazard of the wars';[89] and yet, in his hope that the loss is not irretrievable, he has evoked in his history that independent self-sufficient Scotland which he wished to recapture in reality.

Macbeth, alongside its moving final celebration of reconciliation, also embodies this quite opposite sense of Scottish history, a sense that we normally associate with the genre of epic – a sense of the passing of a heroic age, its fading into a meaner, more mercenary time. As in epic, we witness the self-destruction of a heroic civilization under the pressure of inner contradiction in the face of outer hostility. The heroic note is heard vibrant right at the start of the play in the captain's speech and elegiac at the end in Macbeth's superbly unjust contempt: 'Then fly, false Thanes,/And mingle with the English epicures' (v. iii.7–8).

It is here, in this tension between heroic elegy and the celebration of social order, that we must search for the meaning of *Macbeth* – a tension whose origins, we have seen, lie in Shakespeare's assimilation of two opposed interpretations of that particular transitional moment in Scottish history associated with the reign of Malcolm Canmore. Has history since then been loss or gain? Which society should we choose to live in? What, indeed, makes any civilization authentic to its inhabitants? These problems have a psychological aspect too, caught up in that most common, most difficult of questions: how can it be that we admire such a man as Macbeth and regret his passing? But it is false to associate the heroic in the play with Macbeth and his wife alone; and if we wish to explore these difficulties further, we must begin with that other heroic figure in the play, the feudal monarch Duncan, a character largely re-created by Shakespeare precisely to explore the might-have-been of a vanished heroic past.

THE TRUSTFUL KINGSHIP OF DUNCAN

The Duncane of the chronicles was a weak indulgent ruler, needing great provocation to lead his troops to war, and scorned by the rebellious Makdowald as 'a faint-hearted milkesop, more meet to gouerne a sort of idle moonks in some cloister, than to haue the rule of such valiant and hardie men of warre as the Scots were'.[90] But not so in *Macbeth*. Shakespeare has made his king much older and therefore necessarily dependent upon his thanes; he has made him virtuous, a king under whom (in the nostalgic words of one of his lords) it might indeed have been possible to 'do faithful homage, and receive free honours' (III. vi.36); and he has made him articulate in the practice of a fully developed philosophy of kingship, grounded in the reciprocity of trust. Duncan's faith is in the strength of his weakness.

Duncan's greeting of the victorious Macbeth in I. iv is central to the play, and I want to make three points about it here.

> O worthiest cousin!
> The sin of my ingratitude even now
> Was heavy on me. Thou art so far before,
> That swiftest wing of recompense is slow
> To overtake thee: would thou hadst less deserv'd,

> That the proportion both of thanks and payment
> Might have been mine! only I have left to say,
> More is thy due than more than all can pay.
>
> (I. iv.14–21)

First, Duncan uses a language of indebtedness rather than of reward. He chooses to say that he cannot pay off his captain, and in so doing he defines service in other than commercial terms. Money cannot be its measure, and Macbeth is no mercenary. Because thanks precede payment in Duncan's scheme, payment finds its worth in thanks; the thanedom of Cawdor is a real symbol of what really matters much more to Duncan, the ever-deepening sense of reciprocal indebtedness between subject and king. It is worth recalling the words of Hector Boece in praise of that old heroic Scotland:

> when they are gentlie intreated, and with courteous moderation, they are found to be verie tractable and pliant vnto reason: in priuate bargains & contracts they are so willing to giue euerie man his own, that they will yéeld the more. And so farre is it growne into a custome euen in these our daies, that except there be some surplusage aboue the bare couenant, they will breake off and not go forwards with the bargaine.[91]

There is more to life than market relations; ancient Celtic traditions of generosity, courtesy and hospitality are used here, as so often since, to awaken a richer humanity than may be found in the mere self-interest of English mercantilism.

Macbeth clearly feels the deep call to reciprocate Duncan's words of greeting:

> The service and the loyalty I owe,
> In doing it, pays itself. Your Highness' part
> Is to receive our duties . . . .
>
> (I. iv.22–4)

Nor is his financial language simply the small change of everyday transaction. It expresses precisely the economic relations of the feudalism that Shakespeare is imagining, where property is conceived as debt, trust, duty. As the pun in the word makes clear in l.10 (a pun significantly absent from our twentieth-century vocabulary), *ownership* is something *owed*; and the owing validates the ownership. Therefore the language of debt, where the moral subsumes the financial sense, is the truest to the society that Duncan works for. It is, indeed, his commitment to the politics of trust that leads him fatefully to respond to Macbeth's declaration of loyalty by inviting himself to Inverness – to 'bind us further to you', he explains (l.43). If we remember the importance of place to feudal ceremony – of who goes where to pay homage, for instance – we shall understand properly the symbolic meaning of this journey of king to subject. For Duncan puts himself at the mercy of his most powerful subject, deliberately, at the very moment when he is most flushed with military success. He dies as he had lived, in active furtherance of his vision of a nation bound together, like an extended family, in the reciprocity of debt.

Second, Duncan uses a language of indebtedness not only to man but also to God: he speaks of the *sin* of ingratitude, and he does so because his political vision is also a religious one, binding God and man together in the one great principle of debt. Life itself, as Cawdor discovered, is owed not owned; it is 'the lease of Nature' (IV. i.99), belonging to God and king alike – and this phrase may serve to remind us too of the crucial place that Nature has in Duncan's vision. The delicacy of his words at Inverness says it all:

> This castle hath a pleasant seat; the air
> Nimbly and sweetly recommends itself
> Unto our gentle senses.
>
> (I. vi.1–3)

He has already spoken of being fed by the 'commendations' of Macbeth (I. iv.55), and behind his acknowledgement of the recommendations of the breeze lies the technical feudal term of *commendatio*, the act by which a vassal gives himself in service to his lord in return for protection. So here the breeze shows alacrity in serving the king, and the king in return acknowledges his own appropriate debt of gratitude. Duncan's words elicit a reciprocal elaboration upon the royal theme from Banquo in praise of house-martins, the *guests* of summer whom the breath of heaven has *wooed* to take up home here by their 'loved mansionry' (I. vi.5). Once again, the sense of indebtedness is declared to breed an increased reciprocity and gratitude, and so the web of relationship between man, nature and God, subordinate and superior alike, is consciously woven and reinforced. This moment will prove to be the last in the play that anyone can speak with such affectionate particularity of the world before them; but nevertheless the religious vision that Duncan shares with his countrymen will continue to make itself felt in the poetry of its disturbance.

Third, the language in which Duncan sets forth his debts to man and God is studiedly ceremonious. It invites the returns of courtesy according to the proportions of degree. 'Sons, kinsmen, Thanes,/And you whose places are the nearest' (I. iv.35–6), he begins: his language is a mode of sustaining distinction, of articulating social order, of conferrring upon his subjects their independence, whilst reaffirming their obligation not to abuse it. Cawdor died a studied aristocratic death because he chose to make of his death an opportunity to rededicate the subject, recrown the king and reinstate the deity; and Duncan lives a studied kingly life in order that his every word and deed might do the same. Even his fatigue becomes an occasion for exhortation, as we see when Lady Macbeth advances upon him in what is surely an excessive, perhaps even an ominous welcome:

> See, see! Our honour'd hostess. –
> The love that follows us sometime is our trouble,
> Which still we thank as love. Herein I teach you,
> How you shall bid God 'ild us for your pains,
> And thank us for your trouble.
> (I. vi.10–14)

Duncan emphasizes the extraordinary pains that are the price of the extraordinary privileges of kingship, and he offers the self-sacrificial work that he puts into his relationships as emblematic of what is truly valuable in them. All that he says and does must be exemplary, and it is here that we touch upon his essential heroism – a heroism which, opposite to that of Macbeth, is of service for the public good.

We may therefore say in conclusion of Duncan's vision that it is *sacramental*, that he celebrates the otherness of the world for the *grace* of the relationships which inform it, and that for him the heart of this grace is the sense of *indebtedness*, drawing man, nature and God together so closely that even the smallest word and deed comes to symbolize the totality in which it participates. Both the house-martin and Duncan are guests, and each may image the other since each partakes of the same reciprocities of hospitality and gratitude. Some words of Marcel Mauss from *The Gift* describe perfectly the kind of early feudal society that Shakespeare had in mind for Duncan's Scotland:

> in these 'early' societies, social phenomena are not discrete; each phenomenon contains all the threads of which the social fabric is composed. In these *total* social phenomena, as we propose to call them, all kinds of institutions find simultaneous expression: religious, legal, moral and economic. In addition, the phenomena have their aesthetic aspect . . . . [92]

The whole of such a society is implicit in each of its parts: here too is the key to the extraordinary coherence and richness of metaphor in *Macbeth* – not in the metaphysics of a supposed 'Elizabethan World Picture' (we shall find a quite different metaphoric structure in the Venetian plays, for example), but in Shakespeare's historical interest in the might-have-been of Duncan's rule, in a Christian feudal monarchy whose chief ideological self-defence lay in a rigorously holistic, heavily tabooed distinction between goodness and evil. For, as we shall see in a moment, Duncan's language is so powerful to articulate social order because of the ever-present threat of disorder; and clearly, within such a permanently threatened society, as within the tribal societies studied by Mauss, 'there is no middle path. There is either complete trust or mistrust.'[93] The house-martin will find its antithesis in the raven, Duncan his in Macbeth: the antithetical structure which characterizes this play so markedly is grounded in the political necessities of its primitive society, where religious taboo alone must do the work which is shared in the Histories and the Venetian plays with law and the agents of law. Hence, of course, the great sociological importance of the gift of which Mauss writes (Duncan gives Lady Macbeth a diamond, we remember, in II. i), to incur the reciprocal debt of obligation; and hence too the central importance of ceremony in the act of donation (at II. i.16 Duncan honours her as his 'most kind hostess'), to avert the violence to which the giver at the moment of giving is peculiarly vulnerable. Heroically, Duncan goes through with it; he puts his faith in debt to defuse and marginalize the opposition he fears, and to this end he devotes all the arts and ceremonies of his kingship.

Yet Duncan's kingship from the start of the play is in a state of crisis. He faces two military threats: invasion and civil war, the enemy without and the enemy within. Each reveals a central contradiction between Duncan's reliance upon trust and the facts of the feudal social formation before him – contradictions which are so dramatically powerful because Duncan is apparently aware of them, active before them, but finally destroyed by them as they converge in the murderous figure of Macbeth. First, the civil war reveals that Scotland cannot be ruled only by trust; 'the golden round' (I. v.27) excites desires and ambitions in men that cannot be subdued to a faith in reciprocal indebtedness. We shall consider these desires and ambitions later when we come to Macbeth; but we must not forget that Macbeth's treason has been preceded by that of Cawdor and Macdonwald – the pattern is recurrent. Second, the external aggression reveals (as indeed does the civil war too) that the defence of 'the gentle weal' (III. iv.75) of trust must be by the barbaric arts of war. This is the question I want to consider here.

We first see Duncan in the field behind his own battle-lines, receiving military intelligence. It is one of a subject's duties to fight for his king, even to die for him, to pay 'a soldier's debt' (v. ix.5). The Macbeth that we glimpse through the sergeant's speech in the second scene is doing his duty; and yet the energies that drive him in the art of war are violent, barbaric and dangerous to the art of peace. The sergeant calls him 'Valour's minion' (I. ii.19) and Rosse calls him 'Bellona's bridegroom' (l.55) – talismanic heroic phrases born in the stress of war, praising the soldier's art to the king and yet suggesting too the dangerous subordination of the subject in the soldier. Perhaps an awareness of his danger underlies the extraordinary terms of Duncan's grateful exclamation: 'O valiant cousin! worthy gentleman!' (l.24). It seems here that Duncan is trying to master the threatening power of his strongest subject, to claim the culture of war for that of peace, to maintain the crucial distinction between creative and destructive violence. His words have the courage of a man not afraid of the battlefield; and yet they are haunted by a grotesque comic possibility, lurking in the disjunction between their tones of ceremonious gratitude and the barbaric language of the sergeant. For the gentle weal is dependent upon a worthy gentleman who seemed ready 'to bathe in reeking wounds,/Or memorize another Golgotha' (ll.40–1). It is this contradiction that Duncan cannot articulate, and it will form an essential aspect of the subject-matter of the play. Perry Anderson put the general theoretical point this way: 'There was thus an inbuilt contradiction within feudalism, between its own rigorous tendency to a decomposition of sovereignty and the absolute exigencies of a final centre of authority in which a practical recomposition could occur.'[94] In *Macbeth* we see the material decomposition of authority necessitated by Duncan's reliance upon his thanes and their men for the defence of the realm, and also an ideological decomposition of authority which seeks to turn that reliance into an opportunity for trust. It is the energies and desires generated within Macbeth by this process that will prove fatal to Duncan at the very moment when he has to recompose his authority after the war.

Duncan does his best. Immediately after the battle is won, he tries ceremonially to reclaim the energies of war for peace; and it is an attempt that shows his prudence as well as his courage. He honours all his noblemen, he honours in particular his most powerful subject at the moment of his greatest exhilaration, and yet he insists that order and distinction will be maintained.

> Sons, kinsmen, Thanes,
> And you whose places are the nearest, know,
> We will establish our estate upon
> Our eldest, Malcolm . . . .
>
> (i. iv.35–8)

It is perhaps this that undoes him; for in this play, as Hazlitt observed, 'every passion brings in its fellow-contrary'[95] and faith excites faith-breach. 'They met me in the day of success' (i. v.1), Macbeth writes to his wife: the desires and ambitions of the subject, already inflamed by the excitement and glory of war, are to be inflamed still further by the restraints of peace. It is an old story, always new, always particular; the same force that should defend a society destroys it. We must witness Duncan's diffused authority disintegrate into civil war, before under Malcolm a practical recomposition of a different kind can occur.

THE WEIRD SISTERS: 'IMPERFECT SPEAKERS'

The castle on the heath is as potent an image in the tragic romance of *Macbeth* as it was in *King Lear*; and once again destruction will be by that which is contrary. The weird sisters – figures who should suggest the far north, if H. N. Paul is right[96] – are the contraries of Duncan, or (in the more accurate phrase of Hazlitt) they are his fellow-contraries, embodying precisely those desires and energies which he is unable to articulate and is driven instead to marginalize. Against the exactitude and clarity of the duties that Duncan lives by, the play sets the strangeness and the imperfect speaking of the sisters. If Duncan's vision is sacramental and ceremonious, theirs is fetishistic and obscene. The particularity of their distinctions ('eye of newt, and toe of frog...') is not relationship to the independence of things in the harmony of their pattern; it is a pornographic and promiscuous dislocation, dismembering the body of the world to make it yield talismanic objects of desire. In terms of the antithetical structure of the play, the three of them represent 'the baleful aspect of the sacred, perceived as a disparate but formidably unified force'.[97]

For the sacred *has* two faces, two opposing sets of ceremonies, the mass that celebrates self-sacrificial love and the black mass that might be used for *maleficium*. The laborious art that the sisters weave into their charms is a direct assault upon the total society of Scotland, and the destruction of the whole is clearly implicit in the destruction of the part, Macbeth, at whom they first aim. They are associated with the wayward perversity of man (the First Folio three times calls them 'weyward sisters'), with 'the multiplying villainies of nature' (I. ii.11), and with the infernal 'spirits/That tend on mortal thoughts' (I. v.40–1). Their 'unclean rites',[98] that is, aim to unravel precisely that harmony between man, nature and God that Duncan had struggled to maintain. Whilst Duncan had used ceremony to fashion the distinct relationships of a seemingly all-inclusive social life, and to avert its ever-present threat of violence, the exclusive rituals of the sisters are devoted to the violent powers which lurk in things forbidden and whose origin is the desire to overthrow distinction. They desire what they should not, *because* they should not – and this takes the play into strange areas indeed.

A recognition of the strangeness that surrounds the sisters is crucial to an appreciation of the play. What kind of unholy sorority are they, after all? Clearly they constitute a dangerous alternative to those extended families upon which Duncan builds his kingdom. Yet we never know the extent of their society or their business: always they are engaged upon 'a deed without a name' (IV. i.49). They have bodies and yet dissolve into air; they are women and yet have beards; they are on the earth yet seem not of it. Their outlandishness must have been as baffling to their first audience as it was to Macbeth and Banquo, for there had never been anything like them in the theatre before. 'As in *A Midsummer Night's Dream* and later in *The Tempest*', wrote Muriel Bradbrook of *Macbeth*, 'Shakespeare created a new kind of supernatural drama and one which was very widely and generally imitated.'[99] What are the sisters? Are they witches? destinies? furies? old women? the collective unconscious of Duncan's Scotland? objective correlatives of the minds of troubled men? They call themselves 'Weird Sisters' (I. iii.32) – but the name is no name, characteristically equivocal, baffling where it seems to illuminate.

Although we know more than either Macbeth or Banquo knows, in that we see the historical nature of the contradiction with which the sisters confront them, it is important to admit our ignorance and the strange excitement with which that ignorance is charged. It is the strange excitement of that particular kind of temptation to which so many phrases of our culture bear witness: 'I don't know what came over me', 'I wasn't in my right mind', 'I was beside myself', 'I don't know what possessed me', or (especially appropriate to this play) 'the devil gets into me when I'm drunk'. The sisters, that is, epitomize the purity of perverse temptation; like Goneril and Regan, though with greater purity because of their seemingly non-human status, they are in rebellion against the patriarchal universe and all the distinctions and taboos that sustain it. This rebelliousness has recently attracted the attention of radical critics eager to valorize the experience of the dispossessed and the marginalized in Shakespeare's plays. Terry Eagleton, for instance, is drawn to the 'dark carnival' and 'fruitful darkness' of their subversive potential.[100] But we need to be careful in interpreting such 'history from below'; as Jonathan Dollimore wrote, 'to piece together its fragments may be eventually to disclose not the self-authenticating other, but the self-division intrinsic to (and which thereby perpetuates) subordination'.[101] I think the sisters are self-divided in this way, perverse in their pleasures and parasitic in their ideology. There is, in fact, an interesting paradox

in their embodiment of 'the baleful aspect of the sacred', which
Marilyn French noticed when she wrote that 'they are aggressive
and authoritative, but seem to have power only to create petty
mischief'.[102] Themselves fragments and dedicated to fragments,
they seem to speak on behalf of a 'formidably unified force' which
yet they are never quite seen to command. This paradox has its
basis both in history and psychology. Keith Thomas noted its
historical basis when he compared the *ad hoc* nature of popular
magic belief with the fully articulated scheme of Christianity ('It
was a collection of miscellaneous recipes, not a comprehensive
body of doctrine', he wrote[103]), whilst its psychological basis lies in
the fundamental inconsolability and insatiability of perversion,
whose temptations hold out infinite promise but disappoint at the
last. Like the sisters, their strangeness excites only to betray.

But there is pleasure, of course, in the excited desire to do the
forbidden thing – a fascination which we cannot simply duck in
moral disapproval. The sisters are not merely Evil. Indeed, we are
able to make human sense of these fantastical figures only at this
point of their pleasure, their relish, their glee; and I want now to
characterize that pleasure in terms of its essential paradox, that,
whilst it seems to confer omnipotence, it serves in fact only to
alienate and depersonalize.

First of all, it is obscene. It is, in a specialized sense, that is to say,
a *social* pleasure, a kind of *folie à trois* perhaps, enjoyed by a small
group of people brought together only by that pleasure in rebellion
against the norms of their larger society. The filthy appetites which
the sisters share establish the only constitution of their sorority;
and they are of course appetites absolutely unfit for the ceremonious public stage of Duncan's Scotland, although they remain
parasitically dependent upon it for the intensity of their illicit glee.

Second, it is sadistic. The sisters are, in Hazlitt's fine phrase,
'malicious from their impotence of enjoyment'.[104] That is, there is
something essentially substitutionary about their pleasuring, parallel to the displacement which Masud Khan noticed at work in
pornography. 'The only true achievement of pornography', he
wrote, 'is that it transmutes rage into erotic somatic events.'[105] So
here the sisters have transmuted fundamental rage into sadistic
malice, tending towards a relentlessly sexualized view of the world
(much as de Sade enforced upon his Juliette) – a world where the
potent excitement of violating taboo must disguise the impotence
of creative enjoyment and relationship.

Third, it is fetishistic. 'Here I have a pilot's thumb . . . ' (I. iii.28). The sisters' sexualization of their world proceeds by fragmentation, and here too their imagination seems pornographic; for, as Steven Marcus has observed, 'pornography is not interested in persons but in organs. Emotions are an embarrassment to it, and motives are distractions.'[106] The sisters are fascinated by *bits* of the body, and they pursue these bits with the manic energy characteristic of the pursuit of the obscene. 'I'll drain him dry as hay . . . ' (l.18).

Fourth, it is ruthlessly selfish. ' "Give me" quoth I' (l.5): their lust to appropriate, to consume (that is, to destroy by incorporation into the self) is grounded in a sense of property antithetical to Duncan's, and governed only by the waywardness of caprice. They seem to pursue chestnuts with the same insistent greed with which they pursue Macbeth. They usurp from others the opportunity to give by taking first; and they do so with a terrible frankness that sets at nought the laboured considerations of Duncan.

Fifth, it transcends the bonds of time and place. The sisters can sail to sea in a sieve, and it is this freedom from human limitation that invests them with what Hazlitt calls their sublimity. Marcus observes that in the imagined world of pornography – 'pornotopia', he calls it – the restrictions of time and place do not apply, since its aim is to re-create the primary processes of the unconscious mind 'in which all things exist in a total, simultaneous present'.[107] This is the strange unchanging world which the sisters inhabit, and it will be left to Macbeth and his wife to live out its human implications; for, of course, only that which is involved in time and place can develop, grow or decline.

Sixth, and last, their pleasure (like much of the pleasure of obscenity and all the pleasure of pornography) depends upon a fetishism of language. Their charms are linguistic rather than culinary, we might say – and this perception brings us back again to the essentially substitutionary nature of their pleasure, as they try to recapture in childish rhythm and incantation a state of consciousness lost for ever to the adult. Marcus again suggests the connection with the language of pornography:

in pornography . . . the intention of language including metaphor, is unmetaphoric and literal; it seeks to *de-elaborate* the verbal structure and the distinctions upon which it is built, to move back through language to that part of our minds where all metaphors are literal truths, where everything is possible, and where we were all once supreme.[108]

The temptation which the sisters embody, that is, is illusion: it seems to provide the power to do, and do, and do, but in fact it leads away from the real world and real relationship into alienation and depersonalization. Their highly eroticized sense of desire leads only to dissociation and despair. We may let Masud Khan's words sum it up: 'The genius, if one may use that word, of pornography rests in its confidence-trick.'[109] It is by the means of such a confidence-trick that the language of the sisters seduces Macbeth.

The sisters, then, have only malice to contribute. Their deeds are evil and their imaginations are depraved; and yet we must reckon seriously with them, if only because of their problematical status. For they are neither real nor unreal. If they were real, Macbeth would be their victim; if unreal, he would be his own. But blame is an inadequate response to those temptations that are structural in a society, inadequate to the strange half-life that they live in the shadow of its taboos. The play needs the sisters; they complete its imagined world, and their pleasure is humanly significant within it. Although perverse, it has at its heart those energies of disobedience, rebellion and desire which are essential to the processes of individual and social evolution. What the play shows is how – in a threatened total society, whose distinctions of order, gender and morality are absolute – those energies are driven to the violent extremes of perversity: they become demonized, nec-romantic, occult. Duncan nurtured a vision of a harmoniously unified Scotland; but the sisters reveal instead a hierarchical, patriarchal society that is deeply and rigidly *dissociated*, where evil is *disavowed* and rebelliousness *disowned* – a society that is rigidly defended against change and therefore highly unstable, since all its inner tensions build up into contradictions which then can only lead to violence.

THE TYRANNICAL KINGSHIP OF MACBETH

Why does Macbeth kill Duncan? The familiar isolation of ambition by way of an answer does not begin to match the metaphoric richness of Macbeth's soliloquies in Acts i and ii, and these are the only reliable guide that we have to his motives and their significant connections with the world. Ambition doesn't usually feel like *that*, we might say. A sentence from Wordsworth, describing the neo-Shakespearean villain of his own play *The Borderers*, establishes the keynote: 'he finds his temptation in strangeness. He is unable to suppress a low hankering after the *double entendre* in vice.'[110] The strangeness in Macbeth's mind has been well described by Wilson Knight: 'He himself is hopelessly at a loss, and has little idea as to why he is going to murder Duncan. He tries to fit names to his reasons – "ambition", for instance – but this is only a name.'[111] *Macbeth* is a study of ambivalence in a total society; and the reason why its hero cannot articulate his motives is that they appertain to the disowned aspect of his own ambivalence. Fair is foul, and foul is fair: Macbeth is unable to resist the desire which is the secret face of prohibition, and which has been driven to speak perversely – 'in a double sense' (v. viii.20), with the *double entendre* of vice – precisely because it is secret. It has become disowned and unable to involve itself creatively in life. Macbeth kills Duncan for the sake of what the play calls 'mischief', for the fascinating pleasure that he finds in doing what most he believes to be wrong. The corollary of this, of course, is that Duncan is killed because he is believed to be good. He falls victim to the tragic paradox that, by the perverse logic of ambivalence, in anathematizing temptation and making it seem unnatural he activates it against himself. He succumbs to the contradictions which he himself has helped to create in the minds of his subjects – contradictions whose material base, of course, lies deep in the military dependence of the warring feudal state upon the loyalty of its aristocratic families.

It is on the heath, by the battlefield, that the sisters tempt Macbeth, seeking (it seems) to exploit the dependence of the gentle weal upon war; for it is there and now, in this most marginal place and time, that Macbeth and his country are most vulnerable. As René Girard puts it, 'a special sort of impurity clings to the warrior returning to his homeland, still tainted with the slaughter of war'.[112] When he returns home and re-enters his castle, however, he finds the sisters' temptation redoubled upon him by his wife:

> Art thou afeard
> To be the same in thine own act and valour,
> As thou art in desire?
>
> (I. vii.39–41)

This is the very dream of omnipotence, to destroy the distinctions between heart and hand, desire and deed; and, as Lady Macbeth persuades her husband to act against the king he should defend, she aims to destroy too the distinctions that Duncan had so laboriously drawn between peace and war. What is more, her temptation, like the charms of the sisters, is highly sexualized, in a way that spells destruction for all the gentle courtesies through which Duncan tries to discipline the extended family of his kingdom. For the unruliness of sexuality, the waywardness of what the porter calls lechery, is felt throughout *Macbeth*; and it is just this unruliness that Lady Macbeth seeks to arouse in her husband by the *double entendre* of her references to act, valour and desire. Duncan, when he addressed her as the wife of the Thane of Cawdor (I. vi.20ff.) had, by the intricate dance of his pronouns, distinguished woman from man, family from family, subject from king, each in its rightful place; but here, within the family, fuelled by those same sexual energies that might keep a family and state together, we find a fierce, competitive, highly sexualized spirit bent upon particular ambition and set against the general good, aroused against it precisely because it is good. Sexual and soldierly excitements fuel one another, promiscuously mixed in the mind of Lady Macbeth, and the extended family loyalties of trust by which Duncan had tried to secure his state against the hazards of war and peace are doomed to disappear. Not even his expressed wish to have been Macbeth's 'purveyor' (l.22) can contain the desire to turn his kingdom upside-down, and he will be murdered by the captain who is his cousin.

The murder is a *folie à deux*, created between Macbeth and his wife where neither alone would have done it; and it strikes to the heart of all that they hold sacred in their society. It is the one great central act of violation that, as all the metaphors of child-murder, rape, blasphemy and drunkenness reveal, evokes all the other acts of violation that they can imagine; for they share with their king a common imaginative commitment to the language of the sacramental. There is one crucial difference, however. Duncan's language tends to *realize* the people around him, offering them the time and place to fulfil themselves voluntarily through their responses to him. But, when Macbeth speaks of the wicked dreams that abuse the curtained sleep, of the celebrations of Witchcraft or the preparations of Murther, his images depend for their intensity upon a superstitious *derealization* of the world. His earlier idealiza-

tion of Duncan – his virtues pleading 'like angels, trumpet-
tongu'd, against/The deep damnation of his taking-off' (I. vii.19–
20) – shows the same hallucinatory quality. He has lost his hold
upon those courtesies through which other people can exert their
discipline, and has been led instead into a state of rapt introver-
sion, a private theatricality of the moral imagination which is a
form of self-estrangement. Even in the self-examinations of his
conscience, we sense the contamination of excitement upon him.
So it is that the hallucinated dagger with its gouts of blood – perfect
emblem of the desire and the aversion which are the twin faces of
his ambivalence – comes to serve the stronger passion and
marshall him the way that he was going.

All that the Macbeths can conceive of love and tenderness points
them irresistibly towards Duncan in his bedchamber.

> I have given suck, and know
> How tender 'tis to love the babe that milks me:
> I would, while it was smiling in my face,
> Have pluck'd my nipple from his boneless gums,
> And dash'd the brains out, had I so sworn
> As you have done to this.
>
> (I. vii.54–9)

Through such troubled sensuous poetry, they are daring to
express themselves in the perverse creations of debauchery, and
finding (as Iago finds) that the immediate juxtaposition of images
of goodness and evil, of tenderness and cruelty, of vulnerability
and savagery, generates emotions of great violence. Macbeth, his
energies roused, relishes the dramatization of himself as 'wither'd
Murther' (II. i.52) and as Tarquin about to ravish Lucrece; and the
metaphor of rape is a revealing one. Duncan's lying-asleep at
Macbeth's mercy in his castle is an emblem of trust, of everything
that both would have their civilization to be; and yet trust excites
betrayal, debt exploitation, weakness violence, and faith faith-
breach. The murder of Duncan is no mere political assassination. It
is the very worst thing imaginable: 'most sacrilegious Murther' (II.
iii.68), violating all the bonds between man, nature and God. And
hence – its hour come round at last – the fascination that it holds.

'O horror! horror! horror!' cries Macduff, forced suddenly to face
the physical reality, the moral atrocity and the full imaginative
implications of Duncan's death. 'Tongue nor heart cannot con-

ceive, nor name thee!' (ii. iii.64–5). The thanes too are seized by
the contamination of the excitement caused by the murder, and for
a moment Macduff glimpses into the strangeness of a world in
which he has lost all bearings. Then suddenly he finds the
language he wants, an old language aroused to an assimilation of
the horror he has just seen. 'Confusion now hath made his
masterpiece!' (l.67), he cries, and the elegiac note is prophetic. He
senses what Macbeth most deeply fears, that the future will only
bring anti-climax. 'All is but toys: renown, and grace, is dead'
(l.94), Macbeth will say. It is true in the fullest sense that 'Treason
has done his worst' (iii. ii.24) – which by the paradox of
ambivalence has also been the best, a masterpiece. A terrible
pornographic beauty has been born:

> Here lay Duncan,
> His silver skin lac'd with his golden blood;
> And his gash'd stabs look'd like a breach in nature
> For ruin's wasteful entrance.
>
> (ii. iii.111–14)

But nothing that Macbeth can do in the future will ever be able so
fully to absorb his imagination again. The king has been killed; and
what's done cannot be redone.

The period of Macbeth's kingship has two antithetically related
aspects, embodied at the end of the play in the alternating scenes
of Act v: the degeneration of Macbeth and his wife, and the
gathering resistance of the thanes under Malcolm and Macduff. I
want briefly to outline them both. First, the degeneration of the
Macbeths – a development which is a deepening not of debt and
trust but of fear, mistrust, suspicion. This mistrust has its political
expression in the rapid establishment of a tyranny where one
man's security is bought with the aid of a network of paid
informers and hired assassins, and where even the assassins are
watched in 'mistrust' (iii. iii.2). 'There's not a one of them, but in
his house/I keep a servant fee'd' (iii. iv.130–1): the keynote is not
gratitude but contempt – the contempt reserved for those one fears
or uses and akin to self-contempt in the generally degraded view it
holds of all mankind. Macbeth does not adventure upon relationship; where Duncan visited his thanes, Macbeth must stay put in
Dunsinane. The mistrust has its family expression too in the

widening separation between husband and wife; their lack of issue comes to seem emblematic of the sterility into which their desires have brought their marriage. Their relationship begins to fail even as conspiracy. Macbeth embarks upon a course of debauchery in violence which he cannot bring himself to share with his wife. 'Be innocent of the knowledge, dearest chuck' (III. ii.45), he says to her with grotesque tenderness whilst awaiting Banquo's murder, and in so doing he condemns her to an isolation which leads eventually to her suicide.

But it is perhaps the psychological exploration of mistrust that is most remarkable in the play, as we watch Macbeth himself disintegrate within the disintegration of his kingdom and his family. 'For mine own good', he says, 'All causes shall give way' (III. iv.134–5). His hubris is a vain attempt to code the moral universe in his own desires in order to secure himself against his fears; and as the play goes on, he falls increasingly into the mistrustful anxieties of the paranoid cycle, where the magical sense of omnipotence is haunted by its fellow-contrary nightmare of impotence. As in *King Lear*, the single state of man falls into extremes which (to quote King James once more) 'although they seeme contrarie, yet growing to the height, runne euer both in one'.[113] The copresence of these two extremes is embodied with great dramatic economy in the *double entendre* of the sisters' second group of prophecies, which torture Macbeth with the hope that that which it is impossible to prevent (his defeat) will be indeed prevented by that which is – again – impossible (the movement of Birnam Wood to Dunsinane, the existence of a man not born of woman). For Macbeth, these gnomic gobbets torn from the book of the black arts serve as fetishes; tantalizingly untrustworthy as they are, they encourage him to plunge on through his 'initiate fear' (III. iv.142) into a reckless debauchery of wrongdoing. But, in the manner of fetishes, they cannot adequately replace those recip- rocities of love and trust which Macbeth has already put to the sword; they can do no more than afford a displaced ground upon which the subsequent conflict between desire and terror can be acted out to its inescapable conclusion. Finally, the contamination of this violent conflict infects Macbeth totally; the diminishing returns of his perversity wither him into the image of the 'wither'd Murther' that he had at first invoked; and then, played out, he is killed, a haunting after-image of the soldier in Act I, fighting fiercely still but for what he no longer believes in.

The process of Macbeth's disintegration is complemented by the integration of the thanes' resistance to him. They resist as they must; but we should not think simply of the opposition between them. There is identity as well as difference, and the language of the thanes suggests how deeply they are united with Macbeth in the strife which divides them; for the violence of emotion aroused by the murder of Duncan has caused a general moral panic throughout the community.

> 			Alas, poor country!
> Almost afraid to know itself. It cannot
> Be call'd our mother, but our grave; where nothing,
> But who knows nothing, is once seen to smile;
> Where sighs, and groans, and shrieks that rent the air
> Are made, not mark'd; where violent sorrow seems
> A modern ecstasy . . . .
> 						(IV. iii.164–70)

Here is the same contamination of excitement and theatricality of imagination that we found in Macbeth, as Rosse attempts to picture the masterpiece of confusion that he sees in Scotland.

Yet, as Macduff found an old language to save himself from strangeness when he spoke of 'most sacrilegious Murther', so too do the thanes in their attempt to help their poor country reknow itself. It is an excited, often superstitious language, anathematizing Evil as the inversion of Good and sentimentalizing both because of the excitements that they feel. Their army will 'dew the sovereign flower, and drown the weeds' (v. ii.30), Macbeth is simply 'the tyrant' (l.11) and Malcolm 'the med'cine of the sickly weal' (l.27): Macbeth is the source of all contamination in the realm, it seems, and to kill him has become a sacred necessity; and a regular use of images of purification and purgation accordingly marks the sacrificial way in which the thanes approach their military mission.

> 			Well; march we on,
> To give obedience where 'tis truly ow'd:
> Meet we the med'cine of the sickly weal;
> And with him pour we, in our country's purge,
> Each drop of us.
> 						(v. ii.25–9)

Yet the emotions in Macduff, for one, are clearly not always of this sacrificial cast. 'Revenges burn in them' (1.3), says Menteth of Malcolm and his military commanders, including 'the good Macduff' (1.2). The language of purification is no doubt psychologically and politically valuable to restrain the violent energies of the civil war in which the play (as it began) is ending; and yet it is a language inadequate to what we see. There is a real sense in which Macbeth has become, despite all his tyranny, a scapegoat, bearing all the violence in his society, unifying it by his death and thereby preventing the thanes from understanding those political contradictions and psychological ambivalences that have caused the violence in which they are even now implicated. Duncan perceived the kind of violence by which he was threatened but could not accommodate it in either his language or his statecraft; Macbeth perceived the kind of violence by which he was threatened but could not accommodate its power to excite; but the thanes do no more than name the violence by which they are threatened 'Macbeth' and try to restore the world as it was before.

This desire on the part of the thanes to restore the world that had already failed them serves by contrast to reinforce the aristocratic heroism of Macbeth, a heroism not of service but of hubris.

> I am in blood
> Stepp'd in so far, that, should I wade no more,
> Returning were as tedious as go o'er.
> (III. iv.135–7)

Macbeth does not return, he goes over; he dares those perverse extremes of experience which he cannot resist. With a warrior's recklessness and a thane's conscience, he commits himself to the conflicts that they entail, and in so doing he draws out everything previously disavowed in his society. In daring that which was most forbidden, he sets in train a violent civil conflict that will change it decisively; he becomes the heroic destroyer of a heroic age.

THE PRUDENT KINGSHIP OF MALCOLM

Macbeth traces the coming of age of Malcolm; by the end he is no longer 'the boy' (v. iii.3) whom Macbeth dismisses with such mistaken contempt. He has learned from experience, and it is in the quality of what he has learned that the heroic age of Duncan is finally lost. He brings peace and reconciliation to Scotland, but not the peace that the thanes expect. They hope to restore the trustful community in which they may once more 'do faithful homage, and receive free honours,/All which we pine for now' (III. vi.36–7); but the man they support has developed a political understanding that will make such a return impossible. Indeed, it is an alarming measure of Malcolm's power at the end of the play that we may be tempted in retrospect to disown Duncan's death as the result of his political naïveté. The end of *Macbeth*, therefore, is no mere celebration of order, no mere enactment of justice. It is these things, but troublingly so, inviting us to question the nature of the order and the justice that we welcome by means of the historical perspective in which it places them.

It is the language of Malcolm's last address, delivered at a moment when the thanes (and Macduff in particular) are power-fully exhilarated with military success, that most clearly marks the historical transformation with which the play is concerned. It is an address which, whilst it seems to revive the poetry and the political language of Duncan, does no more than pay them lip-service; we are witnessing the transformation of poetry into rhetoric. We sense in Malcolm a prudent watchfulness very different from Duncan's trust, and are drawn accordingly to appreciate his political skill – an appreciation in which the nature of the Scottish community will need to be redefined. The separate pieces of evidence of this new watchfulness in Malcolm are slight in themselves, as of necessity they must be if he is to be successful; yet considered together they seem to be conclusive. First, whilst Duncan had nurtured a reciprocal indebtedness between subject and king, Malcolm speaks of settling accounts:

> We shall not spend a large expense of time,
> Before we reckon with your several loves,
> And make us even with you.
>
> (v. ix.26–8)

He is debasing the currency of his father's thought, even as he seems to restore it to circulation. The thanes' honours, we might say, will not be free: they will be repayments. Second, whilst Duncan went to visit Macbeth at Inverness, Malcolm more cannily invites the assembled thanes to wait on him, in his coronation at

Scone; and third – and more complexly – he summarily judges Macbeth and his wife as 'this dead butcher, and his fiend-like Queen' (l.35).

The trouble with this judgement is that it is at once true and untrue to everything that we have seen. Its truth is evident and accounts for the unanimity amongst those who have suffered directly from Macbeth's violence. Its falsehood is evident too, but only to the audience fascinated by the same violence in the theatre. As Helen Gardner observes, discussing the obloquy reserved uniquely for Macbeth amongst Shakespeare's dead tragic heroes, 'it is only we, the audience, who can pay a tribute of silent awe';[114] and our wish to pay that tribute, silent though at first it may be, alienates us from Malcolm and the society that he is trying to rebuild. His judgement, although a shrewd banner under which to unite a divided country, is nevertheless deeply pharisaical. It has the quality of a headline in one of today's popular newspapers, apparently closing the ranks of the good against an anathematized evil but in fact exploiting ambivalence and fomenting its dangerousness. The doctor was far wiser than Malcolm in the face of contamination: 'God, God forgive us all' (v. i.72), he prayed. Malcolm, however, locates the enemy not within but without the circle of his thanes, and demonizes it as 'fiend-like'. It is the same ungenerosity of imagination, the same callow melodrama, that he showed in England when testing Macduff (and *perhaps* himself), praising Edward and reviling 'black Macbeth' (IV. iii.52). He has learnt nothing but watchfulness, it seems. We appreciate his fear; we admire his political skill in the management of men in his military campaign; but our relief at the peace, justice and order restored at the end of the play is inseparable from a sense of disappointment at its imaginative impoverishment. In the words of Wilbur Sanders, who describes this anti-climax well, 'royalty of nature once slain, only the meaner virtues of circumspection and prudence can survive'.[115] Duncan was prepared to run the risk of treason for the sake of trust, but Malcolm is not. He promises at the last, by the help of 'the grace of Grace', to perform all needful things 'in measure, time, and place' (v. ix.38–9), but the words lack all conviction: the poetry that unites man, nature and God has shrivelled into a rhetorical figure. It is as though under Malcolm goodness and evil will amount to nothing more than social and anti-social behaviour. For Macbeth has not only killed Duncan; he has also killed the heroic poetry of sacrament and sacrilege.

CONCLUSION: 'THE END IS WHERE WE START FROM'[116]

There is no moral to be drawn from *Macbeth*, no conclusion. Simply there is the opportunity for reciprocal play of mind, the challenge to compare and understand, historically. Macbeth by the end is wholly deprived of the free play of the historical sense. In his extremes of mood, history has become either necessity – 'They have tied me to a stake: I cannot fly,/But, bear-like, I must fight the course' (v. vii.1–2) – or meaningless succession:

> To-morrow, and to-morrow, and to-morrow,
> Creeps in this petty pace from day to day,
> To the last syllable of recorded time;
> And all our yesterdays have lighted fools
> The way to dusty death.
>
> (v. v.19–23)

Life is a tale told by an idiot – but if the sentences of life are determined arbitrarily by either of the fellow-contraries of fate or chance, we suffer a dissolution of the sense of history. In the theatre we share this dissolution with Macbeth.

> We die with the dying:
> See, they depart, and we go with them.

But also we perceive the history of that dissolution, and the quite different history put together by Malcolm; and we remember Duncan.

> We are born with the dead:
> See, they return, and bring us with them.

Here is the heart of the play's capacity to stimulate comparative understanding, to rise above ritual re-enactment of disorder and ritual celebration of the order that succeeds it. It shows that order and disorder are not transcendental absolutes but states within the historical process, always particular in their nature; and it invites us, in the light of the symbols it provides, to a recomposition of that historical process, to a fresh exploration of the value of all that has been lost and gained. We must tell the tale our own way.

　　Macbeth, then, traces the collapse of a heroic 'total' civilization before the violence generated in its own contradictions. Its king had understood the mind's construction, and had seen the sources of that violence in his subjects' sense of military power, in their political ambition and, most particularly, in their psychological ambivalence (their capacity for 'mischief'). Heroically, and not without political skill, he had set himself to defuse that violence by his commitment to the ceremonies of trust – so that life in Duncan's Scotland seems to us worth living. Yet he was unsuccessful. His dependence upon the military support of his thanes, his own privileged position at their head, his very cultivation of their trust – all excited the violence of his most trusted subject and closest kinsman, Macbeth. He was betrayed, and his civilization collapsed into tyranny and civil war. Finally his son, having witnessed a trust and a violence too terrible to dare, established a new, meaner, more watchful regime, characterized by a certain withering of moral and imaginative scope, a desire to centralize political power and therefore a need to buy service. A crisis in authority has brought about a change in its nature.

Such were the complex passages of history that Shakespeare imagined out of the two pictures of Scotland that he found in Holinshed; and his chosen mode of dramatic representation is what I wish to call a tragedy of incomplete catharsis. Certainly the cathartic pattern, as defined by René Girard, is present in the play's re-enactment of disorder and final celebration of order:

> The spectator may shudder with 'pity and fear', but he must also feel a deep sense of gratitude for his own orderly and relatively secure existence. Every true work of art might be said to partake of the initiatory process in that it forces itself upon the emotions, offers intimations of violence, and instills a respect for the power of violence; that is, it promotes prudence and discourages hubris. [117]

We might say that the play's catharsis is its deepest compliment to King James – a compliment much deeper than personal flattery since (after the style of epic) the play enabled its society as a whole to compliment itself, in the figure of its sovereign, upon its own historical progress and comparative security, under the care of a shepherd protected by the heroic powers of his great ancestors. In so far as the play is cathartic, it successfully purges those violent, destructive emotions that in Duncan's Scotland had been disown-

ed and demonized. They are borne away by the scapegoat figure of
Macbeth, so that authority might be restored.

   Yet it is insufficient to speak of the play only in these terms; for
catharsis is peculiarly the subject of *Macbeth* as well as its means of
intervention in history. Certainly we share the catharsis of the
thanes as we leave the theatre ('The time is free'), but we also
observe Malcolm's manipulation of that feeling; and this juxtaposition drives our feeling into an ironic consciousness inimical to true
catharsis. For catharsis depends upon the degree of dissociation
that Duncan had fostered, upon such strict ceremonies of distinction between good and evil, the permitted and the banned; and it is
these distinctions that Malcolm is beginning to erode and the play
to investigate. If catharsis is the heart of *Macbeth*'s compliment to
King James, its ironic consciousness of catharsis is the heart of its
inquiry into history. If the play purges violent, destructive emotions by scapegoating a dead butcher and his fiend-like queen, it
also invites us to see the political expediency which such a process
might serve; and in so doing it traces a decisive shift in human
consciousness. For it traces the emergence from romance of the
recognizably modern world which its Jacobean audience had
inherited from Malcolm and which we in our turn have inherited
from James – a world made known to us by anti-climax, where
authority is vitiated by policy, poetry by rhetoric and morality by
melodrama, a world where the erosion of the sacred has removed
the restraints upon violence and made its irruption ever more
likely. The play is not simply a compliment to King James, that is.
It invites us to challenge the imaginative sufficiency of the
authority which James had inherited from his ancestors, the
sufficiency of his boasted sense of historical progress and political
security: and it does so by the contrasts that it mobilizes between
the present and its imagined past. The might-have-been of Duncan
and the weird sisters – fellow-contraries dangerously dissociated in
the patriarchal monarchy of a more primitive society – are, with
Macbeth and Scotland torn between them, Shakespeare's elegiac
response to the poetry of feudalism still vestigially alive in the
rhetoric of Jacobean Britain. They are his answer to the question,
what might it have been like if the king truly had been the
Husband, the Head, the Shepherd? Certainly, even if such a world
had existed, it now was gone, destroyed by the contradictions in its
material base, its patriarchalism and its heroic aristocratic code. But
its possibilities for the sacred and the sacrilegious remain – still

today in the twentieth century – to fill the spaces of a world where power is perceived as policy and violence in consequence is drained of its imaginative content.[118] *Macbeth* brings into play a set of images that portray the creativeness of a world where property is debt and power is trust, the destructiveness of a world where the violence of ambivalence is disowned; and it does so with no moral to teach, no conclusion to draw. Simply, there is a play-word which at its close enables us to turn back into what Yeats called 'the desolation of reality',[119] reassured and prudent maybe, but also enriched with images to explore that desolation.

> And the end of all our exploring
> Will be to arrive where we started
> And know the place for the first time.

8
Epilogue: Tragedies of Incomplete Catharsis

Thomas Rymer's comments upon *Othello* have often been mocked; and yet, with the sure instinct of hostility, they hit upon something generally true of Shakespearean tragedy – its *dangerousness*.

> What can remain with the Audience to carry home with them from this sort of Poetry, for their use and edification? how can it work, unless (instead of settling the mind, and purging our passions) to delude our senses, disorder our thoughts, addle our brain, pervert our affections, hair our imaginations, corrupt our appetite, and fill our head with vanity, confusion, *Tintamarre*, and Jingle-jangle, beyond what all the Parish Clarks of *London*, with their *Old Testament* farces, and interludes, in Richard the seconds time cou'd ever pretend to? Our only hopes, for the good of their Souls, can be, that these people go to the Playhouse, as they do to Church, to sit still, look on one another, make no reflection, nor mind the Play, more than they would a sermon. [120]

Rymer establishes a connection here between the ritual arenas of theatre and church which enables him to deplore Shakespearean drama as blasphemous; for it does not hold sacred the psychological and social order held sacred by Rymer himself. The plays unsettle the mind and disorder the faculties; they arouse the passions but refuse 'to temper and reduce them to just measure'. [121] They are not, that is to say, cathartic, and the grounds of Rymer's hostility are clearly laid bare in his opening question: 'What can remain with the Audience to carry home with them...?' This subversiveness has, of course, commonly been the praise of Shakespearean drama in the twentieth century, when the value of art has so often been invoked against a psychological and social order felt to be inauthentic. Here, for instance, is Helen Gardner on Shakespearean tragedy:

it shows us a world of dangers within and without, of bewilderment and perplexity in the extreme, in which men voyage into themselves to discover what they did not know of themselves, capacities for good and evil, and encounter a world in which certainties crumble and profound questions are raised to which at the close neither they nor the spectators can provide adequate answers.[122]

The underlying analysis here, save that it is offered in praise not blame, is very similar to that of Rymer: the plays are dangerous because they contaminate their audience with violent passions which the curiously unresolved nature of their endings cannot altogether integrate.

'Something might be true although at the same time harmful and dangerous in the highest degree', wrote Nietzsche;[123] and the dangerous 'truth' to which Shakespearean tragedy attests is that of *ambivalence*. The violent passions in the plays spring from those secret desires at the heart of taboo, as each hero in his turn finds himself succumbing to precisely the temptation which he would most disown. Freud found evidence for ambivalence within the very concept of taboo. 'The meaning of "taboo", as we see it,' he wrote, 'diverges in two contrary directions. To us it means, on the one hand, "sacred", "consecrated", and on the other "uncanny", "dangerous", "forbidden", "unclean".'[124] The moment of Shakespearean tragedy is the moment when taboo fails, the moment when the hitherto unconscious desire impels itself bewilderingly into consciousness, and we witness (in Clifford Leech's words) 'the realization of the unthinkable'.[125] The forbidden is not only the desired: it has also become the desirable; and yet still the violent passions aroused by temptation retain their sacred character. Lear, compelled by rage to curse the whole of creation, invokes 'the great Gods' (iii. ii.49) not simply to bolster his authority but because of the holy terror he feels at the strength of his own desires. Lady Macbeth invokes the 'Spirits/That tend on mortal thoughts' (i. v.40–1), and her husband invokes the imagery of Witchcraft and Pale Hecate, because they already sense the divinity of the afflatus that is coming upon them. Othello, as we shall see, driven by desire to kill Desdemona, dramatizes himself as Justice pursuing ritual sacrifice, whilst Hamlet too, possessed by revenge, sees himself as God's scourge and minister. Each of them is deeply conscious of being upon holy ground; and so we may say that the sacred in the plays has a power quite opposed to that which Rymer demanded of art. It is not only the sacredness of order that they celebrate but also, more strikingly still, the sacredness of transgression; they explore, embody and arouse ambivalence.

The word 'ambivalence' itself was coined by the Swiss psychiatrist Eugen Bleuler in 1910, in his *Vortrag über Ambivalenz*, and it was rapidly assimilated into psychoanalytic thought in order to chart the hazards of the young child's developing relationships with its parents. It belongs, that is to say, to the whole psychoanalytic enterprise of lifting the already weakening taboos that had governed nineteenth-century bourgeois family-life, so that the child's rage and hatred, like its sexuality, might find a voice. There was an affinity here between psychoanalysis and literature, especially the tragic literature (and the theorization about tragedy) that characterized the modernist period; for there too we find the need to lay fast hold upon those violent passions marginalized by a bourgeois society that was suddenly felt to have become inauthentic. So Marlow in *Heart of Darkness* keeps faith with the whispered violence of Kurtz amidst the sham of the sepulchral city where he must also protect the faith of Kurtz's Intended. He is torn between faith and faith. 'Fair and foul are near of kin', wrote Yeats[126] – 'and fair needs foul', he added, directing our attention back once more to that other great tragic period of our literature, the Jacobean period, when an earlier patriarchal order of family and state became inauthentic and tragedy in consequence needed to lay fast hold upon the sacred in both its aspects, the Apollonian and the Dionysiac.

The sacred violence that we see, because it springs from the breach of taboo, is utterly destructive of the individual in the hopes that his culture had led him to entertain. Rage, ambition, jealousy, revenge – in each case the tragic hero is betrayed by the mischief at the heart of his passion. Lear is betrayed in his authority, Macbeth in his fealty, Othello in his romance and Hamlet in the rationalism of his Renaissance idealism. Each dies, the contamination of passion exhausts itself and the world goes on: here, in the punishment of hubris, is the celebration of order. But we do not witness only individual tragedy; for taboo is a social control, and its breach threatens the tragedy of a whole society. It is, as Sidney said, 'the high and excellent Tragedy, that openeth the greatest wounds'.[127] In *King Lear* power has been drawn to the king until the aristocratic houses reassert themselves and civil war breaks out; in *Macbeth* power has been diffused to the aristocratic houses until the king is powerless and a tyrant usurps him – in both cases the delicate balance of feudal reciprocity is destroyed, seemingly for ever. *Othello*, as we shall see, is interestingly different, but in *Hamlet* too the two new mighty opposites of the Renaissance, the idealist and the Machiavel, destroy not only one another but also the very different Denmarks that each might have created in the vacuum made by the passing of the old feudal order. In each case the ideal potential of a community is destroyed and replaced by a meaner world, a world which generally in the audience we sense to be like our own and which we recognize by its contradictions. It is the same method that we saw in the Histories: how shall we assent fully to those ambiguous figures of Bolingbroke, Henry V, Malcolm, Edgar, Fortinbras? The tragedies withhold complete assent from the order in which they close. It is as A. P. Rossiter wrote: 'Shakespeare's tragedies have rejected the "Tudor–Christian" conception of a moral and just world';[128] and we may agree with René Girard that 'the tragic element always springs up amidst the ruins of a mythic framework'.[129] Suddenly, in the absence of a compelling myth of social order, ambivalence may be perceived as 'truth'; marginalized violent passions may be hungered for; the killing of the king may be relished as, three hundred years later, we are told, the Oedipal dream of killing the father was relished; and the catharsis of tragedy will tend always to be incomplete.

Stephen Greenblatt encapsulated the mixed mode of Shakespearean tragedy well when he described a theatre 'that seems to confirm the official line and thereby to take its place in the central system of values, yet that works at the same time to unsettle all official lines'.[130] Catharsis and ironic consciousness of catharsis work against one another to create a new theatre which, in modern parlance, tends always to deconstruct itself. The plays – even by virtue of their form – tend to desacralize taboo, to demythologize ideology and to demystify authority, simply by placing them in their context of the struggle for social power and its legitimation. So in *Macbeth* the thanes' catharsis was raised into ironic consciousness by Malcolm's exploitation of it; so in *King Lear* Shakespeare shockingly made play with a familiar myth of national origin to expose the abiding contradictions within the social order it legitimated. The plays in this aspect are committed to the same adventure as Freud's work three centuries later (and literary deconstruction today): the raising-to-consciousness of the historical processes that it had been the business of myth and taboo to mystify. As at the end of the nineteenth century, in the knowledge of an emergent socialist culture, an intelligentsia explored the contradictions and ambivalences of a bourgeois society to which they mostly belonged, so too at the start of the seventeenth century, writing for the commercial theatre in an emergent bourgeois culture, a metropolitan intelligentsia had explored the contradictions and ambivalences of a residual aristocratic culture upon whose patronage they mostly depended. Belmont is brought to the bar of Venice, we might say, and in the interplay between the two both are judged. The theatre, like the ritual space of psychoanalysis, was thus richly poised between the radical and the conservative, a place (as Rymer feared) of dangerous potentiality, marginal but important by virtue of the questions raised in the course of the play it permitted. But, if all things may be brought into question, what then? What of the sacred? Where will violence find the full measure of itself that it craves? At the end of *Othello* the hero's death brings about no social change: Gratiano pockets the cash, and it will be business as usual. Venice, as we shall study it in the following section, is in part an image of the contemporary world for Jacobean writers; and we may take Bianca – the whore in love, the mercenary with her head full of romance – as one image of the grotesque, contradictory role of theatre in this new mercantilist world. But this too is a contradiction which the play raises to consciousness, and in so doing it creates a hunger – 'the utopian dream of the artist and of the good man',[131] Danby calls it – for a world yet to be born where these contradictions shall be resolved by the resolution of the contradictions in their material base.

Part Three
'This is Venice'

NICK POTTER

9

Prologue: Between Romance and the Real

The funeral bak'd meats
Did coldly furnish forth the marriage table

It is our contention that the Venice plays are quite unlike the Histories and the Tragedies. Where those plays resonate with a sense of the 'sacred' and of the powerful ambivalence of 'taboo', the Venice plays are about the loss of power, or, rather, about the transformation of its meaning. With the disappearance of the 'sacred', power loses its capacity to exalt and becomes the merely pragmatic power of the prince and the merchant. Such power is only exerted; it can confer no blessings on those who cannot exert it, where sacredness disburses its glamour generously.

'Sacredness' and 'holiness' are words that have to do with our sense of our feelings, with the appearance of our feelings to us in a context of structured meanings whose ultimate source is supra-human, the divine or the demonic. The big feelings of tragedy, the 'wounds' of which Sir Philip Sidney speaks, are grounded in the possibility of the sense of the sacred. The Histories, as we have seen, tease us with the play of 'history', or 'chronicle' as a way of picturing human reality, against the older passions of 'pastime' or 'misrule', or their more civilized reworkings in pastoral and tragedy. The Histories and the Tragedies together address the kinds of difficult glory which belong to an age which is passing.

Kate Belsey has pointed to the hermeneutic fissure that separates us from the past:

To read the past, to read a text from the past, is thus always to make an interpretation which is in a sense an anachronism. Time travel is a fantasy. We cannot reproduce the conditions – the economy, the diseases, the manners, the language and the corresponding subjectivity – of another century.[1]

We cannot know the past as it was to itself, any more than we can know what it was to be ourselves at an earlier age. We cannot *recover* the past, we can only *read* it. But, as memory can throw a light on our present being, reading the past is only a flawed exercise when it is aimed in the wrong direction: that is, as an attempt to recover the past as it was to itself.

The present is not created *ex nihilo* but as a rereading of the past,

> For the pattern is new in every moment
> And every moment is a new and shocking
> Valuation of all we have been.
> ('East Coker')

We may not be able to know the past as it was to itself, but we can experience its difference and strangeness. This difference and strangeness is dramatized *within* the plays: we have not needed to hypothesize a contemporary playgoer's experience to say this. What we are arguing is that, just as contemporary criticism addresses the strangeness of the past, the hermeneutic fissure which separates us from it, so Shakespeare's plays are addressing the strangeness of *their* past. In particular they are addressing the disappearance of the sacred. The 'sacred', as a difference and a strangeness, as a *power*, is, they suggest, part of the past. The more familiar, meaner, desacralized world for which the violence is exchanged is the playgoer's 'now'. The funeral bak'd meats do coldly furnish forth the marriage tables.

Hamlet's horror is expressed at the loss of meaning. The elements of the sacrament of death serve as the elements of the sacrament of marriage. They are, that is, not in themselves sacred. They have one meaning in one context and another in another. They have no meaning really attached to them at all; they are mere signifiers. Sacredness thus becomes diffused, its requirements no longer clearly vested in a set of objects and processes. This is part of the problem: sacredness not actually, sensibly present cannot exert the same certain power to structure community or even personal observance. It is one thing to believe that God is everywhere present and well-disposed, another to attend mass regularly.

Historical generalizations are of necessity crude, but sometimes helpful. We are generalizing, and proposing that Shakespeare's plays are a reflection on the emergence of the modern, post-feudal, commercial world. This world, with its different contradictions and gaps, its particular failures to give utterance to the range of human hope and yearning and consolation to the range of human shame and fear, is the world of Venice, or is a world transposed to Venice. What is different about the Venice plays is that they invite their audiences into their present, where the Tragedies and Histories had invited their audiences into their past. What the two sets of plays share, however, is that unspoken articulation of the dream that it might have been otherwise than it was, or might be otherwise than it is.

This reflection that history is 'man-made' is strikingly imaged in the description of Venice itself: a group of artificially extended islands, Venice shows itself to be an aggregation of separate entities, and this is, in turn, reflected in its oligarchic and republican politics and its individualistic understanding of citizenship. The play of Venice conjured by Shakespeare is the play of a world directly in line with our own, drained of the coherences of the sacred and devoted instead to profit.

10

The Merchant of Venice

The Merchant of Venice, it must be remembered, is a play. This may need restating for it has been subjected to exhaustive examination as a source of evidence for historical discussion of English society in the 1590s. To insist that it is a play is to insist that material developed in the course of such discussion is essentially subordinate to and subordinated by the play. This essay will concentrate therefore on the means by which Shakespeare organizes his perceptions concerning English and Italian societies in the sixteenth century into an aesthetic experience. At the same time it is important to be aware of the extent to which misperception of various kinds contributes to the play's possibility. Walter Cohen has closely explored these aspects of the play's possibility in his essay 'The Merchant of Venice and the Possibilities of Historical Criticism'.[2] I am indebted to this essay for a great many insights into the history with which *The Merchant of Venice* plays. In particular, Walter Cohen grapples convincingly with the nature of usury in the play and with its historical sources and implications for Italian and English capitalism in the sixteenth century. He suggests that, 'in *The Merchant of Venice*, English history evokes fears of capitalism, and Italian history allays those fears. One is the problem, the other the solution, the act of incorporation, of transcendence, toward which the play strives.' The key to this view is the argument that the play presents, not a struggle between capitalism and feudalism, but 'a special instance of the struggle, widespread in Europe, between Jewish quasifeudal fiscalism and native bourgeois mercantilism', and that the play distinguishes carefully between usury which calculates a charge from the moment of the loan, and interest which charges from the appointed day of payment. As Auden noted, Shylock demands repayment not usury: this is the bargain that Antonio seals.[3] The fear of usury which, Cohen argues, fuelled English anti-capitalism, is allayed by the play, which thus reveals a pro-capitalist tendency and an 'essentially corporatist defence of absolutism in the 1590s'.

It is extremely important to decide precisely what kinds of social organization are involved in the play, if we are to say how they matter to the play. Shylock has been seen as a bourgeois hero,[4] as an embodiment of capitalism,[5] while others have rejected this kind of class-analysis altogether in favour of a view such as C. L. Barber's, that the play represents the triumph of good Christians over a bad Jew.[6] Cohen's definition of Shylock's practice is more convincing than the unsatisfactory generalizations of the former tendency, and comprehends more of the actual substance of the play than the latter. Clearly the detail of the development of capitalism in England, seen through that development in Italy, is Shakespeare's focus of interest in the play. The questions I wish to pose are, 'What kind of aesthetic experience does the play hope to create?' and 'How does this kind of experience help us to develop a sense of Shakespeare's historical imagination?'

The Merchant of Venice is a play that presents all sorts of difficulties to a modern reader. The world of an Elizabethan play is never immediately accessible; there are always conventions to be understood and ways of thinking and feeling that need to be learned about before we can begin to understand it fully. In addition to these difficulties, however, *The Merchant of Venice* has at its centre one of the most intractable problems for modern criticism: the character of Shylock the Jewish money-lender. Recent history has made it impossible for us to feel comfortable with a stage representation of Jewish characters as pantomime figures with red wigs and huge noses. But is the play really anti-semitic?

Though the Jews had been officially expelled from England in the reign of Edward I, they could live comfortably enough in London if they conformed outwardly to Christianity, and, though in 1588, 1593 and 1595 there were serious 'anti-alien' riots in London, they were not specifically anti-semitic. The only really concrete historical evidence of the play's topicality is provided by the execution for treason in 1594 of Roderigo Lopez. Lopez was a Portugese Jew who had settled in England and had risen to become a physician to Elizabeth I. He had allowed himself to become embroiled in the web of Spanish–English intrigue. His execution lent topicality to Marlowe's *Jew of Malta*, which was played fifteen times in that year. Neither Lopez nor Barabas, however, bear much relation to Shylock: the public image of the one and Marlowe's character, the other, correspond to the popular picture of the Jew as an exotic oriental, plotting the downfall of Christendom on a grand scale – they are figures of luxury and excess, not Old Testament ascetics. To understand the nature of Shylock, we must look at the play more closely.

If London offered a secure home to conforming Jews, the Italian city states of the fifteenth and sixteenth centuries were more liberal still.[7] In Thomas's *History of Italy* (1549), we read,

> Al men, specially strangers, haue so muche libertee there, that though they speake verie ill by the Venetians, so they attempt nothyng in effecte against theyr astate, no man shall controll them for it. . . . If thou be a Iewe, a Turke, or beleeuest in the diuell (so thou spreade not thyne opinions abroade) thou arte free from all controllement.[8]

Antonio spells out why this should be so:

> The duke cannot deny the course of law:
> For the commodity that strangers have
> With us in Venice, if it be denied,
> Will much impeach the justice of the state,
> Since that the trade and profit of the city
> Consisteth of all nations.
>
> (III. iii.26–31)

Antonio's speech is a grim recognition that he is well and truly caught. The very 'libertee' that Thomas speaks of is the snare by which Antonio has been trapped. This 'libertee' confronts a cruel paradox. As Thomas notes, the condition of 'libertee' stretches even to you who 'beleeuest in the diuell (so thou spreade not thyne opinions abroade)'. What happens when the guarantee of 'libertee' *protects* those who want to deprive others of their 'libertee'? The agony of the Venetians in the play is that they can see no way to act on what is presented to us as obvious: Shylock's demands are not just, though they are legally binding. Portia underlines the absolute authority of the law:

> It must not be, there is no power in Venice
> Can alter a decree established:
> 'Twill be recorded for a precedent,
> And many an error by the same example
> Will rush into the state, – it cannot be.
>
> (IV. i.214–18)

Portia's triumph over Shylock is in terms of the law. She discovers a flaw in the apparently perfect paradox which allows her to prise it apart and then vent upon Shylock the full weight of the penalties provided for in law, forgetting, apparently, her fine speech on the nature of mercy only a few lines earlier. Invoking the law seems to be very like calling up a demon: if your intended victim escapes then you must pay the price. The law stands above everybody in Venice, as Portia, Antonio, the Duke all recognize. It is as though we were never allowed to recover our errors of judgement, to say that we were wrong, and to start again. 'There is no power in Venice/Can alter a decree established'. Of course states more advanced than Venice have developed means of appeal and constitutional change such as the House of Lords or the Supreme Court. Shakespeare's Venice has no such device. On the other hand, Portia voices a fear many conservative politicians have echoed: ''Twill be recorded for a precedent,/And many an error by the same example/Will rush into the state'. It is a question of confidence: because, as Antonio says, 'the trade and profit of the city/Consisteth of all nations', the state must appear to be beyond the reach of all organized interest-groups, especially the dominant group, Christian merchants. Turks, Jews and believers in the devil must feel sufficiently confident of their liberty and their protection to conduct their business in the city.

The way in which the play dramatizes the bifurcation of law and justice leads us deeper into the nature of Shakespeare's Venice. Antonio refers to the 'commodity' that 'strangers' have 'with us in Venice', on which depends 'the trade and profit of the city'. The language reveals a startling paradox: 'strangers' may control the fate of 'us in Venice'. This happens because of the 'commodity' that strangers have to promote the circulation of commodities. In a sort of implied pun it is revealed that a commodity deriving from the promotion of commodity-exchange is incommodious. The law itself becomes a 'stranger' to 'us in Venice': Venetian law is alienated and alienating.

The trial dramatizes a frightening inversion of an older 'natural' order when the Duke reveals himself to be helpless before the law to do what is just and, in so doing, reveals himself helpless before Shylock, his title a pathetic parody, a taunting reminder of the power he has lost to the law. This understanding of the law as alienated is related to an understanding of money in the play. Bassanio has already described silver in a striking phrase as 'thou

pale and common drudge/'Tween man and man' (3.2.103–4), a
striking anticipation of Marx's description of the destruction of
feudal relationships by capitalism in *The Manifesto of the Communist
Party* (1848):

> The bourgeoisie, wherever it has got the upper hand, has put an
> end to all feudal, patriarchal, idyllic relations. It has pitilessly
> torn asunder the motley feudal ties that bound man to his
> 'natural superiors', and has left remaining no other nexus
> between man and man than naked self-interest, than callous
> 'cash payment'.[9]

This 'cash payment' nexus not merely replaces other relationships,
but appears as their opposite, as Antonio reveals:

> If thou wilt lend this money, lend it not
> As to thy friends, for when did friendship take
> A breed for barren metal of his friend?
> But lend it rather to thine enemy,
> Who if he break, thou may'st with better face
> Exact the penalty.
>
> (i. iii.127–32)

Antonio's attitude is underlined in his earlier conversation with
Bassanio:

> My purse, my person, my extremest means
> Lie all unlock'd to your occasions.
>
> (i. i.138–9)

This is an interesting remark. The pun 'purse/person', the
participle 'unlock'd' which the two words share, express 'person'
as an extension of 'purse': 'person' is thought of in terms of 'purse'.
This device echoes an alliterative figure in Shylock's famous
lament: 'My daughter! O my ducats! O my daughter!' (ii. viii.15).
We assent to Solanio's estimate of this lament:

> I never heard a passion so confus'd,
> So strange, outrageous, and so variable . . . .
>
> (ii. viii.12–13)

Yet the terms of Shylock's lament belong to the same order as the terms of Antonio's offer to Bassanio, which is right at the opposite end of the play's moral scale.

Figures whereby human relationships are thought of in terms of money, law or trade are quite frequent in the play. They are especially noticeable in the exchanges between Portia and Bassanio after Bassanio has chosen the lead casket:

> A gentle scroll: fair lady, by your leave,
> I come by note to give, and to receive
> > (III. ii.139–40)

where to 'come by note' means to present a bill, and a few lines later where he expresses his disbelief:

> As doubtful whether what I see be true,
> Until confirm'd, sign'd, ratified by you.
> > (ll.147–8)

Portia's speech is full of commercial terminology: 'the full sum of me' (l.157), 'to term in gross' (l.158),

> Myself, and what is mine, to you and yours
> Is now converted.
> > (ll.166–7)

We can bring this back full circle by referring to the Sonnets, especially to Sonnets 4 and 6, in which the image of money is used paradoxically to express not miserly accumulation but generous expansion. The figures in the sonnets and in the speeches of Bassanio and Portia are clear about the relationship between their terms, however. In I. A. Richards' terms commerce and money are the 'vehicle' for the 'tenor' of love, and the shared language of exchange and contract allows the construction of the figures. The figures in turn construct a hierarchy of acts of valuation, revealing ordered priorities in an orderly world. Antonio's contemptuous speech to Shylock reveals this same pattern: 'for when did friendship take/A breed for barren metal of his friend?' (I. iii.128–9). The 'breeding' of usury between friends is 'barren': a paradox based upon precisely this implied ordering of the activities of love and commerce. The disorganization of Shylock's speech is a failure

to structure the figures as these other speeches do. The alliteration
of 'daughter' and 'ducats' only underlines this failure to express
the one in terms of the other, the failure to construct the ordered
hierarchy of the other speakers. It is in this sense that Shylock's
passion is 'outrageous', a judgement which is to have grim
resonances for the trial scene:

> You'll ask me why I rather choose to have
> A weight of carrion flesh, than to receive
> Three thousand ducats: I'll not answer'd yet?
> But say it is my humour, – is it answer'd?
> What if my house be troubled with a rat,
> And I be pleas'd to give ten thousand ducats
> To have it ban'd? what, are you answer'd yet?
> Some men there are love not a gaping pig!
> Some that are mad if they behold a cat!
> And others when the bagpipe sings i' th' nose,
> Cannot contain their urine.
>
> (IV. i.40–50)

This is the apotheosis of unreason: the unreason that Shylock
shows in his conversation with Tubal:

Why there, there, there, there! a diamond gone cost me two
thousand ducats in Frankfort, – the curse never fell upon our
nation till now, I never felt it till now, – two thousand ducats in
that, and other precious, precious jewels; I would my daughter
were dead at my foot, and the jewels in her ear: would she were
hears'd at my foot, and the ducats in her coffin: – no news of
them? why so! (III. i.76–83)

It is this unreason which we hear in his first comments aside on
Antonio:

> How like a fawning publican he looks!
> I hate him for he is a Christian:
> But more, for that in low simplicity
> He lends out money gratis, and brings down
> The rate of usance here with us in Venice.

> If I can catch him once upon the hip,
> I will feed fat the ancient grudge I bear him.
> He hates our sacred nation, and he rails
> (Even there where merchants most do congregate)
> On me, my bargains, and my well-won thrift,
> Which he calls interest: cursed by my tribe
> If I forgive him!
>
> (I. iii.36–47)

It is an unreason that mingles 'high' and 'low' motives with no sense of their relative status, the voice of a world of disorder that we hear, for example, in *Macbeth*: 'Fair is foul, and foul is fair' (I. i.11) or 'nothing is, but what is not' (I. iii.142). The poetry of *The Merchant of Venice* is the poetry of reason and proportion.

The 'purse/person' figure is not merely an expression of one in terms of the other, but is a recognition of their interlocking: 'person' both extends and encloses 'purse' in the pun. Antonio is a merchant: his 'person', his identity and his standing in the community, his role, his 'personality' in fact, depend on his 'purse'. This is revealed in the depth of his despair:[10]

> I am a tainted wether of the flock,
> Meetest for death, – the weakest kind of fruit
> Drops earliest to the ground, and so let me;
>
> (IV. i.114–16)

and later

> Give me your hand Bassanio, fare you well,
> Grieve not that I am fall'n to this for you:
> For herein Fortune shows herself more kind
> Than is her custom: it is still her use
> To let the wretched man outlive his wealth,
> To view with hollow eye and wrinkled brow
> An age of poverty: from which ling'ring penance
> Of such misery doth she cut me off.
>
> (ll.261–8)

Shylock reminds the court:

> Nay, take my life and all, pardon not that, –
> You take my house, when you do take the prop
> That doth sustain my house: you take my life
> When you do take the means whereby I live.
>
> (ll.370–3)

The attitude to wealth in Belmont is entirely different:

> PORTIA. What sum owes he the Jew?
> BASSANIO. For me three thousand ducats.
> PORTIA.   What no more?
>   Pay him six thousand, and deface the bond:
>   Double six thousand, and then treble that,
>   Before a friend of this description
>   Shall lose a hair through Bassanio's fault.
>
> (III. ii.296–301)

This bespeaks not indifference to wealth as much as plenty of it: more importantly, it reveals that wealth is not the means by which Belmont lives, though it is clearly the base on which Belmont is built. Precisely because Belmont's wealth is an unstated (and apparently limitless) store, a clear contrast is drawn between Belmont and Venice: Venice is all about getting wealth, while Belmont is all about having it.

Shylock and Antonio are sutured together in the play as historically inseparable aspects of capitalist development. At the end of the fourteenth century, for example, Jews were imported into Florence to conduct the 'usurious trade' forbidden to Christians by an edict some fifty years earlier, and the Tudor state was run on loans from European bankers.[11] The simple fact was that merchant capital (represented by Antonio) was not sufficiently stable to guarantee the growth of these economies, though it might have seemed more 'honourable'. Shylock tells the story of Jacob and the ewes to justify himself, and Antonio responds contemptuously:

> This was a venture sir that Jacob serv'd for,
> A thing not in his power to bring to pass,
> But sway'd and fashion'd by the hand of heaven.
>
> (I. iii.86–8)

Shylock complains of Antonio's behaviour to him: 'And all for use of that which is mine own' (1.108). 'Use' here is apparently innocent, meaning 'employment', whereas it actually means 'lent out at interest'. A similar confusion unsettles the word 'exploitation', which can mean 'using to the fullest' or taking advantage of a superior position. It is part of the development of our economic vocabulary, whereby meanings are subverted and confused, words are used to yoke together meanings of quite different valuation. The poetry of the sonnets negotiates this instability and exploits it as does the poetry of Belmont, drawing into elegant and paradoxical unities activities and experience apparently quite diverse.

It was this developing vocabulary that transformed an ambiguity and exchange in the meaning of 'to owe' between 'owing' = 'being in debt' and 'owning' = 'being in rightful possession of'. In an earlier feudal society, bound together by the ideology of mutual obligation, 'own' could mean 'what is owed to me' (and 'what I owe'; own = *owen*, literally 'owing'); that is, it could be a way of defining a place in the carefully drawn hierarchy.[12] Shylock is able to insist on 'ownership' without any corresponding sense of 'owing'. That is, the contract is broken: Shylock accepts what is owed to him but does not recognize any debts to others. Further, Shylock sees his property, implicitly, as conferring a freedom, as though you were entitled to do what you liked with what was your property. Property is thus a power, not a responsibility. This is made clear in the trial:

> The pound of flesh which I demand of him
> Is dearly bought, 'tis mine and I will have it:
> (IV. i.99–100)

Through Shylock, law and money are revealed as being part of a system which is inherently arbitrary in its deepest sources. This arbitrariness is in one sense the guarantee of the developing sense of private property: you know it is yours because you can do what you like with it and you are not accountable to anyone else. But if it is arbitrary it is also rigid and inescapable. When Shylock says, ' 'tis mine and I will have it', we recognize the depth of the paradox: Antonio's flesh, which is 'his' because it is 'him', is not his at all; it is Shylock's. Two ways of talking about what is yours – what is yours because it is part of what you are, and what is yours because of particular kinds of social arrangement grouped under the generic title of 'property' – not only are conflated, but one absorbs and erases the other so that there is no contradiction in the statement 'Antonio's flesh is Shylock's'. This is a terrible ironic reversal of Antonio's hyperbolic pun earlier in the play, 'My purse, my person, my extremest means/Lie all unlock'd to your occasions' (I. i.138–9). A change of meanings is being described which is lamented by a sixteenth-century *Discourse on Usury*: 'God ordeyned lending for maintenaunce of amitye, and declaration of loue, betwixt man and man: whereas now lending is vsed for pryuate benefit and oppression, & so no charitie is vsed at all'.[13] This is the mood of the Sonnets: what is yours, if it is not 'used', is actually a kind of deprivation of others.

> From fairest creatures we desire increase,
> That thereby beauties Rose might never die,
> But as the riper should by time decease,
> His tender heire might beare his memory:
> But thou contracted to thyne owne bright eyes,
> Feed'st thy lights flame with selfe substantiall fewell,
> Making a famine where aboundance lies,
> Thy selfe thy foe, to thy sweet selfe too cruell:
> Thou that art now the worlds fresh ornament,
> And only herald to the gaudy spring,
> Within thine owne bud buriest thy content,
> And tender churle makst wast in niggarding:
> Pitty the world, or else this glutton be,
> To eate the worlds due, by the grave and thee.

This sense of property is figurative rather than actual. It is a hyperbolic expression for 'amity'.

'God-like amity', as Lorenzo calls it (III. iv.3), is a paradigm in the play: 'amity', as in the Sonnets, expects nothing in return but the opportunity of further service. As Solanio says of Antonio's love for Bassanio, 'I think he only loves the world for him' (II. viii.50). Amity, love and merchant capitalism are all united by two concepts, 'hazard' and 'bond', in the play. Antonio 'hazards' for Bassanio, Bassanio 'hazards' for Portia, and Portia 'hazards' for Antonio in her gambit in the trial. The merchant 'hazards' in pursuit of wealth, the successful suitor in Belmont must 'give and hazard all he hath' (II. vii.9). 'Hazard' is property in its active aspect; it is the expression of the dynamic relations of people and things (property being, in Shakespeare's presentation in the play, inseparable from person) from which arise 'amity' and 'love' and 'wealth'. From this point of view, the movements and exchanges between people and things in the play are all insights into the nature of 'hazard'. As Antonio reminds us, 'hazard' is not arbitrary but is 'sway'd and fashion'd by the hand of heaven'. So 'hazard' is actually an expression in the world of the gap between God's knowledge of all conditions and men's ignorance and uncertainty, and of the trust in God that men display when 'hazarding'. Antonio's despair can now be more clearly understood: his losses are a judgement; he has not found favour with heaven. This is of course as incomprehensible as success, but much harder to bear.

'Hazard' is, thus, a development of the notion of mutual debt referred to earlier, appropriate to the new economic conditions of expanded circulation of wealth. 'Bond' represents the earlier, static conception, the system of dependences linked by and, in a sense, created by, acts of hazard. Thus Bassanio's hazard leads to the 'ring-bond', which parallels Shylock's insistence on his bond. The bonds of Venice, though, are external and oppressive, where those of Belmont are internal and expressive: the former determine human relations; the latter are determined by human relations. This is revealed in the mechanism of the casket-choice. Portia rebels against what she sees as the constriction of the device – 'so is the will of a living daughter curb'd by the will of a dead father' (I. ii.23–5) – which foreshadows and contrasts with the Venetians' sense of helplessness under their law. Yet in Belmont the casket-choice is wise. Portia's will is fulfilled by her father's will, not curbed by it. 'Law' in Belmont converges with individual will, guiding it and preserving it from being 'wilful' (as Shylock appears, for example, in the trial scene), expressing its worthiest commitments or offering a salutary reminder as the ring-bonds do.

The differences between Venice and Belmont are not merely differences of this kind, for Venice is real in ways that Belmont is not. The play is similar to other Shakespeare comedies in that it involves a movement between two kinds of place. On the one hand there are places such as the enchanted wood in *A Midsummer Night's Dream*, the King's estate in *Love's Labour's Lost*, the Forest of Arden in *As You Like It*; and on the other the city of Athens, the world outside, the court of the Duke. Typically, the comedy is enacted in dramatic space created by our acceptance of a set of conventions which leads us into a 'hyper-reality' developed from what we have already accepted as the play's 'reality'. Both are of course worlds created by poetry, and in that sense equally unreal, but the one is an extension of the other such that we are led further away from reality before returning to it.

What purgation and regeneration may be achieved in the world described in a comedy takes place in this privileged space in which some of the more mundane restrictive conditions are temporarily suspended. The purged and regenerated influences can then be recombined with their world, which is then set back on course. The plays involve a trajectory, curving out into spaces stretching the limits of credibility before looping back into reality once more.

The Merchant of Venice develops this pattern by extending the 'real' elements of the world of Venice, and leaving its characters in the hyper-real world of Belmont. Belmont is a world close to reality but not subject to the complexities of Venice: it is a more rarefied environment. The casket-choice, the indifference to money, the play-acting and above all the association with music, make it a place removed from the kind of reality we associate with Venice. It is 'Colchos' strond' according to Bassanio, the home of the golden fleece. It is a place, paradoxically, where moral fables come true, as they do in the casket-choice. For Belmont is not unreal. At important points a very real weariness threatens its apparent cosiness. Portia's opening line, indeed, is 'By my troth Nerissa, my little body is aweary of this great world' (I. ii.1.). Upon their return to Belmont, Portia and Nerissa enter at the end of Lorenzo's discourse on music, and Portia's comments provide a darker counterpoint to the dominant mood of the scene:

> That light we see is burning in my hall:
> How far that little candle throws his beams!
> So shines a good deed in a naughty world.
>   (v. i.89–91)

Her tone is reflective, and her thought a melancholy one: while it is a comment on the effectiveness of good deeds it is also a statement that the world is 'naughty' and goodness a gleam in the darkness. Nerissa's replies during this exchange have the effect of attempting to leaven Portia's tendency to images of despair: 'When the moon shone we did not see the candle' (l.92). But this practical good sense does not deflate Portia:

> So doth the greater glory dim the less, –
> A substitute shines brightly as a king

Until a king be by, and then his state
Empties itself, as doth an inland brook
Into the main of waters: – music – hark!

(ll.93–7)

There are two movements in this speech: one continuing from
Portia's *tristesse*, which is a sense of relativism which may reflect
some doubt as to the reality of her victory in the court perhaps, and
one picked up by the audience which is an echo of Lorenzo's
declaration of faith in the model of the spheres which is the reverse
side of relativism. Both are expressed in the image Portia chooses
to develop her sense of relativism. It is an image of exhaustion
underlined by the movement from one line to the next –

and then his state
Empties itself, as doth an inland brook
Into the main of waters

– but it is also an image of the lesser swallowed up by but
contributing to the greater, an image of successive enclosure which
is a structural echo of Lorenzo's model of the spheres. This is
clinched by Portia's hearing the music.

Even the music in her state, prompts sombre reflection:

Nothing is good (I see) without respect, –
Methinks it sounds much sweeter than by day

(ll.99–100)

– a thought which curls again around the mood of melancholy
relativism. Nerissa's response is to suggest somewhat drily,
'Silence bestows that virtue on it madam', but Portia is too deep in
her reverie:

The crow doth sing as sweetly as the lark
When neither is attended: and I think
The nightingale if she should sing by day
When every goose is cackling, would be thought
No better a musician than the wren!
How many things by season, season'd are
To their right praise, and true perfection!

(ll.102–8)

This might seem somewhat cosily moralistic (after 'all that glisters is not gold'!), were it not for the insistent note of relativism, which undermines any sense of absolute positive achievement in their victory. Portia's reflections are clearly reaching into a substratum of the play's suggestiveness, resonating at a deeper level of the audience's recognition. This note has the effect of surrounding Belmont with a vaguely felt melancholy, a seriousness which makes Belmont, at this point, seem more real than Venice.

Yet Venice is a more real world: it is a world of law and money and revenge. It is the world of Shylock, and Shylock may claim to be the most misunderstood of Venetians if the stage history of the play is brought in evidence. Nicholas Rowe in 1709 protested that the comic Shylock was a distortion, 'there appears in it such a deadly Spirit of Revenge, such a savage Fierceness and Fellness', while Richard Hole in 1796 went so far as to suggest that we should imagine the situation reversed: what would we think if Shylock had heaped the same indignities upon Antonio? Hazlitt noted of Edmund Kean's performane in 1814, 'his Jew is more than half a Christian. Certainly, our sympathies are much oftener with him than with his enemies. He is honest in his vices; they are hypocrites in their virtues.' Sir Henry Irving in 1879 ensured that Shylock kept 'a firm front to the last, and . . . [had] a fine curl of withering scorn upon his lips for Gratiano, as he . . . [walked] away to die in silence and alone'.

That these constructions could be put upon Shakespeare's words show that there is more to Shylock than the pantomime Jew, but on the other hand they are 'readings' of the play and exploitations of it which indicate ambiguities in it rather than supplying a definitive account of it. Shylock is open to interpretation because of what Rowe saw as the mixed nature of the play: 'tho' we have seen the Play Receiv'd and Acted as a Comedy, and the Part of the *Jew* perform'd by an excellent Comedian, yet I cannot but think that it was design'd Tragically by the Author'.[14]

Shylock is never justified in the play – he is merely presented as psychologically complex, as rounded in a way that a more restricted comedy would not require. Shakespeare takes care to present Shylock as more than a character-type: his motives are intelligible if not sympathetic. The difficulty for later readers has been the relative colourlessness of the Christian community. There is no reason for assuming that an Elizabethan audience would have had the same difficulty. Nicholas Rowe's comments postdate the official readmission of the Jews into England under Cromwell and the later stage history accords well with a Romantic sympathy for potentially tragic figures. The important point here is that Shylock's convincingness makes real for an audience the pressures of Venice. Law and Money are dramatically realized in the vengeful figure of Shylock. The instabilities of the Venetian state are clearly presented in his manipulation of the language of that state, the deepest weakness of which is revealed in the contrast between Portia's complaint of her 'will curb'd' and Shylock's triumphant cynicism in the trial scene: 'But say it is my humour – is it answer'd?' Here is the 'triumph of the will' made manifest: a striking paradox for readers in the wake of the Nazi nightmare, but a paradox to be read very differently here. Shylock is here the manifestation of an attitude to property, to what is your own, that has no other guide than 'will'. Portia's will is guided by the wisdom of Belmont, Shylock's by a mixture of apparently chaotic feelings:

> So can I give no reason, nor I will not,
> More than a lodg'd hate, and a certain loathing
> I bear Antonio, that I follow thus
> A losing suit against him! – are you answer'd?
>
> (IV. i.59–62)

In Venice such beliefs are 'libertees', guaranteed by law in pursuit of money.

Shylock is not, of course, only a money-lender. He is also one of a long line of old men whose daughters are spirited away by agile young men. His theatrical presence is deeply conventional in this sense. Revenge, usury and old age confront a youthful, generous, loving and forgiving world. Where this conventionality is surpassed, it deepens our understanding of these qualities. I have already looked at Shylock's sense of property. His role as the old spoilsport underlines his inflexibility and his wilfulness and 'explains' them dramatically: a good part of the drama derives from the paradox of the power old age here wields. The deepest ambivalences of Shylock's function in the play derive from his discussions with Antonio in Act I. It is here, in Shylock's vitriolic asides (especially I. iii.36–47) and in Antonio's flashing anger and bitter contempt that we see a deeper bond between them than is ever explained by the plot. Some of the presentation, the hatred of Christians, the yoking of 'high' and 'low' concerns ('my daughter, my ducats') are conventional and fit happily with the sources of the play. What Shakespeare has done is to explore that conventional figure and to present it credibly. Shylock is not a stock character: he is dramatically completely convincing. In achieving this, Shakespeare realizes his Venice as a place. The resonances of 'strangers' as a central concept in the life of Venice are focused in Shylock. It is because Shylock has a claim on our understanding that the trial scene appears as a nightmare world-turned-upside-down in which the world that has allowed this to happen stands revealed. Because Shylock is no pantomime figure, this is no pantomime nightmare.

It is this inversion of the world that allows the smooth passage of Belmont into Venice. The trial scene embodies a triple paradox: Shylock has turned Venice inside-out, Portia is a girl playing a boy, and a fairy-tale world intrudes on a real world. This is achieved dramatically through the play's careful handling of fairy-tale and realistic elements in a blend such that Belmont and Venice are not distinct worlds: they are different areas of a dramatic space the outside limits of which are defined by reality and fairy-tale. Belmont is Venice's presiding genius: a 'world' rather than a place. This is most clearly expressed in the play's closing act, a beautifully articulated series of unfolding scenes which constitute a single dramatic action. The last act is perhaps the most consciously 'fabricated' section of the play, more akin to a musical movement or a dance than it is to the realism of Venice. The background of this action is laid by Lorenzo and Jessica, whose mock-solemn litany, 'in such a night', establishes a mood of serious playfulness, a tone of playfulness that reveals a deeper seriousness. Though they place themselves comically in the tradition of legendary lovers, the tradition provides us with a perspective within which to estimate them. The comic placing does not deny them the tradition: it orients them within it.

This figure of orientation within a set or series is a dominant pattern in Belmont, as Portia's will is protected and guided by the casket-choice from being merely wilful. The figure achieves its highest expression in Lorenzo's stately discourse on music, in which a continuity is established stretching from the individual consciousness out to the 'spheres' themselves. Belmont is, of course, the earthly social manifestation of the harmony of the spheres, while Venice protects and guarantees by law the unguided will. Venice and Belmont are not, of course, irredeemably opposed. The act of hazard links the two, expressing as it does a trust in such universal harmony, though it is not as clearly revealed in Venice as it is in Belmont. This places Venice below Belmont in the hierarchy of revealed realities which Lorenzo's speech presents to us, and in which he is training Jessica.

The mood of playfulness revealing seriousness is built upon by successive serious and comic moments within the action: Launcelot Gobbo's scene and Portia's entrance are part of a *chiaroscuro* variation, playing around the deeper resonances of the action, while Gratiano's undisguised sexual pleasure roots Belmont in an older tradition still. The play ends with his pun. It is a pun which echoes some of the accumulated meanings of the last act, especially Lorenzo's disquisition on music, the echoes and contrasts of the ring-bond, the sexual pun itself. It expresses all the circular, closed, formal movements which the last act draws together in a stately dance and which celebrates a rich and various harmony. The sense of fabrication is important. Portia's throwaway gesture to Antonio–

> Antonio you are welcome,
> And I have better news in store for you
> Than you expect: unseal this letter soon,
> There you shall find three of your argosies
> Are richly come to harbour suddenly.
> You shall not know by what strange accident
> I chanced on this letter
>
> (v. i.273–9)

– is an assertion of the autonomy of a dramatically realized world, a fiction, which none the less convinces, an illusion. Just as Venice is a reality the logic of which turns into nightmare, Belmont is a dream the logic of which turns into a hyper-reality. *The Merchant of Venice* is a play which quite deliberately turns its back on reality and hands us its illusion.[15]

To call the last act of *The Merchant of Venice* a dance is not misleading: the image of a dance perfectly expresses the balance of interlocking tensions, the complex and dynamic harmony which Belmont reveals. It is a model of itself that the play reveals in Lorenzo's speech and it is a subtle and attractive model, but we should not be deaf to its silences. It is, for example, silent about the sources of Portia's great wealth, about the saga of exploitation and oppression which was the history of feudalism's extraction of wealth from the vast majority of the population. Shakespeare chooses the court as his reality in the end, and the dance as its most representative activity. This is not dishonest: it is the presentation of a historical situation in its metaphysical and aesthetic aspects, imaginatively conceived. These aspects of history represent a society's best intentions, its best view of itself, and they have a truth.

Schematically the play presents the historical contradiction between the feudal social order and developing capitalism, in its aspects of thought and feeling, as a series of dramatically realized images. This allows Shakespeare to elide history, offering a welcome in Belmont to Antonio, whom it has saved from himself, so to speak. In literary terms the play offers a subtle experience, comedy pushed almost over into tragedy. The tragic elements in the play are pushed almost beyond the point up to which comic resolution is still possible. It does so with enormous tact. Antonio is left partially unresolved at the end of the play, not being taken into the marriage-round, which reminds us of the melancholic undertow in Belmont which does so much to render Belmont solid.

In effect there are two plays, a classic comedy tracing the development of the relationship between Portia and Bassanio to a successful conclusion, and a much more ambiguous tragi-comedy tracing the aversion of tragedy and ending without any clear expression of social renewal and, thus, no guarantee that Venice has been purged. Antonio has rather been saved from it. The success of the play lies in its movement from one world to the other, from Venice to Belmont, without losing sight of Venice. In doing this it is able to reconcile in art what proved to be irreconcilable in history, without straining the credulity of its audience. To an Elizabethan audience the appeal to aspirant townsman as well as to aristocrat and courtier must have guaranteed that both could have seen at least something of that ideal resolution. This is the play's contemporary truth: a temporary stabilization in the long struggle between capitalism and feudalism, a lull in the storm thanks to the prosperity of Tudor England, is crystallized in art in its deepest and purest form. What was temporary and unstable appears as real, elegant and eternal because aesthetically convincing. It is of course, in one sense at least, untrue. Shakespeare denatures merchant capital by personifying it as Antonio and by avoiding a direct confrontation with its nature by contrasting it with finance capital personified by Shylock. Antonio cannot but shine. Thus Shakespeare is able to seal the alliance with Belmont without encouraging his audience to ask too many questions. The device of personification allows the personal relationship between Antonio and Bassanio, becoming a personal alliance between Antonio and Belmont, to imply things about the relationship between one aspect of the development of capitalism and feudalism which are much more difficult to imagine happening in history than they are to assent to in the play. In a very important sense, however, we are not being asked to judge: we are being asked to enjoy an image of a world which offers the ideal with a consciousness of the real as a constantly encroaching and subverting presence. The play's closing gestures are made to an audience about to leave the theatre for the world and are intended to remain as echoes of a vision, and an illusion.

I think that this is the most rewarding aspect of the play for a modern reader. Four hundred years later we are able to draw out its current of melancholy and set against that the defiant elegance of the self-conscious illusion. It is a complex and moving experience, the experience of a social order parading its best image of itself at the height of its power, celebrating its capacity to incorporate the very force that was to destroy it. It is not difficult to see that self-conscious dramatic illusion as an ironic commentary on the status of its own meanings, and that current of melancholy as a note of self-knowledge. As W. H. Auden wrote in 'Spain'' 'History to the defeated/May say alas but cannot help or pardon'. But, then, The Merchant of Venice does not ask for either help or pardon.

11

Othello

'WHAT SHOULD BE SAID TO THEE?'

Thomas Rymer's withering contempt for the drama of an un-polished age, or so he thought it to be, is perfectly expressed in his summary of *Othello* as 'a play about a handkerchief'. Rymer's impatience with what the play amounts to echoes a real difficulty that the characters at the end of the play have themselves.

> LODOVICO. O thou Othello, that wert once so good,
>   Fall'n in the practice of a damned slave,
>   What should be said to thee?
>
> (v. ii.292–4)

That is, 'What should be said *of* you, about you? Not 'What *shall* be said' or '*can* be said', or even 'should *I* say', but 'What should be said?' What does he mean? He means, 'What are the appropriate words, what is the appropriate, the proper title for you, for your deed, for what you have done, for your motives for doing it, for a proper judgement of you and your deed?' He means to resign from any personal titles to say anything himself, in his own part, and to deny any personal titles to anybody else. There is, as it were, an abstract, impersonal judgement, an assessment, an account which may be made or given, to which Lodovico looks, but in vain, because he does not know what it is, or where he might begin to look for it.[16] 'What should be said to thee?' is an expression of hopelessness, and of deep sympathy. The question is a rhetorical question, framed in order to express bewilderment, amazement, a sense of wonder transcending our capacity to speak at all. Like Blake's question in 'The Tyger' – 'What immortal hand or eye/Dare frame thy fearful symmetry?' – it does not expect an answer, that is. The question is put as a means of expressing most forcefully the speaker's sense that an adequate answer cannot be given. Yet we must attempt answers if we are not to fall into a hopeless resignation. What then, should be said to Othello?

First of all let us ask ourselves what sort of 'saying' we require. Do we want an explanation, and, if so, of what kind? Or do we want a judgement, and, if so, of what kind? Let us look at Othello's own response to Lodovico's question

> Why, anything,
> An honourable murderer, if you will:
> For nought I did in hate, but all in honour
>
> (ll.294–6)

That is a curious phrase that Othello chooses: 'an honourable murderer'. It is a paradox, perhaps even an oxymoron, like 'a pleasing pain'. The terms are surely contradictory. And is this an expression of his misery? a self-wounding irony? 'Why, anything', he says, 'if you will'. I am whatever you will have me. But he expands his own account: 'For nought I did in hate but all in honour'. A little earlier he has given an account of what he is doing that we need to bear in mind.

> It is the cause, yet I'll not shed her blood,
> Nor scar that whiter skin of hers than snow,
> And smooth, as monumental alabaster;
> Yet she must die, else she'll betray more men.
>
> (ll.3–6)

The key is that first 'yet'. I think Othello means that justice as he conceives of it would involve what we might call an element of 'poetic justice', or appropriateness, that the punishment should fit the crime, and that the 'cause' of Desdemona's crime is her sexual attractiveness, her desire, her 'body', which should in accordance with the demand that the punishment should fit the crime, have damage inflicted upon it. Yet, though this is the case, Othello will not damage her body. Why not?

We can be more specific about what Othello means in that first line, and paraphrase it thus: 'though her blood is the cause, I'll not shed it', where 'blood' carries the associated meaning of 'desire' or 'passion'. Then what happens? 'Nor scar that whiter skin of hers than snow'. The rhythms of this line are insistent: the accents fall softly yet firmly on 'scar', 'whiter', 'skin', 'hers', 'snow'. 'Scar' and 'skin' close softly together in an alliteration which is echoed faintly in 'snow' and picked up again in 'smooth' in the following line.

These phrases are not really connected as expansion of the 'it' of 'It is the cause'. Othello is not clarifying his initial phrase. Rather these phrases flow out of the way that 'it' has caught in his mind. 'Blood' is not the whole of the cause. How do you find a final, fixed image to express desire? Desire is fathomless, endlessly in pursuit of a receding ideal object, yet the object, though yearned for, cannot be spoken of. You cannot get hold of it to speak of it, for then it is got, not desired. John Donne makes the point in 'The Good Morrow': 'If any beauty I did see/Which I desired, and got, 'twas but a dream of thee.'

Desire is waking in Othello as he sees the sleeping Desdemona, and the rhythms of his language become a poetry of a different kind. This is why he must recall himself: '*Yet* she must die, else she'll betray more men'. 'Though she is beautiful', he means, and he can say that because we feel her beauty, richly, in his language because he feels it. He must dispel the enchantment by reminding himself of the justice of his mission: 'else she'll betray more men'. But this is really the first indication that we have had that Othello may think that he is performing a socially useful service. It has never been mentioned before. He wants to kill her in his rage at her: 'I will chop her into messes . . . Cuckold me!' (IV. i.196). In fact the idea of justice enters only a very little after this explosion, and has much more to do with aesthetic appropriateness than it has to do with moral justice:

> IAGO. Do it not with poison, strangle her in her bed, even the bed she hath contaminated.
> OTHELLO. Good, good, the justice of it pleases, very good.
>
> (IV. i.203–5)

Othello has earlier decided to poison her 'lest her body and her beauty unprovide my mind' (l.201), which is just what they are doing in this scene now. His preparedness is being tested: he has 'provided' his mind, stiffened his resolve, but 'her body and her beauty' are working on him to undo that resolution. He stiffens his resolve again by *inventing* another purpose, the *social* justice to be served by ridding the world of a devil, a temptress. There is of course no warrant at all for this view of Desdemona. But, in a world in which appearance and reality are so paradoxically related, a world in which Iago can say, 'I am not what I am' (I. i.65), and appear to be making sense, how are we to judge people? For

Othello appearance has become a disguise, and beauty the badge of evil and protestations of innocence only further proofs of guilt:

> this is a subtle whore,
> A closet, lock and key, of villainous secrets,
> And yet she'll kneel and pray, I ha' seen her do't.
> (IV. ii.21–3)

The desperation of the situation emerges in Othello's brutal interrogation of Desdemona that follows:

> OTHELLO. Are you not a strumpet?
> DESDEMONA.   No, as I am a Christian:
>   If to preserve this vessel for my lord
>   From any hated foul unlawful touch,
>   Be not to be a strumpet, I am none.
> OTHELLO. What, not a whore?
> DESDEMONA.   No, as I shall be sav'd.
> OTHELLO. Is't possible?
> DESDEMONA. O heaven, forgiveness.
> OTHELLO.   I cry you mercy,
>   I took you for that cunning whore of Venice,
>   That married with Othello: you, mistress,
>   That have the office opposite to Saint Peter,
>   And keeps the gates in hell, ay, you, you, you!
>   We ha' done our course; there's money for your pains,
>   I pray you turn the key, and keep our counsel.
> (ll.84–96)

This scene swings wildly between the language of depravity and the language of piety. Othello's bitter exit speech leaves Emilia and Desdemona confused and bewildered. Yet Othello is convinced that he can penetrate the disguises. His house is really a brothel, and Emilia is the woman who keeps the till, and that brothel is, in turn, hell, and the till-keeper a demonic Saint Peter, a keeper of the gates of perdition.

By what oaths could Desdemona swear her innocence and be believed? What could be said to her? This turns Lodovico's question with which we began into another kind of helplessness altogether. There language failed to meet its object because that object outreached it in its complexity: here, language fails to convince. There the speaking was impossible; here it is ineffective. Speaking has become ineffective because Othello has grasped an interpretative key. He knows now what's what. People say one thing and mean another. And he knows that because 'honest Iago' has told him so. So, when 'her body and beauty' begin to work on him, he knows it to be an evil influence and clutches at the straw this offers him, that women's beauty is a snare for honest men, and pictures himself as a sort of exorcist, cleansing the world of this evil. It is, of course, a sort of madness.

So how are we to take Othello's account of himself, as 'an honourable murderer'? I think we have to grasp it as an extreme paradox, an oxymoron. It is the speech that emerges from a state of extreme exasperation. The figure works by a kind of logical illogicality. The meanings are mutually exclusive. Logically speaking, there cannot be an 'honourable murderer' any more than there can be a 'pleasing pain', because what we mean by 'pain' is the opposite of what we mean by 'pleasing', and what we mean by 'murderer' is the opposite of what we mean by 'honourable'. He does not mean that he is an honourable man who has committed a murder; he means that he is an honourable murderer. The expression emerges from states of experience that we may pray we never find ourselves entering.

Othello has been used to speak of marvels with ease, as he has done with Brabantio and Desdemona:

> of antres vast, and deserts idle,
> Rough quarries, rocks and hills, whose heads touch heaven,
> . . .
> And of the Cannibals, that each other eat;
> The Anthropophagi, and men whose heads
> Do grow beneath their shoulders.
>
> (I. iii.140–5)

But this is a marvel which outreaches language. The word that the play attaches to such phenomena is 'monstrous': Emilia describes jealousy as 'a monster/Begot upon itself, born on itself' (III. iv.159–160); Iago describes his plan as a 'monstrous birth' (I. iii.402); Montano, when he realizes what Iago has done, exclaims, 'O monstrous act' (V. ii.191); Othello says of a cuckold, 'A horned man's a monster, and a beast' (IV. i.62), and exclaims, 'O monstrous, monstrous' (III. iii.433) when Iago relates Cassio's dream to him; in the same scene Iago describes jealousy as 'the green-ey'd monster, which doth mock/That meat it feeds on'(ll.170–1); Othello talks of Iago hiding 'some monster in his thought,/Too hideous to be shown' (ll.111–12); the brawl which Iago has incited is described by Othello as 'monstrous' (II. iii.208). These are things that are 'out of nature', 'extraordinary', and thus disturbing. There is a strong element of the grotesque (a monstrous birth', 'a horned man') and of the paradoxical ('begot upon itself') which links these things with the 'marvels' of, for example, 'men whose heads/Do grow beneath their shoulders'.

In a sense, Othello is a 'monster'. The 'Moor of Venice' is, perhaps, a little like the 'Bearded Lady', or the 'Siamese Twins', fascinating, repelling, compelling wonder and unease. Certainly Brabantio takes Desdemona's attraction to Othello as being out of nature, and Iago works on the suspicion that it might be 'unnatural'. What then is the 'ordinary', the 'comprehensible', the 'natural'?

POETRY AND DISORDER

These categories arise out of the community of experience shared by the members of a social body, which is discoursed about and, in a sense, created, in their language. This is the force of Lodovico's 'What should be said . . . ?'. If we ask, 'By whom should it be said?', the answer offered by the play is 'the state', Venice. What Lodovico is saying is, 'What will our world find appropriate to say?' and the implied meaning is that there is nothing that our world will find appropriate to say, because its available language cannot reach into these areas of experience, they are too 'monstrous', they are 'unspeakable'. We shall wait in expectant silence for the birth that will not arrive. That word 'state' (which Othello uses in his final speech) carries with it associations of 'stateliness', of 'dignity' and of 'appropriateness', of *due dignity* in fact. 'The state' in *Othello* is not the state of George Orwell's *1984*; it is not Lenin's state – 'special bodies of armed men, having prisons etc., at their command':[17] that is, it is not an arrangement separate from the community of citizens, from their sense of community, but is meant to express exactly that community itself. 'The state' here is closer to Hegel's idea that the state constitutes the 'best self' of a society. That 'best self' will be left speechless.

In both *The Merchant of Venice* and *Othello*, that 'best self' is
shown as crucially flawed. We are introduced to it in *Othello* in Act 1.
This act shows us the state confronting a potentially shattering
disruption, an apparently irreconcilable conflict between one of its
leading members and its General, and yet absorbing this threat in
the face of a larger threat, the Turkish fleet. Aroused and disturbed
by Iago and Roderigo, Brabantio arrives at the Duke's palace
talking wildly of witchcraft. He is outraged, and his language
seethes with the shock of disruption, seeking to express and to
convey that shock. It is violent language to meet violence, the
extraordinary, the 'monstrous'. Desdemona herself speaks of her
'downright violence' in loving Othello, which Iago picks up later in
talking to Roderigo: 'with what violence she first lov'd the Moor,
but for bragging, and telling her fantastical lies' (II. i.221–2) – his
version of Othello's

> She lov'd me for the dangers I had pass'd,
> And I lov'd her that she did pity them.
> (I. iii.167–8)

Her feelings have been forceful, and the effect has been disruptive
and shocking. The scene is electric. The Duke has responded to
Brabantio's outrage,

> Whoe'er he be, that in this foul proceeding
> Hath thus beguil'd your daughter of herself,
> And you of her, the bloody book of law
> You shall yourself read, in the bitter letter,
> After its own sense, though our proper son
> Stood in your action.
> (ll.65–70)

It is a pronouncement, a declaration. Yet everything changes
when the Duke realizes that it is Othello who stands in the action.
At this point a peculiar thing happens. The scene becomes
charged with language-awareness. It is as though 'violence' were
about to break out and needs to be managed, negotiated. It is an
intensely sensitive scene. At its heart is Othello's and Desdemona's poetry and the Duke brings it to a successful conclusion
in a series of rhymed homilies, which form is then taken up by

Brabantio (I. iii.199–219). This is concluded by Brabantio's final line, which leads into a speech in prose from the Duke about the arrangements for the expedition. There is then a return to blank verse, but the Duke and Brabantio mark their exits with rhymed couplets of opposite significance:

> DUKE. . . .
>   If virtue no delighted beauty lack,
>   Your son-in-law is far more fair than black.
>   . . .
> BRABANTIO.
>   Look to her, Moor, have a quick eye to see:
>   She has deceiv'd her father, may do thee.
>   (ll.289–93)

The act is concluded with a rich display of scurrilous prose from Iago, bolstering Roderigo, which parodies the Duke's use of *'sententia'*, and then a remarkable verse soliloquy in which Iago begins his plotting, which ends with that startling image

> I ha't, it is engender'd; Hell and night
> Must bring this monstrous birth to the world's light.

The scene is a striking display of virtuosity in which poetry and the language of everyday transactions jostle each other busily. We learn from it the true note of poetry: in Othello's and Desdemona's speeches, in Iago's and even in Brabantio's, we hear the note of eternity in our speech, something being made which will last, whether because it partakes of the order of the heavens, as Othello's does, and Desdemona's which meets Othello's, or of the chaos of rage which perpetually threatens that order, as does Brabantio's.

This scene is a *tableau vivant* of the relationships of kinds of discourse, ways of talking. We see the world defined as the attempt to negotiate the distance and tension between order and chaos, with what appears to be a resolution brought about by order, in the Duke's rhymed *sententiae*. But this is ominous. The starry isolatedness of Othello's language as we track it through the play, what Wilson Knight called 'the Othello music',[18] is fatally unbending and when it breaks is easy prey to the restless savagery of rage:

> I had rather be a toad,
> And live upon the vapour in a dungeon,
> Than keep a corner in a thing I love,
> For others' uses: yet 'tis the plague of great ones,
> Prerogativ'd are they less than the base,
> 'Tis destiny, unshunnable, like death:
> Even then this forked plague is fated to us,
> When we do quicken.
>
> (III. iii.274–81)

This is a repugnant but powerful mixture of infantile rage and pompous self-flattery: Othello 'cheering himself up' that, though he may be a cuckold, so many 'great ones' are. It suggests frustrated rage at the soiling of a dream, a world 'of one entire and perfect chrysolite'. And the dream is sterile, monstrous. If it is a dream of starry perfection, it is also a dream of waste emptiness, of 'antres vast and deserts idle', as well as of 'yond marble heaven', or of a girl made of alabaster, or snow.

This dream of sterile perfection is a dream of art, more specifically of Romance. It is the imposition on the world of a particular kind of heroic story and an attempt to live it, an attempt which proves fatal.

This scene shows both Desdemona and Othello to be taken with the language of Romance, and it shows that condition as being a form of self-definition against Venetian respectability as far as Desdemona is concerned. Othello, it is implied, is to be contrasted with 'the wealthy curled darlings of our nation': he is bracing, clear, distant, adventurous. The paradox is that Othello is revealed by the play to be dedicated precisely to the service of Venice, 'the signiory' as he calls them. The Romance language of military service and adventure is an invention, a mythologizing of other, previous social formations.

Both *Othello* and *The Merchant of Venice* have to do with the perception of a new world erupting from an existing world and threatening to destroy it, but both plays explore the act of perception, or imagining, itself. The 'worlds' perceived by any discourse become clear in the act of contrastive imagination, the act of perception and discourse itself. The worlds about which different discourses talk, from which they claim to derive, to which they address themselves, take shape as acts of those discourses, are precipitates of those discourses. Perception is perception not of an 'out there', but of that which comes to be understood within a definite discourse.

In a consideration of Stephen Greenblatt's *Renaissance Self-Fashioning*, which draws attention to that book's theme of the decipherment of power encoded in ideology, Michael Bristol points out that,

> as with any statement about demystification, this one depends to some extent on an alleged prior condition – here, feudal times – that is both mystified and monolithic, and thus in need of critical decipherment. It is, of course doubtful that any such situation ever existed.[19]

This is not a merely academic objection, though Michael Bristol seems to think that it is. It is a central objection, or rather elaboration. The point is that these perceptions are acts of imagination, acts of construction of expressive images, and that the way in which they work is precisely to render as solid and inflexible that which is fluid and indeterminate – that is, human activity. This is surely what we mean by 'social reality'. It is a kind of art that renders solidity, just as it is art that can dissolve it again, as I have shown *The Merchant of Venice* does in some part. The difference is that we know that art is art: we do not normally think of social reality as art.

Thus 'worlds', 'social formations', 'social realities' are static pictures of what is actually fluid and changeable, pictures which can be judged (and in practice are judged) as they are adequate to various moments in that fluidity and changeableness. They can be imposed from above by the powerful, or they can be raised from below by those who seek to decipher their power and to challenge it. They may also be appealed to, as critical standards, or fled into, as refuges from other pictures, or refuges from a bewildering changeableness.

Such contrastive picturing appears in the great anti-Romance works *Gargantua and Pantagruel* (1532) and *Don Quixote* (1605), for example, as a gleeful upturning of the stiff old world of courtesy in the one, or as a compassionate poignant comedy of bathos in the other. Periods of transition are especially rich in opportunities for the exploration of the complexes of feeling involved in picturing the world. Romance is the survival into Venice of a way of picturing the fluidity of human activity which has become increasingly inappropriate, exactly because that fluidity has allowed the precipitation of a different picture, the commercial city, which still trades on some of the values enshrined by that Romance picture, however pragmatically, and is crucially dependent on that picture to secure the allegiance of its military arm, here Othello.

The Duke's role in this scene is to stand between two kinds of language and to negotiate a peace. But he does not compose a quarrel. Othello's language merely confronts his audience immovably, presenting an impregnable orderliness, cool and high and distant. Brabantio gives up the fight: he does not change his mind. In fact very little notice is taken of Brabantio's right to feel aggrieved. The Duke's evident relief encourages him to smooth over any difficulties. As long as Brabantio does not want to fight and seems prepared to console himself with bitter grumbling, then a few *sententiae* can bridge the gap between this uneasy peace and the more pressing business of the Turkish fleet. The point is that justice is not being done. The Duke has begun by claiming that justice will be done and has concluded by smoothing over rather than resolving the contradiction that has erupted. The feeling in the scene is that the situation would have been handled differently had the Turkish fleet not been so threatening, and had it not been the Venetian General who stood in the action. Justice is considered here pragmatically.

A similar, though more extended, pragmatism is at the heart of the scene in which Emilia and Desdemona discuss adultery:

> marry, I would not do such a thing for a joint-ring; or for measures of lawn, nor for gowns, or petticoats, nor caps, nor any such exhibition; but, for the whole world? ud's pity, who would not make her husband a cuckold, to make him a monarch? I should venture purgatory for it. (IV. iii.71–6)

This is in answer to Desdemona's horror and astonishment that any woman would commit adultery at all. Her hyperbole, 'Wouldst thou do such a thing for all the world?' (l.67) is taken literally by Emilia: 'The world is a huge thing, it is a great price,/For a small vice' (ll.68–9). In Desdemona's view virtue is priceless, it is absolute: in Emilia's view high prices introduce new considerations. Her view is supported by a view of marriage which stresses the individualistic and competitive side of relationships.

> Let husbands know,
> Their wives have sense like them. . . .
> . . .
> And have not we affections?
> Desires for sport? and frailty, as men have?
> Then let them use us well: else let them know,
> The ills we do, their ills instruct us so.
>
> (ll.93–103)

This is a curious irruption of *sententia* in a scene over which Othello's murderous presence hovers. It is part of the dangerously fragmented, 'monadic' world of the play in which people's talk is frequently grotesquely discontinuous. Emilia's discourse belongs to the world of sexual comedy, and this is heading quickly towards tragedy.[20] Desdemona's 'Good night, good night', dazed, distracted, is more eloquent than any rejoinder. She is bewildered by Emilia's view of relationships.[21]

In both these cases a debate is introduced only to be set aside, and that debate is between two views of human relationships. On the one hand, both Brabantio and Desdemona insist on the absolute nature of the obligations to be borne by persons in relationships, the command laid upon a person by their relationship to another, their duty. This is not only selfish – Brabantio hints at the difficult pain of parenthood:

> God bu'y, I ha' done:
> Please it your grace, on to the state-affairs;
> I had rather to adopt a child than get it;
>
> (I. iii.189–91)

His sense of grief is here, surely, only just under control. He has tried to do his best by the child he has loved for so long and she has served him by becoming herself. We cannot side with Brabantio, but we can feel compassion for him and wish to help him. The proper relationship between parents and children is a subtle and delicate management of the competing claims of affection, which is so deeply the subject of *King Lear* and which lies at the heart of Belmont. In *Othello* we are reminded of the difficulties only to see them swept aside. Similarly, Desdemona's bewildered 'Good night, good night' does not suggest debate at all, but conveys rather a sickening sense of the gulf that separates people's ethical outlooks.

Such a view suggests that a distinction may be drawn between the 'idealists' and the 'pragmatists' in the play. Emilia and the Duke express in different ways a view that the 'right' or 'good' is not absolutely commanding, but to be discovered in specific situations in the negotiation between competing claims, rather than applied externally, from outside the situation itself. It is useful to bear in mind here the rigorous authority of Justice in *The Merchant of Venice* and the counterposed claims of mercy, in Portia's famous speech. The situations are quite different. Mercy tempers Justice; it does not displace it. That we are capable of falling short of our ideals does not mean that we should dispense with them: because human situations are often more complicated than will fit easily into our ethical insistences is not a reason for abandoning the latter. Taken together, the plays suggest that what is right may be unattainable, but is none the less right and to be sought. On the one hand our own complexity, and on the other a compassion for that complexity, ought to guide us. One of the alternatives is to see morality as a sort of 'cover', as Iago does.

Iago is best seen as a critic of Venice. Accounts of Iago have too often taken a metaphysical turn[22] where perhaps a category familiar to criminologists is more appropriate. Individuals who do not feel incorporated into their society may evolve a strategy which Robert Merton has called 'Innovation'.[23] The institutionalized goals of a society are accepted by the Innovator, but the institutionalized means of achieving those goals are either rejected, or seen as in some way unnecessary to the achievement of those goals. This may involve a particular interpretation on the Innovator's part of the nature of those goals. For Iago the getting and having is all that matters, the deserving is all hypocrisy and cant.

The Innovator can only be effectively answered if it can be shown that by 'cheating' you do not win. If a society cannot demonstrate that the nature of its goals is such that they cannot be won by any other means than those institutionalized within that society, then the Innovator's criticism may be said to have some force. For example, you cannot 'win' a game of chess by cheating, for by playing outside the rules of the game you are no longer playing the game at all, and cannot therefore be said to have 'won'. But, if 'winning' means being perceived to have got the better of your opponent, then, as long as your cheating has gone unnoticed, you have 'won'. If, for example, it really does seem that in-stitutionalized signs of achievement of goals, or the consequent

effects of achievement of goals (such as wealth, power, status) are
things that can be exercised and enjoyed whether or not they have
been achieved by the appropriate institutionalized means, then the
Innovator may have a point. In the world implied by the scenes I
have just considered, it may seem that there is some justification
for such a view. This would help to explain Iago's peculiar silence
at the end of the play. Is this the heroism of the only 'honest' man
in the play? Iago may have come to believe this. Where in the play
can we find the means to refute him?

THE IDEALISTS

> LODOVICO. O thou Othello, that wert once so good,
> Fall'n in the practice of a damned slave,
> What should be said to thee?
> OTHELLO.   Why, anything,
> An honourable murderer, if you will . . . .
>   (v. ii.292–5)

Othello's self-judgement appallingly collapses our categories of
judgement. How can a 'murderer' be 'honourable'? The oxymoron
threatens the whole basis of discrimination and leads us into the
heart of Othello's experience. I want to suggest that we can see the
play in terms of another oxymoron: the convergence of two
outsiders, the Innovator and the Moor of Venice. This very title
itself implies an oxymoron: 'the Venetian Moor'.[24] Definitions of
kind collapse, as they do not do in 'the Merchant of Venice'. Is
Othello a Moor living in Venice? naturalized as a Venetian citizen?
in which case how is he still a Moor? Barbara Everett reminds us of
the fierceness with which the issue of nationality lighted on the
Moors in Spain, an issue in which the Elizabethan court was
indirectly involved. Othello may serve Venice and be devoted to
it, but he is not 'of' it. Indeed, this is Iago's trump card:

> OTHELLO. And yet how nature erring from itself –
> IAGO. Ay, there's the point: as, to be bold with you,
> Not to affect many proposed matches,
> Of her own clime, complexion, and degree,
> Whereto we see in all things nature tends;

> Fie, we may smell in such a will most rank,
> Foul disproportion; thoughts unnatural.
>
> (III. iii.231–7)

When we see this convergence sealed in the dreadful compact
with which this scene concludes, all the careful structure of
difference that constitutes the world Othello serves, and that the
play has shown already to be founded more on pragmatic
negotiation than on any commitment to principles, collapses
utterly, compressed in their embrace. Out of this unnatural
embrace comes Iago's 'monstrous birth'. This is not merely the
murder considered as the physical termination of the life of
Desdemona, but as the destruction of the 'persons' of both
Desdemona and Othello.[25] For Iago, 'person' means 'person-for-
others', and he is convinced that this conceals a 'real' life of hunger
for domination and sexual indulgence. His language is the language of pornography, a language of rich and diverse innuendo
and alternative naming, which manages to suggest that a (frequently 'polymorphously perverse') sexuality lies at the heart of
the world. This is similar to the world that Lear glimpses:

> Behold yond simp'ring dame,
> Whose face between her forks presages snow;
> That minces virtue, and does shake the head
> To hear of pleasure's name;
> The fitchew nor the soiled horse goes to't
> With a more riotous appetite.
>
> (IV. vi.117–22)

Such a vision never really coheres into a focal, culminating act,
but remains diffused and refracted in suggestion. Steven Marcus
quotes some random passages from *The Romance of Lust* in his
study of Victorian pornography *The Other Victorians* to illustrate his
concept of 'pornotopia', the 'no-place' into which the world
becomes transformed by the operations of pornography. He
comments,

> Relations between human beings also take on a special appear-
> ance in pornotopia. It is in fact something of a misnomer to call
> these representations 'relations between human beings'. They
> are rather juxtapositions of human bodies, parts of bodies,
> limbs, and organs; they are depictions of positions and events,
> diagrammatic schema for sexual ballets.[26]

In Iago's world, everyone is talking about the same thing, but
under all kinds of concealment. 'Person' in such a view, is an
encipherment of sexual greed and the craving for power. Iago is
determined that they will not get away with such a deception. He
spends the whole play in a kind of excited rage, fuelling his
outrage and his anticipation, until he has got Othello into the same
condition in III. iii, in which he displays a hideously fascinating
control, managing Othello's rage like a skilful rider. His role in the
deliberations over the method of the murder is terrifying: he is
guiding and shaping Othello's passion like a lover, and, when the
murder is done, he is spent:

> Demand me nothing, what you know, you know,
> From this time forth I never will speak word.
>   (v. ii.304–5)

The murder is the last moment of an act, not the act itself, which
is a strange and terrible seduction of which the murder is only the
climax. The deepest paradox of this situation is that these three,
Othello, Iago and Desdemona, really are the play's 'idealists'. It is
they who refuse to accept the world as it presents itself and
abstract and idealize. It may seem odd to consider Iago an idealist,
but he is. His 'ideals' are not lofty ethical goals, but they are
thought-pictures, abstractions which reduce the complexity of the
real to the intensity of the ideal. Steven Marcus refers to the work
of Max Weber on methodology in the social sciences to clarify this
point:

> An ideal type, Weber remarks, is not 'average' of anything. It
> is formed rather by 'the one-sided *accentuation* of one or more
> points of view and by the synthesis of a great many diffuse,
> discrete, more or less present and occasionally absent *concrete
> individual* phenomena, which are arranged according to those
> one-sidedly emphasized viewpoints into a unified *analytical*
> construct'. In substance, he states, 'this construct is like a *utopia*
> which has been arrived at by the analytical accentuation of
> certain elements of reality'.[27]

It is in this sense that all three are 'idealists', insisting on the truth
of their absolutes, which, to refer to Weber again, 'cannot be found
empirically anywhere in reality'.

THE MISSING MIDDLE GROUND

'Person' can be thought of as a particular 'moment' of the whole ensemble of discourses about what it is to be a person available to a community. I want to suggest that Iago exploits a deficiency in the way that Venice handles the differences between sets of discourses. What I have described as Venice's 'pragmatism', 'diplomatic' or 'negotiated' relationships between sets of discourses, does not permit the growth of a fully intercursive relationship in which the possibilities of discussion and translation may be developed, but works actively to keep separate the differences it defines. Iago's vision cannot be simply dismissed. The play is constantly aware that love is physical as well as spiritual. Cassio's awkwardness with Iago in Cyprus is revealing:

> IAGO. ... our general cast us thus early for the love of his Desdemona, who let us not therefore blame: he hath not yet made wanton the night with her, and she is sport for Jove.
> CASSIO. She is a most exquisite lady.
> IAGO. And I'll warrant her full of game.
> CASSIO. Indeed she is a most fresh and delicate creature.
> IAGO. What an eye she has! methinks it sounds a parley of provocation.   (II. iii.14–22)

Which is right? How can we imagine a person who can be spoken about in both ways? The language of courtesy and the language of coarseness disallow each other, and yet there seems to be no middle ground on which sexual love can be talked about as both physical and spiritual. For the play this appears to be a paradox beyond the capacity of language to mediate. Poor Desdemona is caught between irreconcilable opposites, denatured because that nature is quite literally 'unspeakable'. Is she Cassio's 'most exquisite lady' or Iago's 'white ewe' of the first scene of the play? This paradox becomes acute in the bedchamber scene.

Othello's determination that the murder should be bloodless converges with Desdemona's laying out the wedding-sheets to suggest that the wedding-night murder will be bloodless, that Desdemona's virginity will be taken bloodlessly. Othello's 'Be thus, when thou art dead, and I will kill thee,/And love thee after' (v. ii.18–19) introduces another, more sinister, paradox. Her sexual identity appears insuperably problematic, to be approached either in a near-miraculous manner (that is, that she will remain intact), or in a near-diabolic, necrophiliac manner. Here extreme idealizations, demi-goddess or inert object, are poised to destroy the girl. As a 'signifier' she is being torn apart by the stress of the 'signifieds' others insistently attach to her. The pathos of her sad little ritual, laying out the wedding-sheets, singing distractedly, is the pathos of bewilderment. She is here the entire victim, who in our first meeting with her appeared as determined as Cordelia in *King Lear* to declare her vision of authenticity.

Othello, on the other hand, is riven by the process of significa- tion, split by his obstinately tenacious grip on his Romance vision of crystalline perfection. Love is the flaw in that vision. In the bedchamber Othello tries to speak a tempest of meanings that rages around Desdemona's sleeping form, a tempest released by the fracturing of that vision. Othello is a guardian, a warrior who protects peace. His Romance values are a way of talking about that job, its stresses and its fulfilments. Power, for Othello, confers responsibility, which is one of the great meanings of the idea of civil or military service. He is a figure of moral strength and also of violence, the figure of the responsible warrior, because that violence is guided by that moral strength. When the moral strength is subverted, the violence spills over. Desdemona has become the heart of that moral strength, the focal centre of authority in the light of which power is exercised responsibly. She has become Venice for Othello. When his belief in her is upset the effect is to destroy his role and his identity:

> O now for ever
> Farewell the tranquil mind, farewell content:
> Farewell the plumed troop, and the big wars,
> That makes ambition virtue: O farewell,
> Farewell the neighing steed, and the shrill trump,
> The spirit-stirring drum, the ear-piercing fife;
> The royal banner, and all quality,
> Pride, pomp, and circumstance of glorious war!
> And, O ye mortal engines, whose wide throats
> The immortal Jove's great clamour counterfeit;
> Farewell, Othello's occupation's gone!
> (III. iii.353–63)

Like Macbeth, the guardian of the state has become a murderer to strike at its heart. Behind this lies a deeper paradox still, which is the state's dependence on the very violence that threatens it, but channelled and ordered by the ideology of military service expressed by Othello in this speech. This appears as one of many potentially unstable collocations negotiated by Venice in the complex polity of its ideological life.

Iago and Cassio break off their conversation thus: 'Well, happiness to their sheets! . . . Come, lieutenant, I have a stoup of wine' (II. iii.26–7). This is not a resolution, but an agreement to differ based on a diplomatically chosen image which is not a real middle ground because it is the kind of compromise which only holds because it says so little. The alternative in the face of such hopeless contradictoriness is the agony of the oxymoron, the figure that embraces contradictoriness itself. To an extent, of course, all figures do this: this is 'poetry'. Where it fails is 'monstrosity'. The uneasy peace, the middle ground that is not, is the agreement to differ.

Civilization in Venice, then, is the function of a kind of diplomacy at the social and at the personal levels of our being. The silences and rifts are acknowledged, for the pressures of concealing them would be intolerable, and they appear in the penumbral world of the language-gesture in which Iago is most at home. The allusion, the pun, the linguistic doublenesses which are the material of sexual banter, are a temporary way of admitting what diplomacy excludes from the full light of day. Ironically enough, Iago has in his own way idealized what is no more than a language-paradigm in the same way that Othello has. The doublenesses of language are a quite subtle way of accommodating difficult contradictions. Iago's insistence on singleness is, in effect, an idealization which attempts to resolve these contradictions into one set of their component propositions, denying the others altogether. Iago rationalizes downwards while Othello rationalizes upwards.

THE TRAGEDY

Though the evidence for the view is slight enough, it may be suggested that Desdemona, despite her *naïveté*, might have offered a way onto that missing middle ground, as so many Shakespea-

rean heroines do, especially in the comedies. This is only speculation, but it raises a point. Desdemona's *naïveté* is crucially disabling. If she were a Viola, or a Rosamund ... If there were anyone in
the play who could see into the tightening whirlpool ... And that is
exactly the point. That is precisely where the tragedy lies. The
world of Venice has evaded its middle grounds so that it has
effectively isolated each ground which is free to negotiate with any
other ground, 'free from all controllement', and condemned to
enclosure. The play's tragedy is so avoidable and yet so inevitable,
and that is where its character for an audience lies. The excruciat-
ing experience is that of being the only one who holds all the clues
yet is incapable of intervening: we can only watch as the action
destroys the people in front of us as we know it will. We watch
with a terrible knowledge of what they could have been if their
potential had only been given scope to unfold. If Othello and
Desdemona could have learned from each other, and Emilia and
Desdemona from each other, then perhaps the awful rigid Venetian distinctnesses would have yielded, and diplomacy have been
replaced by interaction.

The fascinating image Venice presents geographically, erected
on islands in a lagoon, is a terrifying image of the vision of the
play. 'This is Venice/My house is not a grange', says Brabantio,
and yet the play goes on to show with the claustrophobic logic of
the closet-drama that a grange, ironically, might have been safer.
The perpetual paradox of the play is the paradox of the modern city
as Dickens explored it in, for example, *Bleak House*, that people are
pressed so close together and are yet so entirely ignorant of what is
happening in each other's lives, and so sealed from each other. In
this, Venice is the emblematic city.

Yet the play has no illusions. Venice is a real world and it works
well enough. *Othello* is a tragedy *in* Venice, not *of* Venice. At the
end of the play, Lodovico reminds us just how capable Venice is of
mopping up:

> Gratiano, keep the house,
> And seize upon the fortunes of the Moor,
> For they succeed to you.
>
> (v. ii.366–8)

The priorities of Venice are not affected by what has happened.

Our deepest shocks as an audience are the result of Othello's degradation. We are drawn into the squalor of his abjection. He becomes absurd, ridiculous. What is shocking and riveting is the coherence of the picture: the Noble Moor demanding 'ocular proof', sneaking and peeping at Cassio from his hiding-place. Iago guys Othello in all these dreadful scenes as Maria and Sir Toby guy Malvolio, but Malvolio is all pretence, so we laugh. Surely Othello was not all pretence?

Othello is not pretending: he is 'acting'. Not 'acting' as in 'performing', though: he is 'acting' as in 'acting-as-though' the stories, the 'pomp and circumstance of glorious war', were not just an idealized and temporary view. He is not fooling himself about that view either; he is no Don Quixote. His version of 'civilization' has no way of speaking the complex of feelings really involved in loving somebody. It cannot make the distinctions and assist the necessary self-education. In the end the Romance posture is a form of pretence, though not fraudulent and self-aggrandising as much as an effort to be better and to feel yourself and your world to be better, but which does not involve the right kinds of efforts.

Leavis and Eliot are unfair to Othello at last.[28] The clumsy manoeuvres of the last scenes of the play take us through a sort of stumbling, imperfect effort at self-seeing on Othello's part which it is not enough to see as 'cheering himself up', or as 'self-dramatization' only, though it is certainly that too. My contention is that there is heard a note of real clarity at the end:

> 　　　　　　　　　set you down this,
> And say besides, that in Aleppo once,
> Where a malignant and a turban'd Turk
> Beat a Venetian, and traduc'd the state,
> I took by the throat the circumcised dog,
> And smote him thus.
>
> 　　　　　　　　　　　　(v. ii.352–7)

This is not as easy as it seems. I think we have to imagine that this is where it all began, and that a story hangs thereby. Perhaps the merchant rewarded the young Othello by bringing him to Venice. Whatever it is, it will be romantic, and it will contain Othello's history. His real history, that is: the set of circumstances within which he has recast his own vision of things. It would reveal how that version of things revealed itself to him, and why he reshaped his life in its light. It is a clear moment in Othello's wandering final words, free from hyperbole, elaborate similes. It is simply a memory, etched on his mind. It is inexpressibly sad. It is the origin and the terminus of Othello's history and his story. It is immensely revealing in a suggestive way, and it is simply the truth. It is perhaps the only 'round unvarnish'd tale' that he tells.[29]

THE PLAY

I think the point about the play is that we must see Othello as hopelessly wrong, and yet wish he were right. It is not that the one might or ought to displace the other. Our pleasure in understanding consists in holding the two positions at once. The price we pay is the recognition that he is hopelessly wrong, and the world not at all as he thinks it. This may be salutary. Be that as it may, it is a necessary part of the feeling of pleasure in understanding.

The force of the play can be felt in Othello's 'in Aleppo once'. 'There was a time', or 'there could have been a time', is such a powerful feeling in the play, set as it is in the sober and practical city of Venice. That is the story-teller's 'once', and we know it never happened quite like that. But, then, that is art. It is always a sort of might-have-been, which is consoling:

> Remaining a perpetual possibility
> Only in a world of speculation.
> ('Burnt Norton')

For an Elizabethan audience, I suggest, the play offered an *elegy for an imagined past* – not for the past as it really was, though that is part of it, but for the past as it might have been, richer, more grand, more intense. This elegy is acted out in Desdemona and Othello's tragedy: it is part of that tragedy that the aspirations that are their downfall should be exactly towards this sort of *imagined past*.

There is, in the end, a bleakness about Shakespeare's two great Venetian plays which is interesting. Venice, it seems, was generally regarded as prodigious, in its way,[30] and yet Shakespeare always places in it more tantalizing prodigies in comparison with which, especially in the wake of their withdrawal or their demise, Venice seems coldly permanent. It is not in any way a shabby

world, but it is a world in which there is no place for the high
Romance values towards which Othello aspires. And these values
are not themselves uncomplicated, for it is their unyielding opacity
that plays such an important part in Othello's downfall. And yet
always that yearning for such a world, 'of one entire and perfect
chrysolite', is part of the complicated way in which we come to
terms with our world. We know all about the inadequacies and
impracticalities of these ideal worlds which pose themselves as
supplying the lustre our world may seem to lack, but that is their
point. The Elizabethan world which had just given way to the
Stuarts had consolidated the Tudor pacification in England, and it
must still have been possible to imagine that peace bought at the
expense of colour. This is a paradoxical expression of relief when
that sense of elegy is presented, as it is in *Othello*, as hopelessly
tragic. It is possible to say that the world may be safe, but it is
dreary, and mean that the world may be dreary, but it is safe.

This reminds us that Othello's Romance values are at least in
part a search for beauty. They represent an attempt to transform
the world. As such they are clearly related to the activity of art, and
through Bianca we see the close parallels with passion as a
transforming feeling. It is this complex for which Venice has no
place, and that is envied and hated by Iago as imposture. Art and
passion and beauty are perversely mirrored in Iago's mad hate,
and their proper relationship to life is thus clearly defined. Life can
no more be made up of art or passion or beauty than it can be of
their opposite, destructive impulses, epitomized in Iago. That
opposition is the structure of the tragic action. Art and passion and
beauty exist in tension with life, enriching it and illuminating it,
but they and life exist as contraries in Blake's sense in *The Marriage
of Heaven and Hell*; they give each other life and vitality. Without
that tension the states themselves lose their vitalizing energy and
become empty shells, husks of meaning. Passion and beauty are
conditions to which we aspire: art is the means by which
imaginative spaces are opened up, strictly outside real life and
history, existing in definite though flexible relationships to life and
history, which enable us to image our longing in relation to our
life. These spaces opened up by art construct a ground from which
we are enabled to look about us, backwards to the past, around us
in the present, forwards to the future, with a vision that we cannot
so well develop from the point of our involvement in real life. Life
is shaped most often by tensions and conflicts in which we have to

take sides and make choices, lose things in order to gain things. At its best, art shapes this difficulty not so that we withdraw from tension and choice, but so that we see it so much more clearly and richly.[31]

Art may not be able to solve any of our complexities of feeling, but it can shape them movingly, so that for a while we can live through them in all their contradictoriness, but *shaped*, not chaotic. And it is not only 'our' complexities of feeling. The art of the past has an engaging habit of enclosing its own audience within it by implication so that when it is our turn to attend we add, as it were, an outer circle to them, bringing 'our' complexities of feeling into a closer relationship with 'theirs', both in their resemblances and in their differences. In this way 'their' imagined past becomes more clearly part of 'our' imagined past, so that that 'for a while' is really endlessly revolving, gathering to itself new meanings, while at its heart that tragic elegy is perpetually replayed: 'And say besides, that in Aleppo once . . . .'

12

Epilogue: 'This is Venice'

Both *Othello* and *The Merchant of Venice* reveal a view of Venice as a particular kind of social world. Both plays offer a tension between the 'idealists' and the 'real' world of law and commerce and political expediency. *The Merchant of Venice* dramatizes law as the constituent structure of Venice, *Othello* the expediency and negotiation which is both controlled by law and made necessary by it if commerce is to be effectively carried on. Law and expediency are, in a sense, opposites. The Duke in *The Merchant of Venice* expresses himself helpless before the law; in *Othello* the Duke sets the law aside in the interests of political expediency. In *The Merchant of Venice* the law must be protected because it guarantees commerce; in *Othello* Othello must be protected because he guarantees commerce. Commerce is thus the middle term in which law and expediency meet. There is a paradoxical flavour about such a term, and we are perhaps reminded of the multiplying paradoxes of both plays, or even the downright contradictions and plain nonsense of Iago, or the sinister wilfulness of Shylock. Iago and Shylock represent a challenge to Venice precisely because they exploit the structure of Venice. Both law and expediency are dishonest in terms of each other. Law represents a rigidity which denies flexibility, expediency a flexibility which denies the absolute nature of moral values. Belmont shows us an ideal image of the ordering of the complexity of human responsiveness, neither losing touch with values, nor denying the confused nature of existence. Law in *The Merchant of Venice* and Othello's Romance idealizations in *Othello* deny the ordinary, the mixed, the confused. Their rigid purities cannot compromise, so they break – others or their adherents. Expediency, on the other hand, is no better. Portia speaks of tempering one virtue, justice, with another, mercy. Emilia speaks of letting go one's sense of being bothered about doing 'wrong' in order to get something one wants. Yet Portia wins by a legal trick and the last act is shot through with melancholy, and Emilia dies for her intransigent stand against the horror of her husband's crime. The plays do not simply set one social or moral world against another.

Portia and Othello are both figures that arise from a dramatic meditation on the meaning and value of the fairy-tale world of Romance: the Princess in the Tower and the Saracen Knight perhaps. The point is that they are real people, caught in different ways in a tension between their world and the other world, Venice. Taken together, the plays bid a rich and subtly complex farewell to their world, and cautiously and resignedly acknowledge the other. Portia cannot simply be taken as an absolutist *deus ex machina*, protecting the native merchant from the foreign usurer – unless we play down the complexity of the poetry of the last act, in particular its melancholy pointing the contrast between Venice and Belmont as real and imagined worlds; and, whatever uncertainty *The Merchant of Venice* may have about the absolutist model as a workable possibility, *Othello* vividly challenges its desirability.

Othello explores Venice as psychologically 'commercial': it is interested in the disparity between public discourse and private discourse and suggests that public discourse is not deeply unified, but is an area of negotiation and jostling between private discourses. Nowhere in the play is there an attempt to state or define in debate a constitutive discourse. Only on two occasions do we come near to such attempts: the Duke's assertion of Brabantio's right to justice is one, which is immediately subverted, and Lodovico's hopeless bafflement, 'What should be said to thee?', is the other. I have already suggested that Othello and Desdemona are the victims of this situation. In Desdemona's bewildered conversation with Emilia, in Iago's exchange with Cassio about Desdemona, we see that there is little attempt in Venice to keep discourse under scrutiny, to argue out meanings and to win them or stand by them. Conflict is to be avoided; every Venetian has a right to his or her opinion; the law guarantees it, 'the trade and profit of the city' depend upon it. This is what makes Lodovico's implicit appeal to the state so hopeless. In the sense in which he appeals to it, it does not exist. In the same way, in the sense in which Othello believes he serves it, it does not exist. Because of this, it does not sustain Othello's Romance language; it merely makes use of it, and therefore cannot nourish it. That language therefore dies, becomes rigid, brittle and sterile. To live, a language needs to be engaged in a continual struggle for meanings and testing of meanings. Otherwise those 'meanings' do not mean anything: they are no use in actual situations, they only work in imagined worlds, they become dead tokens, like Revolutionary *assignats* or Confederate dollars, they cannot be exchanged for anything. The world changes beyond their capacity to mean. Like a miser, Othello hoards meanings, but devaluation and revaluation, the minting of new currencies, new forms of credit, the miser's enemies, turn his wealth into scrap. The meditations on money in *The Merchant of Venice* apply with equal force to the terms of Othello's vision in *Othello*.

In a way this can be seen as a development of the meditation in *The Merchant of Venice* on the meaning of Belmont in the last act. The 'naughty world', catalysed and exploited by Iago, completely extinguishes the candle at last. The 'candle' is not just Desdemona, or Othello, or both of them, or love, or goodness. More subtly, it is a way of understanding what it is to be a person. *The Merchant of Venice* exposes a vision of 'person' as an articulation of a world, not to be understood apart from that world, a moment in the weave of that world. Against that is placed the wilful individuality of Shylock. Though Othello expresses values that belong to the world implied by Belmont, he is more like Shylock in his mode of personal being. Because there is no world of which he may be an articulation, no weave of which he may be part, except in his imagining, he is as wilfully individual as Shylock. In both cases Venice's lack of what I have called 'intercursiveness' brings tragedy to the fore. In Belmont discourses interpenetrate as wit and poetry and vision. But to seek full existence as a person in Venice is to risk isolation, and impoverishment and sterility, and that kind of getting things hopelessly wrong which is so close to madness in *Othello*. Belmont can harmonize tensions in its poetry, or can at least postpone the inevitable until the tensions that might have produced tragedy have become tamed and transformed. In *Othello* that poetry has petrified. Those who seek full existence as persons through commitment to some absolute value become foolish, pitiable, ridiculous or terrifying, or tragic. For surely Othello is tragic in the last resort of his being to his beginning? From III. iii onwards he is torn by such a tumult of different passions that we in turn fear him, are disgusted by him, pity him, fear for him, are terrified by what is happening to him, and, at the end, find him so far beyond our capacity to feel that we must agree with Lodovico's helplessness: 'What should be said to thee?' This is the ultimate blankness of Venice. It does not exist in such a way that it could have anything to say that 'should be said'.

There is an instructive parallel to be drawn between Cassio's drunkenness and Othello's 'madness'. In both cases conscious control slips and inchoate passionate feeling erupts. Iago even encourages the suggestion that this happens during sleep, in his account of the night he has spent in Cassio's bed. The point seems to be that in Venice control is external, and is exerted as restraint, as repression. This can be contrasted with the model offered by Belmont of a shaped, 'curb'd' feeling, managed not repressed. This external control in Venice is epitomized in the rule of law, and the dangers and inadequacies of such a model are revealed by Shylock's trap. More subtly still, *Othello* suggests that such a model, failing to encourage the intercursiveness of differences, traps people in their mutually alienated selfhoods, which imprisonment it presents as the preservation of individual rights. The duke's resort to expediency exposes 'law' still more fully. The only validation of law in Venice is 'the trade and profit of the city'. If this is to come into conflict with the rule of law, the law must give way. Ultimately Venice is ruled by commerce and profit. What lies exposed to view is the deepest question a civilization has to face: its right to claim the loyalties of its members and servants, which, in time of war, becomes the rightfulness of its claim to continued existence.

To read these plays as propaganda, or compliment, or as a kind of reassurance, is to miss the point of 'play'. I have in mind here the three senses in which we have made use of this word: that is, 'play' as drama, 'play' as game, and 'play' as 'looseness of fit', a flexibility language enjoys which permits the construction of figures, the possibility of poetry. To 'play' or 'replay' history in these plays is not necessarily to affirm or to challenge history's real outcomes. It is rather to celebrate a marginal *consciousness*, an awareness of unrealized possibilities, which may only exist as 'play'. This could so easily become fantasy, but is prevented from so becoming by a consistent grasp of 'reality' – that is, the appearance in the plays of history's real outcomes – and the playing of possibility across this grasp like a kind of light. 'Possibility' is not the same as 'possibilities': the latter are settled imaginative structures, the former more a sense of the richness and diversity of things as they are imagined, which hints at difference and otherness. As worlds settle into place this sense becomes fugitive and may disappear. It seems daydreaming, or naïveté, or a wilful refusal to adapt to 'reality' as it is said to be from time to time. Consider the distance between Antony's distraught musings:

> Sometime we see a cloud that's dragonish,
> A vapour sometime, like a bear, or lion,
> A tower'd citadel, a pendent rock,
> A forked mountain, or blue promontory
> With trees upon't, that nod unto the world,
> And mock our eyes with air. Thou hast seen these signs,
> They are black vesper's pageants.
> EROS.   Ay, my lord.
> ANTONY. That which is now a horse, even with a thought
> The rack dislimns, and makes it indistinct
> As water is in water
>   (*Antony and Cleopatra*, IV. xiv.2–11)

and Hamlet's:

> Do you see yonder cloud that's almost in shape of a camel?
> POLONIUS. By th'mass and 'tis – like a camel indeed.
> HAMLET. Methinks it is like a weasel.
> POLONIUS. It is backed like a weasel.
> HAMLET. Or like a whale.
> POLONIUS. Very like a whale.   (*Hamlet*, III. ii.367–73)

The feeling in the first is that 'we are such stuff/As dreams are
made on' (*The Tempest*, IV. i.156–7), 'insubstantial pageants', and
is a sober and moving reflection that our dreams of ourselves and
of others are not always realizable, cannot always be made 'real'.
The feeling in the second is of a powerful arbitrariness that brings
close Nietzsche's fearful 'weightlessness' of things. Antony's
mood is closer to the Venice plays, though that fearful powerful
arbitrariness breaks out in them too.

The reflection I wish to stress is that there is no reason for
assuming that the 'real' is any more than those dreams that *are*
realizable, those versions of things that really do gather people's
assent and so become substantial, in the sense that people's belief
in their reality is their substance. When this happens, the unrealized dreams become merely dreams, and 'the rack dislimns'.
These plays dramatize that poignancy and give paradoxical substance to those dreams, because we are moved by them, and that is
their substance.

And there you'll find me, if a jot
    You still should care
For me, and for my curious air;
If otherwise, then I shall not,
    For you, be there.
        (Thomas Hardy, 'My spirit
        will not haunt the mound')

The Venice plays bring into sharp focus the ambiguity and richness of this experience, and what relevance it has for us:

Whatever we inherit from the fortunate
We have taken from the defeated
What they had to leave us – a symbol:
A symbol perfected in death.
        ('Little Gidding')

Whatever the weakness and dangers of Venice as a model of civilization, neither play lets us feel that there is any alternative. Venice is, in Eliot's terms, 'the fortunate': what haunts us is a complex vision of a world seen as it turns from us to go, whose poetry and passionate danger leave us with a richly ambiguous symbol, 'a symbol perfected in death', and we are the better for having come within its influence.

Conclusion
Nick Potter

I

The situations that occur in history can be seen from two points of view, one situated within, the other without. This latter perspective can be thought of as investigating the 'structural' or 'objective' aspects of a historical situation, while the other can be thought of as investigating its 'subjective' or 'emblematic' aspects.

When a society poses itself a problem, it does so not only in terms of analytical language, but also in terms of a language of images designed to mobilize not so much knowledge *about* that problem as knowledge *of* it, a language that engages intuition and feeling as well as reason. In our study of Shakespeare's plays we have been conscious of their twofold engagement: on the one hand with their present, and on the other with the past. In both cases that engagement is with the 'emblematic' as well as with the 'structural'. What excited the imagination of the dramatist was the imaginative aspect of history, history as emblem. Our interest, therefore, is also in the emblematic aspect of the history of the time. From this point of view we have seen the period as being dominated by the phenomenon of the Renaissance.

The Renaissance in England appears as an efflorescence associated with Reformation and giving way to revolution, restoration, and Reason. Its place is as a part of the Tudor pacification, a celebration of the virtues of prosperity and of the opportunities arising from it. It is itself an intensification, a concentration of energies and a dissolving of constraints upon inquiry. It chose the theatre as one of its chief voices, or platforms, as it were. The persistence of theatrical metaphors and allusions in Shakespeare's work gives us a clue as to why this should be. If the world is a stage, the stage may be a world. That rhetorical trope should take the place of logic is characteristic of an open-mindedness towards the possibilities offered by the world that we associate with the Renaissance. A later thinker, struggling against the Age of Reason, pointed towards a similar paradox in a different image:

> To see a world in a Grain of Sand,
> And a Heaven in a Wild Flower,
> Hold Infinity in the palm of your hand,
> And Eternity in an hour.
> (Blake, 'Auguries of Innocence')

By Blake's time the vision had retreated to poetry. The image of man acting and speaking, strutting and fretting his hour upon the stage, had become man listening to himself talk in his mind, building Jerusalem in his head rather than in the theatre.

The theatre is like an illusionist: it is persuasive. Reality and illusion pass into each other. The dominant metaphor is one of a proliferation of surfaces, appearances. And, if the stage is a world, perhaps all the world's a stage. The persuasiveness of theatre lies in its mischievous erosion of our sense of social reality: boys play girls who play boys who pretend to be paupers and turn out to be princesses played by actors. In this unfolding there is no guarantee of an ending, a final turning-out of the truth. Every 'ending' is an interim report on the state of the game. But, if the edges are blurred, in the centre real clarity emerges, sometimes startlingly. People go mad, kings are killed, evil seduces us. Though it is only play, it never quite goes away. The feelings and the sense of threat have been real. The actors unmask *after* the play, not in the middle of it. In the theatre we are helpless. We are also free. Play and destiny interweave magically, leaving us unsure.

To the extent that the Renaissance can be seen as confident, this play is a giddy excitement extending the boundaries of inquiry and experience. To the extent that that confidence is coupled with fear of presumption, this play relieves that fear with images, consoles it with causes and with company in the shape of its heroes.

This theatre did not erupt fully fledged with the Renaissance. It emerged, as we have suggested, out of an intense and imaginative process of integration and the creative use of opportunities presented by residual tradition and source material. What is new is the depth of play, the radical extent to which it involves the world in its revelry. The microcosm becomes increasingly voracious, giving birth in turn to ever larger, more daring worlds.

From the point of view of the emblematic once again, we have also tended to see the period in terms of two kinds of confrontation as imaged in the plays as we have discussed them. First, there is the aspect of confrontation amongst different ruling groups or within ruling groups, a competition for political dominance. From the Chronicle plays to *The Merchant of Venice* the political relations of a society are a manifest concern of the plays. Secondly, there is a kind of confrontation more difficult to characterize, but which we may for the sake of convenience call 'cultural'.

This aspect of confrontation may be thought of in terms of a set of oppositions, between court and country, town and village, church and grove. This is not meant to imply a settled analytical viewpoint. It is an attempt to describe a coherence and an extension belonging to phenomena that appear in the plays as elements of 'revelry' and the excitements of disorder. Structurally speaking, the period is one in which a growing Puritan movement attacks 'pastime' or 'holiday', a traditional country ideology, in the name of the dignity of labour.

There is an intangible borderline that divides an older culture, belonging to the village, the countryside and pre-Christian religious forms, that holds 'work' to be a necessary evil, from a culture, belonging to the town and to certain Christian religious forms, that holds 'work' to be dignifying. The first proclaims 'pastime', 'revelry', 'misrule', as a celebration of an image of freedom from work, while the second initiates proceedings against 'pastime', 'revelry', 'misrule' – indeed, against the entire ideology of 'holiday' – for precisely the reason that it is a repudiation of work. 'Holiday' is not a real rebellion against work, though: it is a statement that work, however necessary, is not the most important aspect of human existence. It became important during the Tudor period to change this public view and to overturn or to suppress 'pastime'.

The court, it must be stressed, straddles this division uneasily. In its emblematic aspect, especially through the Christmas 'misrule' festivities, the court is seen as the source and promise of 'pastime', as well as the agency of the imposition of the necessity of work. This role was changing through the sixteenth century and the court was increasingly being seen as being involved in serious pursuits which, if not exactly work, were no longer 'pastime'. The curious alliance with the country whereby the court, and sometimes the manor, could be admired and envied and resented at the same time, was breaking down. The court was more frequently seen as the place of responsibility and government, as it is in Shakespeare's comedies, for example. Even in Belmont they do not simply 'fleet the time carelessly' any more. There is a heavy weight of state responsibility, however far in the background it may appear.

The watchfulness of the Tudor state reveals its awareness of its own continuing instability, which appears in these plays not only as political instability, but as this deeper, emblematic conflict of 'orderliness' and 'misrule'. This can be taken to suggest that Shakespeare sees the political conflicts as being importantly related to this emblematic conflict, and, indeed, often as less important than the emblematic, at least for this purpose. Certainly the images that call forth his creative powers most strongly are images of disorder that so shake the single state of character and audience that 'nothing is but what is not'. For convenience it can be said that the central axis of the vision of the plays lies not along the divisions amongst the classes contending for dominance, but along this fault-line of English society itself: order and misrule, town and village, work and holiday, an old world and a new struggling to be born. The political sense of the plays is that the divisions that shake the body that rules release the often terrible energies held in temporary check by the different kinds of societies the plays are concerned with, and to which 'holiday' pays a due and cautious deference.

II

Renaissance theatre has two real sources: the tradition of morality drama, and a tradition of popular mime, such as mummers' plays, which parallels this development and interweaves with it. In both the element of ritual and ceremony is evident. The theatre is an enactment of something, and the audience is in attendance at the enactment. In terms of its institutional status in Tudor and Jacobean England, the theatre must be seen as being comparable to the church in its liturgical aspect, and the church in its ecclesiastical aspect as being comparable to the emergent state. That is, the first two are charged with the enactment of socially important experiences, and the last two with the organization of the material social relationships within which the former can take place. Tudor and Jacobean drama is urban, and courtly: the village as a social institution is not involved with it except in the important sense that its traditions persist in fragmentary form in its popular theatrical elements. This is clearly a relationship in which conflicts and

friction are inevitable. The religious and the secular, the sacred and
the profane, the town and the village, the permitted and the
unpermitted that belong to each offer the theatre a uniquely
privileged ground in that it has itself no readily apparent body of
permitted and unpermitted: it is an area of ritual enactment
without clear allegiances, a temple and priests waiting for a god.

We are presented in many of the plays with a disturbing implied
image: the courtly is brought into the inn-yard, the mummers
mime a Christian sanctity. At the same time, the inn-yard is
brought into the court and the clergy celebrate the May. The first is
an image of desecration; the second, one of sacralization. What is
implied is that what is important, what is sacred, is to be derided,
and what is profane is to be elevated. This is the element of revelry
that the plays involve, and it may represent a simultaneous
struggle and compromise, a difficult synthesis of town and village,
court and country, church and grove, which is a political and a
cultural and a social effort. It may be a hegemonic struggle, to
defeat a surviving cultural independence, to absorb it, or it may be
the effort to win a common understanding which will enrich itself
through embracing contraries. Whichever, the place of the theatre
seems to be defined as an enactment of a play of possibilities. If the
priests of the theatre are waiting for their god, the attempt is to
conjure him through a shaped open-endedness, a structured and
structuring play. If the god has arrived, or was already there, then
the theatre is an active pantheon, not merely housing its gods, but
articulating their complex relatedness. For, if the sacred is derided
and the profane elevated, it is also true that, as though within an
embracing Christian mystery that through subjection we rise, that
scorn and derision ennobles, through that topsy-turvy giddiness
we do not lose sight of sacredness and profaneness themselves. If
'fair is foul and foul is fair' the confusion depends on fairness and
foulness; and, though we get confused, the plays do not extinguish
either, but present both all the more vividly for our uncertainty as
to where they are really to be found in our world.

III

What do we get from a study of the plays? The answer to this
question involves first considering another: what is it that we

study? We have all tried to *interpret* the plays on which we have written: we have tried to recover the set of meanings and the feelings which lie behind the text, whether unconsciously or consciously. We have accepted that there is a deliberateness involved. The texts were meant: that is, they were fashioned. They did not come about of their own accord. We have tried to make specific sense of these perceptions, that the texts were fashioned and that sets of meanings and feelings are involved with them in terms of each play. The question that has lurked behind our every attempt has been, what was Shakespeare up to?

A text may be seen as a structure of anticipated responses – that is, a structure made out of language, a structure of words and phrases, cadences and silences, sounds and meanings, which, it is imagined, will evoke certain sets of responses. The structure of those responses, their sequence and interaction, is the end, the purpose and the termination of the text. It is, in its enactment, a speaking that is heard. And there is a mystery. Who is speaking? A man who left Stratford-upon-Avon one day in the company of a group of players, who owned property in Stratford, who left his wife his second-best bed, who had a share in the Globe Theatre .... The sparseness of the facts of Shakespeare's life is an emblem of their ambiguous help towards an answer to this question. 'Shakespeare' is a story we tell to explain the imaginative acts that fashioned these texts that structure our responses and reveal what they have to reveal in so doing.

We cannot reduce the texts to the meanings or feelings evoked, or to those which, we theorize, stimulated the imaginative acts that led to their fashioning. They are 'plays', of and with their meanings, dramatic articulations of them, and they have their existence in their activity and in the history of their activity that is the responses and interpretations which have occurred in connection with them and which we read backwards towards their source, their 'having been intended', against which we can gauge their completeness.

'It is impossible to say just what I mean': Prufrock's complaint applies, more or less, in all ages. The exasperated anguish with which we struggle to say just what we mean, to speak ourselves, as individuals or as communities, is not new. The task of the poet is sometimes that of the scribe: making shapely our different attempts. And not only in a spirit of self-effacing recording but in a joyous celebration of the attempt which transcends the disappointment of failure. This also is an intention, a fashioning.

But the celebration is not indifferent to the particularity of the attempt. The condition of the celebration is that the attempt should have been worthwhile. What we have noted in our study has been a certain consistency of concern, or 'attempt' perhaps. On the one hand there has been noted a heterogeneity, a 'gallimaufry' of anticipated responses which renders even tragedy subversively comic in its resistance to confinement within any particular harmony or resolution. On the other hand, and paradoxically, there has been noted a resolving harmony, a quiet attestation to the inevitably mixed nature of the world in which meanings are to be made.

Michael Bristol, in *Carnival and Theatre* (1985) has pointed to the work of René Girard, Roger Caillois, Victor Turner and others who have seen in 'carnival' and 'festivity' a set of 'informal mechanisms' contributing to the survival of communities. May we see these plays in such a context? On the other hand, we have traced, especially in the tragedies and the Venice plays, the emergence of an anguished individual consciousness. Perhaps the plays are closer to Nietzsche's views, expressed in *The Birth of Tragedy* (1872), that the pain of existing is expressed in the frenzy of worship and the despair of normality in 'festivity'? Freud's later suggestion that there may exist a 'death-instinct', opposite to the 'life-instinct', expressed in *Beyond the Pleasure Principle* (1920), is perhaps an attempt to come to terms with a similar feeling. The survival of the community may be served by such activities; they may even be a purging of such destructive and self-destructive impulses; but the plays often suggest an alignment with the point of view of existing individuals who, in disgust and despair at the ordinary, release their pent-up yearning for the exalted in a frenzy of self-loathing, desire and despair. This orgiastic release is also a part of what we have been able to trace as the plays' emotional 'sub-text'. Subversive or supportive, conciliatory or combative: how can we describe 'Shakespeare's' motives?

IV

The question is, do these plays tend to support a view of the Elizabethan and Jacobean theatre as an 'ideological state apparatus', as the French philosopher Louis Althusser has called those institutions which are charged with the maintenance and promotion of ideology?

In general, what can we say that the plays propose? They appear at last to propose that form of society we might have expected them to propose – that is, the form of society in which they were produced: commercial, urban, English society as it was under the Tudors. Not without regret is this proposed, but, as we have argued, the effect of these plays is to turn their audiences out into a reality which the plays demand for their particular functioning: they do not challenge that reality; they assume it and they depend upon it. In this special sense, given the privileged position of the theatre as a producer of collective experience, they can be said to propose that reality. But, again, how does that proposition really come about? Is it a motive that we can assign to Shakespeare, or does it properly belong to 'Shakespeare'?

This must be clarified. There is behind all writing a figure that Wayne Booth, in *The Rhetoric of Fiction*, called the 'implied author', the character made up by the reader from his or her reading, induced into the text while appearing to be deduced from it. This 'implied author' may or may not fit with the actual author, the person whose deliberations issued in the text. We may never know how much of what we argue a text 'means' was 'meant' by the actual author. It is in the light of this doubt that a distinction is needed between Shakespeare and 'Shakespeare'. This not to deny the importance of Shakespeare. Though we have not addressed ourselves systematically to the question, we feel that the owner of New Place was not indifferently involved in his writing, ready to turn a compliment or a satire, depending on whose hand was on the purse-strings. It is only that we are aware of the mystery of authorship in the sense in which we want to talk about it. How meanings come to be meant, how meanings are discovered in the business of searching for means of expression of other meanings, these are only too familiar difficulties:

> And what you thought you came for
> Is only a shell, a husk of meaning
> From which the purpose breaks only when it is fulfilled
> If at all. Either you had no purpose
> Or the purpose is beyond the end you figured
> And is altered in fulfilment.
>
> ('Little Gidding')

Of course it would make a sort of sense to say that the owner of New Place would be bound to propose the sort of society from which he profited, and that in fact, as Marx and Engels said in *The German Ideology*, 'the ruling ideas in any epoch are nothing more than the ideal expression of the dominant social relationships, the dominant social relationships grasped as ideas', but this is too easily cynical a conclusion. Why should not the owner of New Place have felt only dismay at his profit, while helplessly returning to it? We have only our doubts and our suspicions. The evidence of the writing will only ever be evidence of 'Shakespeare' and will not help us to relate him to his shadowy counterpart. The ideological aspect of the plays, then, consists in a proposition of a form of society which is not in any simple way a positive proposition.

This proposition is an effect of the plays. It is a part of their intention. But it is not at all the whole of their intention. What was referred to earlier as our 'helplessness' in the theatre is a surrender to its excitements. The plays are not interested in the past or in other societies simply to confirm the presence of contemporary reality. The worlds conjured by Othello, envisioned by Duncan, or by Henry V, worlds such as Belmont, or Falstaff's, are real worlds of the imagination, human possibilities if not political possibilities, which enrich our knowledge of our present. This is the answer to the question posed by 'Burnt Norton':

> But to what purpose
> Disturbing the dust on a bowl of rose leaves
> I do not know.

These are some of the passages we did not take, doors that history never opened: the past not as gone, but as haunting the present with its suggestion of what might have been. In the theatre we surrender to the excitements of the past and of the 'other'. This is not the interest of the antiquary but that of the artist obsessed with a risky playfulness that is enticing. While the fault-line of English society may be an occasion for sober reflection in reality, in the theatre it is exhilaratingly dangerous.

V

What has attracted us to these plays is the daring of the poetry. In play, as in jest, we approach the acknowledgement of what we would disavow. Collectively, individually, we are drawn to the replaying of what we have to put from us but which never leaves us. Fears and wishes haunt us in these plays: the wish to impose a spurious and illusory unity upon class-divided society to further our pursuit of our own ends, or to justify it to ourselves, as much as the wish to kill the father, the political and social as much as the individual psychological. Generosity and selfishness, goodness and wickedness, self and other, reason and desire, are seen as subtly complicit in our vision of these plays, and the plays themselves as a continual, ironic, paradoxical stand taken by the spirit in the business of making its meanings to itself and to others, having its say amid the 'play' of these differences. Scribe, prophet, jester – the poet may be all or any of these. We have only attempted to find our way along the clue of the texts, forwards and backwards, towards our own time and towards an elusive, tantalizing, permanent absence which is clear though never near – 'the Bard', 'the Swan of Avon', Shaksper, Shakeshaft, 'Shakespeare'. He himself was aware of the ironies implicit in naming and hoping thereby to pin down. Picasso's cartoon reminds us of the tenuousness of the outline and also of its firmness. In the play of identity and differences is the daring of the poetry.

The propositions of literary-critical activity are not those of history, or of politics, or of sociology, or of linguistics. They are the propositions that arise as a result of a process of inquiry occasioned by particular texts. What we get from a study of the plays is what we get by untying the meanings and feelings involved in the texts. When we have done this we have also isolated the 'play' that is writing: the specific activity of the text, the life those meanings and feelings have in that particular involvement. We have participated in the plays: we have involved other ways of talking about our world with them; we have thrown all into play; we have recovered a state of 'innocence'.

> 'No, no, let us play, for it is yet day
> 'And we cannot go to sleep;
> 'Besides in the sky the little birds fly,
> 'And the hills are all cover'd with sheep.'
> (Blake, *Songs of Innocence*, 1789)

We leave the theatre, and inquiries such as this, for a different, later world:

> Then come home, my children, the sun is gone down,
> And the dews of night arise;
> Your Spring & your day are wasted in play,
> And your winter and night in disguise.
>
> (Blake, *Songs of Experience*, 1794)⁻

Neither one of these two 'Nurse's Songs' is *right*. As Blake put it in *The Marriage of Heaven and Hell*, 'Without Contraries is no progression'. In this consideration of history and play we hope to have made a similar point.

Notes

NOTES TO THE INTRODUCTION

1. We have regularly invoked Eliot's *Four Quartets* throughout this book in our contention, against a certain crude materialism, that the material history of man is a matter not only of the things that have been done but also of the things that have been imagined, desired or regretted.

2. The phrase, referring to the birth of modern historiography, is to be found in the title to F. Smith Fussner's *The Historical Revolution: English Historical Writing and Thought 1580–1640* Routledge and Kegan Paul, 1962), where an account of the subject may be found.

3. The Folio ending to *Love's Labour's Lost*, a valedictory note characteristic of the comedies as players and audience go their separate ways.

4. Raymond Williams, in the Afterword to Jonathan Dollimore and Alan Sinfield (eds), *Political Shakespeare: New Essays in Cultural Materialism* (Manchester University Press, 1985) p. 238.

5. John Danby, *Shakespeare's Doctrine of Nature: A Study of 'King Lear'* (Faber and Faber, 1949) p. 18.

6. G. Wilson Knight, *The Imperial Theme*, Prefatory Note to the Third Edition (Methuen, 1951) p. vi. The whole of Wilson Knight's criticism on Shakespeare exemplifies this approach in an extreme form.

7. Jonathan Dollimore, 'Shakespeare, Cultural Materialism and the New Historicism', in Dollimore and Sinfield, *Political Shakespeare*, p. 10. This collection of essays may serve as an introduction to this new critical methodology.

8. D. W. Winnicott, *Playing and Reality* (Penguin, 1974) p. 83. This is an ideal introduction to the work of the British school of object-relations psychoanalysis to which we refer here.

9. William Wordsworth, *Home at Grasmere*, ed. Beth Darlington (Cornell University Press, 1977) MS D, ll. 576–7.

10. See J. Huizinga, *Homo Ludens: A Study of the Play-Element in Culture*, tr. R. F. C. Hull (Routledge and Kegan Paul, 1949) esp. ch. 2. What is really required, of course, is not a list of the plurality of meanings that 'play' has had in various cultures but a historically specific account of the particular meanings that have been contested in each; it is one of the key-words of our own culture.

NOTES TO PART ONE   THEATRES OF HISTORY: CHRONICLE PLAYS

1. See E. M. W. Tillyard, *Shakespeare's History Plays* (Chatto and Windus, 1944); G. Wilson Knight, *The Olive and the Sword* (Oxford University Press, 1944); Lily B. Campbell, *Shakespeare's Histories* (Huntington Library, 1947); Derek Traversi, *Shakespeare from 'Richard II' to 'Henry V'* (Hollis and Carter, 1957).
2. Tillyard, *Shakespeare's History Plays*, pp. 320–1.
3. See Graham Holderness, 'Readings in the Shakespeare Myth', in Peter Widdowson *et al.* (eds), *Popular Fictions* (Methuen, 1986).
4. Alan Sinfield and Jonathan Dollimore, 'History and Ideology: the Instance of *Henry V*', in John Drakakis (ed.), *Alternative Shakespeares* (Methuen, 1986).
5. Ibid., p. 225.
6. James H. Kavanagh, 'Shakespeare in Ideology', in Drakakis, *Alternative Shakespeares*, p. 148.
7. See Leonard Tennenhouse, 'Strategies of State and Political Plays', in Jonathan Dollimore and Alan Sinfield (eds), *Political Shakespeare: New Essays in Cultural Materialism* (Manchester University Press, 1985).
8. See, for example, Irving Ribner, *The English History Play in the Age of Shakespeare* (Princeton University Press, 1957); and Moody E. Prior, *The Drama of Power* (Northwestern University Press, 1973).
9. See F. Smith Fussner, *The Historical Revolution* (Routledge and Kegan Paul, 1962), and J. G. A. Pocock, *The Ancient Constitution and the Feudal Law* (Cambridge University Press, 1957).
10. See Graham Holderness, *Shakespeare's History* (Gill and Macmillan, 1985).
11. See, for example, for the first view, Traversi, *Shakespeare from 'Richard II' to 'Henry V'*; Alvin B. Kernan, 'The *Henriad*: Shakespeare's Major History Plays', in his collection of essays *Modern Shakespearean Criticism* (Harcourt, Brace and World, 1970); and, for the second, Edna Boris Zwick, *Shakespeare's English Kings, the People and the Law* (Associated University Presses, 1974).
12. See Anne Barton, 'The King Disguised: Shakespeare's *Henry V* and the Comical History', in Joseph G. Price (ed.), *The Triple Bond* (Pennsylvania State University Press, 1975). See also Paul Dean, 'Chronicle and Romance Modes in *Henry V*', *Shakespeare Quarterly*, 32 (1981); and 'Shakespeare's *Henry VI* Tetralogy and Elizabethan Romance Histories: The Emergence of a Genre', *Shakespeare Quarterly*, 33 (1982).
13. See Peter Ure (ed.), *The Arden Shakespeare: King Richard II* (Methuen, 1956) pp. li–lvii.
14. See Tillyard: *Shakespeare's History Plays*, pp. 250–1; H. M. Richmond, *Shakespeare's Political Plays* (Random House, 1967) p. 130; F. W. Brownlow, *Two Shakespearean Sequences* (Macmillan, 1977) p. 108.
15. Ure (ed.), *King Richard II*, p. lv.

16. Paul Alpers, 'What is Pastoral?', *Critical Inquiry*, 8 (Spring 1982) 457.
17. See William Empson, *Some Versions of Pastoral* (Chatto and Windus, 1935).
18. See Louis Adrian Montrose, 'Of Gentlemen and Shepherds: the Politics of Elizabethan Pastoral Form', *ELH*, 50 (Fall 1983) 432.
19. Peter V. Marinelli, *Pastoral* (Methuen, 1971) p. 9.
20. Renato Poggioli, 'The Oaten Flute', *Harvard Library Bulletin*, 11 (1957) 151.
21. See Raymond Williams, *The Country and the City* (Chatto and Windus, 1973).
22. For other views of this relationship see Charles R. Forker, 'Shakespeare's Historical Plays as Historical-Pastoral', *Shakespeare Studies*, 1 (1965); William W. E. Slights, 'Nature's Originals: Value in Shakespearean Pastoral', *Shakespeare Survey*, 37 (1984); and James C. Bulman, 'Shakespeare's Georgic Histories', *Shakespeare Survey*, 38 (1985).
23. Samuel Daniel, *The Civil Wars* (1595), ed. Laurence Michel (Yale University Press, 1958) p. 67.
24. See Andrew Gurr (ed.), *The New Cambridge Shakespeare: Richard II* (Cambridge University Press, 1984) pp. 10–11.
25. For a thorough investigation of the sources of the Tudor chronicles, see H. A. Kelly, *Divine Providence in the England of Shakespeare's Histories* (Harvard University Press, 1970).
26. See Benjamin Williams (ed. and tr.), *Chronique de las Traison et Mort de Richard Deux Roy Dengleterre* (FSA, 1846); John Webb (ed. and tr.), *Translation of a French Metrical History of the Deposition of King Richard II* [Jean Creton], *Archaeologia*, xx (1819); and Daniel, *The Civil Wars*, ii.13ff. (p. 104ff. in Michel edn).
27. See Graham Holderness, 'Shakespeare's History: *Richard II*', *Literature and History*, 7:1 (1981).
28. Henry C. Lea, *Superstition and Force: Essays on the Wager of Battle* (Lea, 1866) p. 155.
29. G. D. Squibb, *The High Court of Chivalry* (Oxford University Press, 1959) p. 22.
30. See Maurice Keen, *Chivalry* (Yale University Press, 1985) p. 177.
31. Arthur Underhill, 'Law', in *Shakespeare's England* (Clarendon Press, 1916) p. 390.
32. Donna B. Hamilton, 'The State of Law in *Richard II*', *Shakespeare Quarterly*, 34 (1983) 16.
33. For the complicity of recent accounts in this view, see Laurie E. Osborne, 'Crisis of Degree in Shakespeare's *Henriad*', *Studies in English Literature*, 25:2 (Spring 1985); and Harry Berger, Jr, 'Psychoanalyzing the Shakespeare Text', in Patricia Parker and Geoffrey Hartman (eds), *Shakespeare and the Question of Theory* (Methuen, 1986).
34. Simon Shepherd (ed.), *Thomas of Woodstock* (Nottingham Drama Texts, 1977); and Daniel, *The Civil Wars*, i. 26 (p. 78 in Michel edn).
35. Tillyard suggested that the chronicle of Jean Froissart might have

coloured Shakespeare's vision with a mediaeval decor (see Tillyard, *Shakespeare's History Plays* pp. 252–3); but Froissart's chronicle is no simple mediaeval tapestry – see for example his account of the Mowbray–Bolingbroke quarrel: *The Thirde and Fourthe Boke of Sir Johan Froyssart*, tr. Lord Berners (1525; Da Capo Press, Theatrum Orbis Terrarum, 1970) iv. xcviii.

36. See Tillyard, *Shakespeare's History Plays*, pp. 257–9; Traversi, *Shakespeare from 'Richard II' to 'Henry V'* pp. 12–13; Campbell, *Shakespeare's Histories*, p. 194; M. M. Reese, *The Cease of Majesty* (Edward Arnold, 1961) pp. 231–2; S. C. Sen Gupta, *Shakespeare's Historical Plays* (Oxford University Press, 1964). Quotation from Wilbur Sanders, *The Dramatist and the Received Idea: Studies in the Plays of Marlowe and Shakespeare* (Cambridge University Press, 1968) p. 160.

37. See 'The Order of Battle in the Court of Chivalry', *Black Book of the Admiralty* (Rolls Series) pp. 325–6.

38. See n. 35 above.

39. See Keen, *Chivalry*, ch. 8.

40. Ibid., p. 27.

41. See John Bellamy, *The Tudor Law of Treason* (University of Toronto Press, Routledge and Kegan Paul, 1979).

42. See J. G. Bellamy, *The Law of Treason in the Later Middle Ages* (Cambridge University Press, 1970).

43. See Reese, *The Cease of Majesty*, p. 232; Sanders, *The Dramatist and the Received Idea*, p. 161; Robert Ornstein, *A Kingdom for a Stage* (Cambridge, Mass., 1972) p. 110; H. R. Coursen, *The Leasing Out of England* (University Press of America, 1982) p. 43.

44. S. Schoenbaum, '*Richard II* and the Realities of Power', *Shakespeare Survey*, 28 (1975) 10; and see also Moody E. Prior, *The Drama of Power* (Northwestern University Press, 1973) pp. 144–15.

45. See Gurr (ed.), *Richard II*, p. 20.

46. Diane Bornstein, 'Trial by Combat and Official Irresponsibility in *Richard II*', *Shakespeare Studies*, 8 (1975).

47. The juxtaposition is central to pastoral convention: see, for example, Torquato Tasso, *Jerusalem Delivered*, tr. Edward Fairfax (1600; Centaur Press, 1962), bk vii. pp. 166–7.

48. cf. *The Winter's Tale*, iv. iv.445–7; and *King Lear*, i i.180–1.

49. A similar technique is employed in *Thomas of Woodstock*: see n.34 above.

50. Renato Poggioli, 'Naboth's Vineyard, or the Pastoral View of the Social Order', *Journal of the History of Ideas*, xxiv:1 (1963) 9.

51. For an analogous argument see Ronald R. Macdonald, 'Uneasy Lies: Language and History in Shakespeare's Lancastrian Tetralogy', *Shakespeare Quarterly*, 35 (1984).

52. 'Gardeners' in the Quarto text; 'Gardener and 2 servants' in the Folio.

53. Daniel, *The Civil Wars*, iii.65 (pp. 145–6 in Michel edn).

54. See *3 Henry VI*, ii. v.1–54; and *Richard II*, iii. iii.147–54.

55. See David Young, *The Heart's Forest* (Yale University Press, 1972).

56. See Forker, 'Shakespeare's Historical Plays as Historical-Pastoral',

Shakespeare Studies, 1; Slights, 'Nature's Originals: Value in Shakespearean Pastoral', *Shakespeare Survey,* 37; and Bulman, 'Shakespeare's Georgic Histories', *Shakespeare Survey,* 38.

57. Sir Philip Sidney, *A Defence of Poetry,* ed. Jan van Dorsten (Oxford University Press, 1966) pp. 65–6.
58. Bertolt Brecht, *Messingkauf Dialogues,* tr. John Willett (Eyre Methuen, 1965) pp. 63–4.
59. For the factual details of the Essex connection see Ure (ed.), *King Richard II,* pp. lvii–lxii; and Gurr (ed.), *Richard II,* pp. 6–9. For discussion see Holderness, *Shakespeare's History,* pp. 131–44; and Dollimore and Sinfield, 'History and Ideology: the Instance of *Henry V'*, in Drakakis, *Alternative Shakespeares.*
60. See Tillyard, *Shakespeare's History Plays,* pp. 264–304.
61. Tennenhouse, 'Strategies of State and Political Plays', in Dollimore and Sinfield, *Political Shakespeare.*
62. Ibid., p. 121.
63. Ibid., pp. 121–12.
64. Tillyard, *Shakespeare's History Plays,* pp. 298–9.
65. Tennenhouse, 'Strategies of State and Political Plays', in Dollimore and Sinfield, *Political Shakespeare,* p. 125.
66. A similar view emerges from C. L. Barber, *Shakespeare's Festive Comedy: A Study of Dramatic Form and its Relation to Social Custom* (Princeton University Press, 1959).
67. See Tillyard, *Shakespeare's History Plays,* p. 261; A. R. Humphreys (ed.), *The Arden Shakespeare: The Second Part of King Henry IV* (Methuen, 1966) p. xxiii; Wilbur Sanders, *The Dramatist and the Received Idea* (Cambridge University Press, 1968) pp. 190–2.
68. See below, pp. 122–3.
69. See J. L. Kirby, *Henry IV of England* (Constable, 1970) pp. 55–6.
70. To ensure dynastic continuity Henry entailed the crown: see Raphael Holinshed, *Chronicles of England, Scotland and Ireland* (1577, 1587; AMS Press, 1965) III. 8.
71. Tennenhouse, 'Strategies of State and Political Plays', in Dollimore and Sinfield, *Political Shakespeare,* p. 122.
72. See Humphreys (ed.), *The Second Part of King Henry IV,* pp. 237–40.
73. Louis Althusser, *Lenin and Philosophy,* tr. Ben Brewster (New Left Books, 1971) pp. 203–4.
74. Ribner, *The English History Play in the Age of Shakespeare;* A. P. Rossiter, *Angel with Horns and Other Shakespeare Lectures,* ed. Graham Storey (Longmans Green, 1961).
75. Pierre Macherey, *Towards a Theory of Literary Production,* tr. Geoffrey Wall (Routledge and Kegan Paul, 1978) p. 79.
76. Barber, *Shakespeare's Festive Comedy,* p. 216.
77. Derek Cohen, 'The Rite of Violence in *Henry IV, Part One'*, *Shakespeare Survey,* 38 (1985) 78.
78. See S. L. Bethell, *Shakespeare and the Popular Dramatic Tradition* (1944; Octagon Books, 1970); and Robert Weimann, *Shakespeare and the Popular Tradition in the Theatre,* ed. R. Schwarz (Johns Hopkins University Press, 1978).

79. See Raymond Powell, *Shakespeare and the Critics' Debate* (Macmillan, 1980) pp. 7–8, 71–2.
80. J. Dover Wilson, *The Fortunes of Falstaff* (Cambridge University Press, 1947) p. 22.
81. Dipak Nandy, quoted in Humphreys (ed.), *The Second Part of King Henry IV*, pp. lx–lxi.
82. Thomas Carlyle, *On Heroes, Hero Worship and the Heroic in History* (1841; World's Classics, Oxford University Press, 1935) p. 144; Charles Knight, *Studies in Shakespeare* (Routledge, 1868) p. 183; W. B. Yeats, 'At Stratford-on-Avon' (1903), in *Essays and Introductions* (Macmillan, 1961) p. 108; Una Ellis-Fermor, 'Shakespeare's Political Plays', in *The Frontiers of Drama* (Methuen, 1945) p. 44; J. H. Walter (ed.), *The Arden Shakespeare: King Henry V* (Methuen, 1954) p. xxi. G. B. Shaw, *Dramatic Opinions and Essays* (1907), and Sidney Lee (ed.), *Henry V* (Renaissance edn, 1908), quoted in Michael Quinn (ed.), *Shakespeare's Henry V: A Collection of Critical Essays* (Macmillan, 1969) pp. 56 and 59; Gerald Gould, 'A New Reading of *Henry V*', *English Review*, 1919, repr. in Quinn, *'Henry V': Critical Essays*, pp. 81–94.
83. Walter (ed.), *King Henry V*, pp. xiv–xxi; and Zdenek Stribrny, '*Henry V* and History', in Arnold Kettle (ed.), *Shakespeare in a Changing World* (Lawrence and Wishart, 1964), quoted from Quinn, *'Henry V': Critical Essays*, p. 187.
84. See H. A. Kelly, *Divine Providence in the England of Shakespeare's Histories* (Harvard University Press, 1970); and above, pp. 13–19.
85. Holinshed, *Chronicles*, III, 133.
86. Ibid., p. 65.
87. Ibid., pp. 66–7.
88. Ibid., pp. 73–4.
89. *The Famous Victories of Henry V*, in Geoffrey Bullough (ed.), *Narrative and Dramatic Sources of Shakespeare* (Routledge and Kegan Paul, 1962) IV; and Thomas Dekker, *The Shoemakers' Holiday*, ed. D. J. Palmer (Ernest Benn, 1975).
90. Barton, 'The King Disguised', in Price, *The Triple Bond*.
91. See, for example, Traversi, *Shakespeare from 'Richard II' to 'Henry V'*; Honor Matthews, *Character and Symbol in Shakespeare's Plays* (Chatto and Windus, 1962); and Stribrny, '*Henry V* and History', in Kettle, *Shakespeare in a Changing World*.
92. Walter (ed.), *King Henry V*, p. xvi.
93. See Andrew Gurr, '*Henry V* and the Bees' Commonwealth', *Shakespeare Survey*, 30 (1977).
94. In pursuit of his father's advice: see *2 Henry IV*, IV. v.212–15.
95. Holinshed, *Chronicles*, III, p. 71.
96. Daniel, *The Civil Wars*, ed. Michel, p. 166.
97. Further evidence for this view is set out by Karl P. Wentersdorf, 'The Conspiracy of Silence in *Henry V*', *Shakespeare Quarterly*, 27 (1976).
98. William Hazlitt, *Characters of Shakespeare's Plays* (1817; Everyman's Library, 1906) p. 158.

99. See Walter (ed.), *King Henry V*, pp. xiv–xvii.
100. Gary Taylor (ed.), *The Oxford Shakespeare: Henry V* (Oxford University Press, 1982) p. 56; and cf. Lawrence Danson, 'Henry V: King, Chorus and Critics', *Shakespeare Quarterly*, 34 (1983).
101. See also II. i and IV. vii.
102. Restored in Taylor (ed.), *Henry V*, p. 243. See Jennifer Kraus, 'Name-calling and the New Oxford *Henry V'*, *Shakespeare Quarterly*, 34 (1985).
103. Norman Rabkin, 'Rabbits, Ducks and *Henry V'*, *Shakespeare Quarterly*, 28 (1977) p. 286.
104. Walter Benjamin, *Understanding Brecht* (New Left Books, 1977) p. 4.

NOTES TO PART TWO   THE TRAGIC ROMANCES OF FEUDALISM

1. *The Political Works of James I*, ed. C. H. McIlwain (New York, Russell and Russell, 1965) p. 292.
2. The phrase is from J. W. Draper, 'The Occasion of *King Lear'*, *Studies in Philology*, 34 (1937) 185. The idea is discussed more fully in the sections on *King Lear* and *Macbeth* below.
3. W. R. Elton, *'King Lear' and the Gods* (San Marino, 1966) p. 243; see also pp. 241–5.
4. *The Political Works of James I*, p. 62.
5. Perry Anderson, *Lineages of the Absolutist State* (New Left Books, 1974) p. 135.
6. See J. G. A. Pocock, *The Ancient Constitution and the Feudal Law: A Study of English Historical Thought in the Seventeenth Century* (Cambridge University Press, 1957) ch. 1, pp. 21–9, and the whole of ch. 3, for a discussion of the stimulus brought to historical thought by the need to compare two different coexisting systems of law.
7. Ibid., pp. 59–63.
8. Gordon J. Schochet, *Patriarchalism in Political Thought: The Authoritarian Family and Political Speculation and Attitudes Especially in Seventeenth-Century England* (Basil Blackwell, 1975) p. 9.
9. A sense of the scope of these is given in D. R. Kelley, *'De Origine Feudorum*: The Beginnings of a Historical Problem', *Speculum*, 39 (Apr 1964) 207–28.
10. Keith Thomas, *Religion and the Decline of Magic: Studies in Popular Beliefs in Sixteenth- and Seventeenth-Century England* (Penguin, 1973) p. 672.
11. Robert Burton, *The Anatomy of Melancholy* (Everyman's Library edn, 1932), I,65. Keith Thomas refers to these pages in the passage just quoted.
12. Ibid., p. 64.
13. William Hazlitt, *Works*, ed. P. P. Howe (London, 1930–4) IV,260. W. R. Elton's *'King Lear' and the Gods* has been the most thorough modern attempt to argue the play's pagan setting.

14.   John Danby, *Shakespeare's Doctrine of Nature: A Study of 'King Lear'* (Faber and Faber, 1949) p. 138. Elton, *'King Lear' and the Gods*, ch. 1, lists several Christian interpretations dating from the 1940s and 1950s. Danby's understanding of the play is not in fact historically specific.

15.   References throughout are to the Arden edn, ed. Kenneth Muir (Methuen, 1972). However, my understanding of the play's textual history rests upon the account given in Gary Taylor and Michael Warren (eds), *The Division of the Kingdoms: Shakespeare's Two Versions of 'King Lear'* (Oxford University Press, 1983): namely, that the Folio version of the play (written *c.* 1609–10) is Shakespeare's own revision of the Quarto version (written *c.* 1605–6), and that the commonly received composite text of Folio and Quarto is quite without authorization, an eighteenth-century invention. Accordingly, although using the Arden text for reference in the absence of anything more generally accessible, I have nevertheless aimed at an understanding of the Folio version and have not drawn upon material only to be found in the Quarto.

16.   Quoted in G. B. Harrison, and R. F. McDonnell (eds), *'King Lear': Text, Sources, Criticism* (New York, Harcourt, Brace and World, 1962) p. 117.

17.   Samuel Johnson, *Works*, VIII (Yale University Press, 1968) 703.

18.   Elton, *'King Lear' and the Gods*, p. 188. Elton's attempts to grapple with the Christian elements of the play are curious blemishes on the monolithic structure of his pagan reading; see esp. p. 338.

19.   Rosalie Colie, 'Reason and Need: *King Lear* and the "Crisis" of the Aristocracy', in R. L. Colie and F. T. Flahiff (eds), *Some Facets of 'King Lear': Essays in Prismatic Criticism* (University of Toronto Press, 1974) p. 191.

20.   W. W. Greg, 'Time, Place, and Politics in *King Lear*', in J. C. Maxwell (ed.), *Collected Papers* (Oxford University Press, 1966) p. 322. I assume the Gloucester of I. v.1 is the person and not the place.

21.   A. C. Bradley, *Shakespearean Tragedy* (Macmillan, 1905) p. 261.

22.   Bronislaw Malinowski, 'Myth in Primitive Psychology' (1926), republished in *Magic, Science and Religion and Other Essays* (Souvenir Press (Educational and Academic) 1974). These phrases are from pp. 100 and 126. Further page references to this essay appear in the text where possible.

23.   Well-documented accounts of the history of the Brutus myth may be found in T. D. Kendrick's *British Antiquity* (Methuen, 1950), esp. in chs 3 and 5–7; in Edwin Greenlaw's *Studies in Spenser's Historical Allegory* (Johns Hopkins Press, 1932), ch. 1; in R. F. Brinkley's *Arthurian Legend in the Seventeenth Century* (first published by the Johns Hopkins Press, 1932, and reprinted by Frank Cass, London, 1967), ch. 1 and also pp. 206–12; and also in Elton, *'King Lear' and the Gods*, pp. 241–5.

24.   *Gorboduc*, I. ii.259–61, in T. W. Craik (ed.), *Minor Elizabethan Tragedies* (Everyman's Library, 1974).

25. Spenser's letter to Raleigh, in J. C. Smith and E. de Selincourt (eds), *The Poetical Works of Edmund Spenser* (Oxford University Press, 1912) p. 408. For an account of Spenser's scepticism about the historicity of the Brutus myth, see Kendrick, *British Antiquity*, pp. 126–32.
26. Claude Lévi-Strauss, *Structural Anthropology*, tr. C. Jacobson and B. G. Schoepf (Penguin, 1977) p. 209.
27. Edmund Spenser, *The Faerie Queene*, ii. x.1 and ii. ix.56.
28. *The Political Works of James I*, p. 37.
29. Glynne Wickham, 'From Tragedy to Tragi-Comedy: *King Lear* as Prologue', *Shakespeare Survey*, 26 (1973) 36. This essay too discusses the relationship between *King Lear* and the Brutus myth.
30. Gillian Beer, *The Romance* (Methuen, 1970) p. 2.
31. See Lawrence Stone's *The Family, Sex and Marriage in England 1500–1800* (Penguin, 1979) ch. 5: 'The Reinforcement of Patriarchy'.
32. Maynard Mack, *'King Lear' in our Time* (Methuen, 1966) p. 5.
33. Bruno Bettelheim, *The Uses of Enchantment: The Meaning and Importance of Fairy Tales* (Penguin, 1978) p. 239.
34. Daniel 4:25, 27. For the tradition of the Abasement of the Proud King, see Mack, *'King Lear' in our Time*, pp. 49–51, and L. H. Hornstein, *'King Robert of Sicily*: Analogues and Origins', in *PMLA*, 79 (1964) 13–21.
35. Michael Long, *The Unnatural Scene: A Study in Shakespearean Tragedy* (Methuen, 1976) p. 163.
36. With the shape of *King Leir* in mind, John Kerrigan comments in 'Revision, Adaptation, and the Fool in *King Lear*', 'The play constantly provokes its audience to predict a return from "the worst", only to disappoint.' See Taylor and Warren, *The Division of the Kingdoms*, p. 225.
37. The best discussion of this is to be found in the essay by J. A. Barish and M. Waingrow, ' "Service" in *King Lear*', *Shakespeare Quarterly*, 9 (1958) 347–55. See also W. H. Auden's essay 'Balaam and his Ass', in *The Dyer's Hand* (Faber and Faber, 1963) pp. 107–45.
38. Samuel Daniel, *A Panegyrike Congratvlatory Deliuered to the Kings most excellent maiesty at* Burleigh Harrington *in Rutlandshire* (Scolar Press, 1970) stanza 26.
39. Mack, *'King Lear' in our Time*, p. 65.
40. See Gary Taylor, 'King Lear: The Date and Authorship of the Folio Version', in Taylor and Warren, *The Division of the Kingdoms*, p. 451, n. 168.
41. P. B. Shelley, Preface to *Prometheus Unbound*, in Thomas Hutchinson (ed.), *Shelley: Poetical Works* (Oxford University Press, 1967) p. 207. Shelley is aiming to revitalize and to radicalize that tradition of romance of which Shakespeare is critical in *King Lear*.
42. See Elton, *'King Lear' and the Gods*, pp. 267–70, for a fuller account of the relationship between Spenser and Shakespeare here.
43. By J. W. Draper in 'The Occasion of *King Lear*', *Studies in Philology*, 34 (1937) 185.
44. J. W. Draper suggests this too: 'Perhaps it was composed as direct

propaganda to develop a public sentiment in favor of the Union' (ibid., p. 185.

45. Gary Taylor comments, in 'Monopolies, Show Trials, Disaster, and Invasion: *King Lear* and Censorship', 'In electing to dramatize Lear's reign, Shakespeare was presumably paying James a compliment, for James (whose great ambition was to unite the island of Britain into one kingdom) pictured himself as the anti-type to Lear (who had divided it). But the very existence of such a perceived relationship between Lear and James opened up the possibility of other, less flattering comparisons between them' (Taylor and Warren, *The Division of the Kingdoms*, p. 104). A fascinating list of these comparisons may be found on pp. 102–5, suggesting possible reasons for the possible censorship of the Quarto.

46. See the opening sentence to ch. 18 of Fulke Greville's *The Life of the Renowned Sir Philip Sidney*.

47. William Wordsworth, *Poetical Works*, ed. E. de Selincourt (Oxford University Press, 1940–9) iv,73.

48. John Donne, 'A Nocturnall upon S. Lucies Day', where the extinction of the light of romance (unlike in *King Lear*) leads to Christian consolation.

49. Danby, *Shakespeare's Doctrine of Nature*, p. 50 and 46.

50. James H. Kavanagh, 'Shakespeare in Ideology', in John Drakakis (ed.), *Alternative Shakespeares* (Methuen, 1985) pp. 156–7.

51. Marvin Rosenberg, *The Masks of King Lear* (University of California Press, 1972) p. 34.

52. Barish and Waingrow, ' "Service" in *King Lear*', *Shakespeare Quarterly*, 9, p. 349.

53. See *King Lear*, iv. iv.24, and Luke 2:49. Such Christian language gathers around Cordelia throughout the play.

54. See *King Lear* v. iii.321. Kent does not distinguish here between his God and his king.

55. Bettelheim, *The Uses of Enchantment*, p. 238.

56. Janine Chasseguet-Smirgel, *Creativity and Perversion* (Free Association Books, 1985) p. 12.

57. William Wordsworth, *The Prelude* (1805 version) x.830. The phrase first appears in *The Borderers*. See *The Borderers*, ed. Robert Osborn (Cornell University Press, 1982) Early Version, iii. v.33, where a neo-Shakespearean villain is speaking the language of Godwinian anarchism.

58. M. Masud R. Khan, *Alienation in Perversions* (Hogarth Press, 1979) p. 16: 'The inconsolability of the pervert is matched only by his insatiability.'

59. See Melanie Klein, 'Envy and Gratitude', in *Envy and Gratitude and Other Works 1946–63* (Hogarth Press, 1975) pp. 176–235. I follow her argument here that envy is the primary two–person relationship out of which the three-person relationship of jealousy may develop.

60. Joseph Conrad, *Nostromo* (Penguin edn, 1963) p. 303.

61. Marilyn French, *Shakespeare's Division of Experience* (Sphere, 1983) p. 227.
62. Chasseguet-Smirgel, *Creativity and Perversion*, p. 10.
63. Wordsworth, *The Borderers* (1842 version), ll.1529–30.
64. *The Political Works of James I*, p. 38.
65. G. Wilson Knight, *The Wheel of Fire* (Methuen, 1954) p. 160. See the whole of ch. 8: '*King Lear* and the Comedy of the Grotesque'.
66. French, *Shakespeare's Division of Experience*, p. 241.
67. Danby, *Shakespeare's Doctrine of Nature*, p. 209.
68. Edmund Burke, *Reflections on the Revolution in France* (Everyman's Library edn, 1910) pp. 93–4.
69. Joseph Conrad, *Lord Jim* (Penguin edn, 1949) p. 66.
70. *The Political Works of James I*, p. 68.
71. Ibid., pp. xlii–xliii.
72. Holinshed, *Chronicles*, I, 443.
73. Malinowski, 'Myth in Primitive Psychology', in *Magic, Science and Religion*, p. 113.
74. Wilbur Sanders, *The Dramatist and the Received Idea: Studies in the Plays of Marlowe and Shakespeare* (Cambridge University Press, 1968) p. 326.
75. Long, *The Unnatural Scene*, p. 236.
76. Glynne Wickham, 'Hell-Castle and its Door-Keeper', in *Shakespeare Survey*, 19 (1966) 70.
77. See E. M. W. Tillyard, *Shakespeare's History Plays* (Chatto and Windus, 1944) p. 315. See also pp. 315–18.
78. See H. N. Paul, *The Royal Play of 'Macbeth'* (New York, 1950) p. 7ff.
79. Ibid., p. 40.
80. M. C. Bradbrook, 'The Sources of *Macbeth*', *Shakespeare Survey*, 4 (1951) 39.
81. *The Political Works of James I*, p. 271. These quotations are from the 1603 address.
82. Ibid., p. 25.
83. Ibid., p. 272.
84. Holinshed, *Chronicles* (New York,) v, 269.
85. A. P. Rossiter, *Angel with Horns and Other Shakespeare Lectures*, ed. Graham Storey (Longmans Green, 1961) p. 210.
86. Holinshed, *Chronicles*, v, 25–6.
87. Ibid., p. 24.
88. Ibid., p. 282.
89. Ibid., p. 25.
90. Ibid., p. 265.
91. Ibid., p. 25.
92. Marcel Mauss, *The Gift: Forms and Functions of Exchange in Archaic Societies*, tr. Ian Cunnison (Cohen and West, 1966) p. 1.
93. Ibid., p. 79.
94. Perry Anderson, *Passages from Antiquity to Feudalism* (New Left Books, 1974) p. 152.
95. Hazlitt, *Works*, IV, 191.

96. Paul, *The Royal Play of 'Macbeth'*, p. 255ff.
97. René Girard, *Violence and the Sacred*, tr. Patrick Gregory (Johns Hopkins University Press, 1977) p. 58.
98. Wilson Knight, *The Wheel of Fire*, p. 139. The phrase captures perfectly the obscene nature of the sisters' connection with the sacred.
99. Bradbrook, 'The Sources of *Macbeth*', *Shakespeare Survey*, 4, p. 42.
100. Terry Eagleton, *William Shakespeare* (Basil Blackwell, 1986) p. 5.
101. Jonathan Dollimore, 'Shakespeare, Cultural Materialism and the New Historicism', in Jonathan Dollimore and Alan Sinfield (eds), *Political Shakespeare: New Essays in Cultural Materialism* (Manchester University Press, 1985) p. 15.
102. French, *Shakespeare's Division of Experience*, p. 242.
103. Thomas, *Religion and the Decline of Magic* p. 761.
104. Hazlitt, *Works*, iv,189.
105. Masud Khan, *Alienation in Perversions*, p. 223.
106. Steven Marcus, *The Other Victorians: A Study of Sexuality and Pornography in Mid-Nineteenth-Century England* (Weidenfeld and Nicolson, 1966) p. 281.
107. Ibid., p. 270.
108. Ibid., p. 280.
109. Masud Khan, *Alienation in Perversions*, p. 221.
110. Wordsworth, *The Borderers*, p. 65.
111. Wilson Knight, *The Wheel of Fire*, p. 121.
112. Girard, *Violence and the Sacred*, p. 41.
113. *The Political Works of James I*, p. 38.
114. Helen Gardener, 'Tragic Mysteries', in David Bevington and Jay L. Halio (eds), *Shakespeare, Pattern of Excelling Nature* (Associated University Presses, 1978) p. 94.
115. Sanders, *The Dramatist and the Received Idea*, p. 258. See also pp. 255–65 for an account of the relationship between Duncan and Macbeth similar to the one advanced here, but within a moral rather than a historical context.
116. This line, and the two following couplets, are from T. S. Eliot's 'Little Gidding'.
117. Girard, *Violence and the Sacred*, pp. 291–2.
118. I have in mind here Cassirer's description of the modern state, quoted in Sanders, *The Dramatist and the Received Idea*, p. 68: 'The political world has lost its connexion not only with religion or metaphysics but also with all the other forms of man's ethical and cultural life. It stands alone – in an empty space.'
119. W. B. Yeats, 'Meru', in *The Collected Poems of W. B. Yeats* (Macmillan, 1950) p. 333.
120. Thomas Rymer, *A Short View of Tragedy*, in Curt A. Zimansky (ed.), *The Critical Works of Thomas Rymer* (Yale University Press, 1956) p. 164.
121. John Milton, Introduction to *Samson Agonistes*, the best and most representative definition of catharsis in the period.
122. Helen Gardner, 'Tragic Mysteries', in Bevington and Halio, *Shake-*

speare, Pattern of Excelling Nature, p. 90.

123. Friedrich Nietzsche, *Beyond Good and Evil: Prelude to a Philosophy of the Future*, tr. R. J. Hollingdale (Penguin, 1973) section 39, p. 50.
124. Sigmund Freud, *Totem and Taboo*, in the Pelican Freud Library, vol. 13 (Penguin, 1985) p. 71.
125. Clifford Leech, *Tragedy* (Methuen, 1969) p. 65.
126. W. B. Yeats, 'Crazy Jane Talks with the Bishop', in *Collected Poems*, p. 294.
127. Sir Philip Sidney, *A Defence of Poetry*, ed. Jan van Dorsten (Oxford University Press, 1966) p. 45.
128. Rossiter, *Angel with Horns*, p. 261.
129. Girard, *Violence and the Sacred*, p. 205.
130. Stephen Greenblatt, 'Shakespeare and the Exorcists', in Patricia Parker and Geoffrey Hartman (eds), *Shakespeare and the Question of Theory* (Methuen, 1985) p. 184.
131. Danby, *Shakespeare's Doctrine of Nature*, p. 138.

NOTES TO PART THREE   'THIS IS VENICE'

1. Catherine Belsey, *The Subject of Tragedy* (Methuen, 1985) p. 2.
2. Walter Cohen, 'The Merchant of Venice and the Possibilities of Historical Criticism', *ELH*, 4:9 (Winter 1982) 765–89.
3. W. H. Auden, *The Dyer's Hand* (Faber and Faber, 1963) pp. 227–8.
4. See, for example, Erich Auerbach, *Mimesis* (Princeton University Press, 1953).
5. See, for example, John W. Draper, 'Usury in *The Merchant of Venice*', *Modern Philology*, 33 (1935) 37–47. See also E. C. Pettet, '*The Merchant of Venice* and the Problem of Usury', *Essays and Studies* 31 (1945) 19–33; and Paul N. Siegel, 'Shylock, the Elizabeth Puritan, and Our Own World', in *Shakespeare in his Time and Ours* (Notre Dame University Press, 1968).
6. C. L. Barber, *Shakespeare's Festive Comedy: A Study of Dramatic Form and its Relation to Social Custom* (Princeton University Press, 1959). See also Frank Kermode, 'The Mature Comedies', in John Russell Brown and Bernard Harris (eds), *Early Shakespeare*, Stratford-upon-Avon Studies no. 3 (Edward Arnold, 1961), and L. C. Knights, *Drama and Society in the Age of Jonson* (London, 1937).
7. See Brian Pullan, *The Jews of Europe and the Inquisition of Venice 1550–1670* (Basil Blackwell, 1983).
8. In John Russell Brown (ed.), *The Arden Shakespeare: The Merchant of Venice* (Methuen, 1959) p. 93n.
9. Karl Marx and Friedrich Engels, *The Manifesto of the Communist Party*, in Lewis S. Feuer (ed.), *Marx and Engels: Basic Writings on Politics and Philosophy* (Fontana, 1969) p. 51.
10. R. F. Hill, '*The Merchant of Venice* and the Pattern of Romantic Comedy', *Shakespeare Survey*, 28 (1975), argues persuasively for a view that Antonio's melancholy arises from his contemplating 'the loss of a friend ... without whom existence is meaningless',

distinguishing his sense of Antonio's love for Bassanio from Graham Midgley's view that Antonio is a latent homosexual – *Essays in Criticism*, x (1960) 119–33. I believe that Antonio's melancholy arises from his sense that he is the 'black sheep' of his 'flock' – that is, merchants of Venice – and that he has earned heaven's disapproval in some way.

11. For a full account of the role of usury in the development of the European economies of this period, see, for example, Benjamin N. Nelson, 'The Usurer and the Merchant Prince: Italian Businessmen and the Ecclesiastical Law of Restitution, 1100–1550', *Journal of Economic History*, Supplement 7 (1947), and *The Idea of Usury: From Tribal Brotherhood to Universal Brotherhood* (Princeton University Press, 1949). See also Brian Pullan, *Rich and Poor in Renaissance Venice: the Social Institutions of a Catholic State, to 1620* (Oxford University Press, 1971); R. H. Tawney, *Religion and the Rise of Capitalism* (London, 1926); and Immanuel Wallerstein, *The Modern World-System: Capitalist Agriculture and the Origins of the European World Economy in the Sixteenth Century* (New York, Academic Press, 1974).

12. Cf. *Macbeth*, I. iv.10–11: 'To throw away the dearest thing he ow'd/As 'twere a careless trifle'.

13. Sir Thomas Wilson, *A Discourse upon Usury*, ed. and introd. R. H. Tawney (1925) N7. I owe this reference to John Russell Brown, Introduction to his edn of *The Merchant of Venice* (p. liv).

14. *The Merchant of Venice*, pp. xxxiv–xxxv.

15. I disagree with Walter Cohen in '*The Merchant of Venice* and the Possibilities of Historical Criticism', *ELH*, 4:9: 'The aristocratic fantasy of Act v, unusually sustained and unironic even for Shakespearean romantic comedy, may ... be seen as a formal effort to obliterate the memory of the preceding.' The deeper point is that the illusion rises above the reality and encloses it.

16. A difficulty shared by twentieth-century critics. As Helen Gardner noted, the play is for them 'a work of obviously supreme artistic power and beauty which does not satisfy their characteristic concerns and strongly resists their characteristic methods' – '*Othello*: A Retrospect, 1900–1967', *Shakespeare Survey*, 21 (1968) 1–12.

17. V. I. Lenin, *Selected Works* (Moscow, 1968) p. 268.

18. G. Wilson Knight, 'The Othello Music', *The Wheel of Fire* (London, 1930).

19. Michael D. Bristol, *Carnival and Theatre* (Methuen, 1985) p. 14.

20. For a discussion of 'tragi-comic' ambiguity in the play see, for example, Barbara Heliodora C. de Mendonca, '*Othello*: A Tragedy Built on a Comic Structure', *Shakespeare Survey*, 21 (1968) 31–8; Susan Snyder, *The Comic Matrix of Shakespeare's Tragedies* (Princeton University Press, 1979); S. Rogers, '*Othello* – Comedy in Reverse', *Shakespeare Quarterly*, 24 (1973) 210–220.

Emrys Jones, in *Scenic Form in Shakespeare* (Oxford University Press, 1971), argues that Shakespeare utilizes scenic structures from *Much Ado about Nothing* and *The Merry Wives of Windsor* in *Othello*. Barbara Everett, in ' "Spanish" Othello: the Making of Shakespeare's Moor', *Shakespeare Survey*, 35 (1982) 101–12, comments, 'It may be . . . worth noting that two of the primary dramatic locations of *Othello*, the street and the harbour-side, are those for centuries recognisable as belonging to Roman comedy and to the Greek New Comedy before it.'

21. I believe that Emilia's views have more serious implications than Dr Johnson thought: 'the virtue of *Aemilia* is such as we often find, worn loosely, but not cast off, easy to commit small crimes, but quickened and alarmed at atrocious villainies' – W. K. Wimsatt (ed.), *Dr Johnson on Shakespeare* (Penguin, 1969) p. 143. It is a question of the stability of the rest of the world in which one lives and acts.

22. For the variety of approaches to Iago see, for example, Leah Scragg, 'Iago – Vice or Devil?', *Shakespeare Survey*, 21 (1968) 53–66; Bernard Spivack, *Shakespeare and the Allegory of Evil* (Columbia University Press, 1958); Sidney R. Homan, 'Iago's Aesthetics: *Othello* and Shakespeare's Portrait of an Artist', *Shakespeare Studies*, 5 (1971) 141–8; S. E. Hyman, *Iago: Some Approaches to the Illusion of his Motivation* (Athenaeum, 1970); Terence Hawkes, 'Iago's Use of Reason', *Studies in Philology*, 58 (1961) pp. 160–9: William Empson, ' "Honest" in *Othello*', *The Structure of Complex Words* (Chatto and Windus, 1951) ch. 11.

23. R. K. Merton, *Social Theory and Social Structure* (Free Press, 1957).

24. I am aware that I am not broaching the 'colour' question. 'Alienness' is more the issue in what I have to say. Coleridge's anxious concern that Shakespeare could have meant Othello to be a 'veritable negro', and M. R. Ridley's reassurance that 'there are more races than one in Africa, and that a man is black in colour is no reason why he should, even to European eyes, look subhuman', are, I suppose, for all their difference, consequences of European imperialism. See T. Hawkes, *Coleridge on Shakespeare* (Penguin, 1969) pp. 187–8, and M. R. Ridley (ed.), *The Arden Shakespeare: Othello* (Methuen, 1962) p. li.

The issue is considered in, for example, K. W. Evans, 'The Racial Factor in *Othello*', *Shakespeare Studies*, 5 (1971) 124–40; Everett, ' "Spanish" Othello', *Shakespeare Survey*, 35; G. K. Hunter, 'Othello and Colour Prejudice', in *Dramatic Identities and Cultural Tradition: Studies in Shakespeare and his Contemporaries* (Liverpool University Press, 1968); Eldred Jones, *Othello's Countrymen: the African in English Renaissance Drama* (Oxford University Press, 1965); G. M. Matthews, 'Othello and the Dignity of Man' in A. Kettle (ed.), *Shakespeare in a Changing World* (Lawrence and Wishart, 1964).

25. The question of the social construction of the person has been treated with special reference to the Renaissance in, for example, Belsey, *The Subject of Tragedy*; Jonathan Dollimore, *Radical Tragedy* (Harvester Press, 1984); Stephen Greenblatt, *Renaissance Self-Fashioning* (University of Chicago Press, 1980).

The emphasis on 'person' here derives from the work of Søren Kierkegaard and Gabriel Marcel. See, for example, H. J. Blackham, *Six Existentialist Thinkers* (Routledge and Kegan Paul, 1952), for an introduction to their thought. See also the entry on 'Person' in Karl Rahner (ed.), *Encyclopedia of Theology* (Burns and Oates, 1975) for a similar emphasis.

26. Steven Marcus, *The Other Victorians: A Study of Sexuality and Pornography in Mid-Nineteenth-Century England* (Weidenfeld and Nicolson, 1966) p. 274.

27. Ibid., p. 267.

28. F. R. Leavis, 'Diabolic Intellect and the Noble Hero: or the Sentimentalist's Othello', *The Common Pursuit* (London, 1952); T. S. Eliot, 'Shakespeare and the Stoicism of Seneca', in *Selected Essays 1917–1932* (Faber and Faber, 1932).

29. See, for example, Giorgio Melchiori, 'The Rhetoric of Character Construction in *Othello*', *Shakespeare Survey*, 34 (1981) 61–72, or Gardner, '*Othello*: A Retrospect', *Shakespeare Survey*, 21, for the different view that Othello takes hold of his soldierly existence at this point and asserts its dignity through an 'act of justice' (Gardner).

30. Mainly for its political stability. See Brian Pullan, 'The Significance of Venice', *Bulletin of the John Rylands Library of Manchester*, 56 (1973–4) 443–462.

31. I am re-emphasizing a view expressed by John Russell Brown that the play demands an openness of response from us to 'whatever the plays offer, however strange that may seem' – *Discovering Shakespeare* (Macmillan, 1981) p. 5. Jane Adamson, in '*Othello*' as *Tragedy: Some Problems of Judgement and Feeling* (Cambridge University Press, 1980), has pointed out that the play is precisely *about* people's over-insistent attempts to make sense of things, to see what they want to see (pp. 3–5).

Index

Entries in **bold** type indicate passages of detailed discussion. References to the notes indicate authors unnamed in the text.